Gardening for All Seasons

THE COMPLETE GUIDE TO PRODUCING FOOD AT HOME 12 MONTHS A YEAR

The New Alchemy Institute Staff

GARY HIRSHBERG AND
TRACY CALVAN, EDITORS

BRICK HOUSE PUBLISHING COMPANY
Andover, Massachusetts

Published by Brick House Publishing Co., Inc.
34 Essex Street
Andover, Massachusetts 01810

Production Credits:

Publisher: *Jack Howell*
Editor: *Jim Bright*
Copy Edited by *Carol Beckwith*
Designed by *Mike Fender*
Produced by *Bookwrights, Inc.*
Illustrated by *Ann Wickham*

Library of Congress Cataloging in Publication Data

Main entry under title:

Gardening for all seasons.

  Bibliography: p.
  Includes index.
  1. Vegetable gardening.   2. Food crops.
3. Food.   4. Indoor gardening.   5. Aquaculture.
I. New Alchemy Institute.
SB321.G28   1983   635   83-2598
ISBN 0-931790-56-5

The excerpt on pages 53 and 54 is from pages 143–144 of *Tomorrow is Our Permanent Address: The Search for an Ecological Science of Design as Embodied in the Bioshelter* by John Todd and Nancy Jack Todd. A Lindisfarne Book. Copyright © 1980 by John Todd and Nancy Jack Todd. By permission of Harper & Row, Publishers, Inc.

Contents

*We dedicate this book to the spirit
of self-reliance in all of us.*

Preface

CONSIDER THE PIECE of Iowa corn that travels to your dinner table. Its journey begins in an enormous cornfield of many hundreds or thousands of acres, where a steady dose of chemical fertilizers is applied. The fertilizers, made from raw materials that were mined in Venezuela (or some other distant country), are enough for the corn plant, but they put nothing back into the soil. Because the corn plant is part of a monoculture plantation, it is highly vulnerable to all manner of pests and requires a steady dose of potentially toxic pesticides and herbicides to ensure its marketable quality. When the corn is harvested at last, the machinery that is employed removes nearly all the plant matter while compacting the soil, so that the soil's water-holding capacity is diminished, and the likelihood of erosion from wind and rain is enhanced. Finally, the ear of corn travels an elaborate, energy-intensive route through storage, sorting, packaging, shipping, and eventual delivery to your grocer. This journey may take it as many as 1500 miles.

Some experts estimate that at least 15 to 20 calories of fossil fuel energy are invested for every calorie of corn energy that is delivered to your local market. This is a dramatic change from the situation at the turn of the century, when we received about one calorie of food energy from every fossil fuel calorie we invested. Viewed on a national or global scale, these figures are staggering. If calories were dollars, economists would have a word to describe this system—*bankrupt*.

That we are facing enormous problems in our entire food system is not news to most readers. Our soils are depleting at unprecedented rates. (According to a 1977 U.S. General Accounting Office report, we are losing an average of 15 tons of topsoil per acre of farmland each year.) Operating costs are putting more farmers out of business than at any time since the Great Depression. It seems that our exclusive focus on annual productivity and big-business farming over the last few decades is finally catching up with our culture. The key question is whether we can reverse these trends in time to leave some sort of agricultural resource base to sustain future generations.

While "experts" are proposing and experimenting with all manner of technologic, economic, and political formulas to reverse these trends, there remains a simple action agenda available to consumers everywhere: *Produce your own!* We don't mean to imply that home food production can replace the farm belt, but research at our Cape Cod center over the last twelve years has convinced us that families can meet a significant portion of their food needs *in their own backyards.*

Gardening For All Seasons was written to celebrate this belief. Much of the text originally was prepared as a series of booklets for members of the Cape and Islands Self-Reliance Corporation on Cape Cod and Martha's Vineyard in Massachusetts. Information that the New Alchemy staff assembled for those booklets represents 12 years of data-gathering at our Cape Cod farm. When at last the long job of compiling, editing, and coordinating was completed, it occurred to us that what we'd done was assemble a useful book for people throughout the country and the world who enjoy gardening and raising a portion of their own food.

Many individuals have contributed to this text. Over 200 staff members and apprentices have worked in New Alchemy Institute gardens and aquaculture systems since our founding in 1969. Each of the contributing authors has provided simple guidelines from data that was gathered over many years by many hands. Much of our early work appeared in *The Journal of the New Alchemists* Numbers 1 through 7. In 1980 we began publishing a quarterly newsletter, *The New Alchemy Quarterly*, which gives brief reports on our research. And most recently, we completed a series of how-to texts on water-pumping windmills, backyard fish farming, tree crops, and greenhouse gardening.

In all our research and our writings, we have sought to demonstrate that a marriage of modern technologies and old ideas of ecological stewardship can result in new, productive human-support systems. Indeed, our name derives from the early Alchemists who wove together diverse natural elements to produce new and valuable results. In the same way, we New Alchemists—along with many other concerned groups and individuals in the late twentieth century—have sought to weave diverse ecological elements into systems for food, energy, shelter, and waste treatment that do not pollute or require the burning of fossil fuels. Whenever possible we combine intensive agriculture, aquaculture, tree crops, and renewable-energy techniques, as in our ''bioshelters.'' Bioshelters are advanced solar-enclosed environments for food and energy production and biological waste treatment in cold climates.

Whether under a bioshelter solar envelope or not, our approach to efficient intensive food production emphasizes the *integration* of food-growing and food-production techniques. For instance, nitrogen-rich water from our aquaculture systems is used as a warm, nutrient-rich irrigant for our food plants. This not only improves vegetable growth, but also acts to relieve the fish systems from excess nitrogen buildup. Often the waste or excess vegetable matter is returned to the fish pond as feed for herbivorous (plant-eating) fish. Some of the hervibores' wastes are consumed by omnivorous fish that inhabit the same ponds. Other fish wastes provide nutrients for the pond algae, which act to purify the water and produce dissolved oxygen for the fish. Furthermore, the presence of algae darkens the water, increasing the pond's ability to absorb sunlight, which in turn warms the water and leads to increased fish growth.

In these and countless other ways we are able to mimic the complexity, and thus the resilience, of natural ecosystems. We've found that the more niches we can build into our food systems, the healthier and more sustainable these systems become.

All our work at New Alchemy begins with the premise that individuals and families can take steps to increase their self-reliance and improve their local environments. In the context of rising costs due to our reliance on imported foods and nonrenewable energy sources, these home improvements can result in significant financial savings as well. But our work also addresses community-, municipal-, and regional-scale food and energy systems. Our bioshelters can be adapted to single-family residences or to commercial-scale microfarms. Our farmscape plans can be adapted to backyards or forests, and our gardening schemes apply to window boxes as well as row crops.

This book is directed primarily toward individuals or families who seek to meet more of their food needs. The introductory chapter provides an overview of these steps, and each subsequent chapter offers concrete information on a variety of food-growing techniques. We have written this text so that each food-growing approach can be understood and initiated on its own or, as you'll read in the final chapter, in tandem with other methods, as we do at our 12-acre Cape Cod center.

This text does not claim to provide all the answers in home food production. For in-depth exploration we hope readers will refer to some of the valuable references that are listed along the way in Resource sections and chapter Bibliographies. Our main objective is to acquaint you with the realities and the rewards of growing and producing food at home.

Gary Hirshberg and Tracy Calvan

Acknowledgments

PRODUCTION OF THIS BOOK has been a true committee process, and it would be folly to try to acknowledge everyone who made *Gardening for All Seasons* possible. Nevertheless, a few key staff members have played vital roles that we feel cannot be overlooked. Merryl Alber and Earle Barnhart performed well beyond the call of duty in the final stages as editors and excalibur cross-checkers. Claire Howes, New Alchemy's Business Manager, endured through more than a few budgetary and scheduling headaches; she deserves our deepest thanks for her patience and spirited support. And Jane Palmer, who typed much of this manuscript at least several times, somehow managed to maintain a sense of humor (and a sharp proofreading eye) when most of us would probably have packed it in.

From here, it becomes difficult to thank adequately each of the more than 200 New Alchemy staff and volunteers who have given of themselves to the noble, though often tedious, work of researching the systems described throughout this book. You know who you are, and we are deeply grateful.

Finally, none of what appears on these pages would be possible without the ongoing help and dedication of our thousands of supporting members, who over the years have given us reason to believe in ourselves. To all our members, thank you.

Gary Hirshberg and Tracy Calvan

Chapter 1

Meeting Nutritional Needs with Good Food

Merryl Alber and Greg Watson

We've learned not to assume that all our readers share a common idea of just what constitutes food, let alone what qualifies as "good" food. Even among our health-conscious associates, there lurk a number of bona fide junk-food junkies who'd plant Twinkie® gardens in their solar greenhouses . . . if only they could find the seeds!

Think of the many definitions we use for "food" in our computerized society. Our great-grandparents probably would have trouble identifying some of the meals we're served on airlines, for example, not to mention the ones we actually order in fast-food restaurants and concoct for ourselves with convenience-store purchases. For some time now, vast numbers of Americans have poured all manner of strange items into their bodies in the joyful pursuit of eating. The heightened awareness of our poor dietary habits is a relatively recent—but encouraging—development.

Today's converts to diet-consciousness are motivated beyond the traditional concern about excess weight. With nearly epidemic rates of cancer and heart disease around us, we have grown more alert to the amounts of sugar, chemical preservatives, stabilizers, and other questionable elements present in the processed foods we once blindly consumed. Many of us want to increase our control over what goes into our bodies—or perhaps more important, over what has been *added* to what goes into our bodies. In the wake of the recent Tylenol® scare, most individuals have decided they'd rather not offer their bodies as repositories for everything the FDA allows on the shelves. For us, this includes the countless chemicals that have somehow become an integral part of our modern food chains.

Food quality is a major issue for many, especially in the context of wax-covered vegetables, ice cream that doesn't melt, and tomatoes that bounce. Many diet-conscious consumers are also motivated by political concerns—a desire to support small farmers, for instance, or to keep food dollars within the local economy. There are ethical issues, as well: the high costs of transporting food from distant points and the ridiculous fact that up to 20 calories of fossil-fuel energy are invested for each calorie of food energy consumed by a typical American in the early 1980s. These are exactly the types of unconscious yet destructive habits that are depriving our children of the abundant resources and relatively healthly biosphere that many of us enjoyed as youngsters.

If you share any of these concerns and thus are motivated to grow your own food, to buy locally, or just to buy *selectively*, the way to begin is with some basic nutritional information and a brief, matter-of-fact discussion about our modern food system. This introductory chapter, written by Merryl Alber and Greg Watson, should get us all off to a good start as we try to gain more control over that stuff called food, on which we all survive.

THE EDITORS

Nutritional Needs

THIS INTRODUCTORY CHAPTER is designed to help you determine whether you are (a) eating high-quality foods and (b) taking advantage of the home gardening and food-prodution opportunities that are available to you.

FIVE ESSENTIAL NUTRIENTS

To maintain good health, you must obtain from your food the fifty-or-so elements that are essential to human life. These nutrients include both simple materials, such as minerals, and complex compounds, such as vitamins, that you are unable to produce in sufficient quantities yourself.

Nutrients may be divided into five categories: carbohydrates, fats, proteins, vitamins, and minerals.

Carbohydrates serve as the major source of energy for your body. The energy they contain was originally captured by the food plant from the sun. Carbohydrates include sugars, starches, and cellulose. They are found in fruits, in legumes and other vegetables, and in breads and cereals.

Fats function as energy storage and often are the carriers of fat-soluble vitamins. Butter, lard, oil, margarine, eggs, nuts, and meat all have high amounts of fat, originally stored by the food plant or animal from which they are derived. In your body, fats are either used immediately for energy or are stored and indirectly serve as insulation.

Protein is found in milk, cheese, eggs, meats, nuts, soy, vegetables, beans, and grains. Protein supplies important structural materials for your body. It is needed for the growth and repair of body tissues and necessary cell components. Proteins are also components of highly specialized chemicals, such as enzymes, antibodies, and hormones.

Vitamins are important for controlling maintenance and repair of the body and for growth and regeneration. They act as catalysts and coenzymes, critically important but needed only in very small amounts. Some vitamins can be made within your body from other simpler food products, but many can be obtained only from particular plants or from animals who previously made or ate them. Vitamins are a diverse group of compounds and are found in a wide range of foods.

Minerals include phosphorus, calcium, iron, copper, magnesium, zinc, and approximately twenty other elements. They are important for regulating nerve and muscle activity, clotting blood, and as components of enzyme activities. Like vitamins, minerals are needed in relatively small amounts and are found in varying proportions in a wide range of foods. A well-balanced diet that includes a variety of vegetables will help ensure that you get enough vitamins and minerals.

HIGH-QUALITY FOOD IN THE RIGHT QUANTITIES
Eat All Parts of a Food

All the nutrients from the food you eat are constantly being absorbed, stored, and used by your body. Some nutrients, particularly minerals and vitamins, are so closely interrelated in their bodily functions that their effectiveness is markedly improved when they are eaten together. Thus it is just as important to eat the right *proportions* of nutrients as it is to eat some of each kind of nutrient. Many nutritionists believe that a diverse diet which is high in vegetables but has less animal protein will ensure adequate amounts of both vitamins and minerals.

"Whole foods" are foods prepared with very little modification from the proportions found in the living plant or animal. A diet consisting mainly of whole foods usually is well-balanced and will provide you with adequate nutrients. The advantage is that the whole food is more likely to contain the full range and normal proportions of materials necessary for life. For example, whole grains are a high-quality source of carbohydrates because they have not had their nutrients stripped away in a refining process, and their fiber encasing remains intact. Whole grains can provide fiber, protein, certain B vitamins, vitamin E, and a good many minerals *in addition to* carbohydrates. The milling and fractioning that refines white flour removes many valuable nutrients as well as the fiber encasing, or *bran*. A diet deficient in fiber will leave you more susceptible to intestinal disorders, elevated cholesterol levels, and colon cancer.[1]

Eat Fresh Food

The benefits of choosing fresh food include maximum vitamin content and maximum flavor. The food value of stable nutrients such as proteins and carbohydrates doesn't change much if they are stored or cooked; however, the more delicate properties of vitamins and flavors do degrade over time. Minerals vary in their stability; some are tightly bound into the food structure, whereas others are easily washed out by cooking.

Eat a Blend of Foods

Your body can adjust to a certain amount of variation in its food supply by accumulating extra amounts of many nutrients and saving them for later use. Carbohydrates are stored as fat and minerals are stored in fluids and bones, for example. Nutritionists have determined the approximate daily requirement, in terms of amount and proportions, for each nutrient. They suggest that a fat intake that provides 25 to 30 percent of your calories—and not more—is compatible with good health. Excess fat, especially in the form of cholesterol, has been linked to heart disease and stroke. Cutting down on fat consumption by substituting carbohydrates such as starches will not only lower the risk of circulatory disease, but also allow for an increased intake of other, more valuable, nutrients.

Unlike most other nutrients, excess protein is *not* stored by the body: it is broken down and either used immediately as an energy source or converted to fat. The nitrogen content of excess protein is excreted. Proteins are essential to numerous body functions, but many people have misconceptions about how much protein is necessary in the diet. Furthermore, a surprising number are unaware of how to obtain that necessary protein. The average American eats about twice the protein that he or she can utilize for structural growth and maintenance. Carbohydrates and fats are the foods that our bodies use preferentially over other sources of energy, so high-cost protein should not be eaten just to supply energy.

Protein is so often associated with meat, fish, eggs, and other animal products that we tend to forget that there are other sources available. Protein is also found in many plant products. Combining protein from several sources will often enhance its food value. For example, combining rice with beans, oatmeal with milk, or peas with corn can provide all the essential protein components necessary in your diet. Frances Moore Lappé popularized this concept (called "protein complementarity") in *Diet for a Small Planet.*[2] She provides this intriguing example: 1½ cups of beans have the usable protein equivalent of a 6¼-ounce steak; 4 cups of rice have the usable protein equivalent of a 7-ounce steak; yet when combined, the beans and rice produce a dish containing the usable protein equivalent of a 19-ounce steak. This represents a 43-percent increase!

Throughout the world people have developed traditional diet combinations of grains, legumes, nuts, and dairy products that provide protein complementarity. In China, for example, soybean products such as tofu are eaten along with rice, while Mexicans often mix corn with beans. In India, rice and beans are important components of the traditional fare, and in the Mideast, people combine wheat breads with chick peas. To reiterate: Large amounts of animal protein in your diet are unnecessary; you can meet your protein requirement far less expensively by using sources other than meat. If you'd like to learn more about protein complementarity, we recommend Lappe's book, *Diet for a Small Planet.*

Vitamins and minerals are both crucial to your health. Calcium, for example, is the main component of bones and teeth, and iron is essential to blood cells. Many diseases and a variety of minor symptoms are associated with vitamin and mineral deficiencies. Only recently have some of the trace minerals been recognized as essential nutrients. Fruits and vegetables are important sources of vitamins and minerals (as well as proteins and carbohydrates). They can be the major components of your diet. Green vegetables are generally low in calories but high in vitamins and minerals. As a rule, the fresher the vegetable and the richer its color (i.e., dark green, deep yellow or red), the more vitamins and minerals it contains. Canning, freezing, and even cooking vegetables can decrease their nutritional value; in particular, vitamin C is easily destroyed by heat. So whenever possible, buy vegetables in season and serve them fresh—with as little cooking as necessary.

Although vitamin and mineral tablets have become popular as a supplement to the diet, there is controversy concerning whether they are in fact as valuable to the body's functions as similar nutrients eaten together in their natural whole-food form. Nutritionally, food plants contain vitamins and minerals in varying proportions in all parts of the plant. For example, the outer skin of most fruits is higher in vitamins and minerals than the inner flesh. The nutritional value of fruit and vegetable skins, peels, and other food "scraps" is often significant, so don't pare and peel it all away! Find ways to utilize these things in your method of home food preparation.

Nutritive Value of American Foods contains a detailed list of many specific foods. You'll soon be an authority yourself!

Quality and Cost Depend on Where the Food Comes From

Many consumers across the country are choosing to shorten the distance between the site of food production and the site of food consumption—that is, themselves. Fresh home-grown food is likely to provide the best-tasting and most nutritious source of food, and home production eliminates the high transport and handling costs of commerical sources. Therefore balancing your diet and decreasing your food costs are two worthwhile projects that can go hand-in-hand. Shifting your diet to include more nutritious foods that you can produce at home is relatively easy and well worth the effort, for both your health and your pocketbook.

FRESH FOOD, STORED FOOD, AND TRANSPORTED FOOD
Where Do You Get Your Food?

As a mental exercise, begin at home and think outward to where your food comes from:

- If you grow fresh sprouts, some comes from within your house.
- If you grow greenhouse lettuce, some comes from a residential greenhouse, probably attached to your house.
- If you grow fresh vegetables, some comes from your backyard garden or your own nearby community-garden plot.
- If you buy from a local produce market, roadside stand, farmers' market, or pick-your-own-produce farm, these close-to-home sources of fresh foods were probably grown in your own region.

• If you buy food in a grocery store, it may have come from as close by as your neighbor's market garden or from as far away as Mexico or China. It may even have been in storage for several years!

The American food industry is large and complex. It not only serves as the major source of food for most of the 230-million American citizens, but also accounts for more than 50 percent of the world's total grain exports. Because of the industry's enormous size and complex structure, most of our food changes hands as many as four or five times as it makes its way from the farm to the consumer's cupboard. Each time that food is handled by middlepeople (truckers, processors, packagers, wholesalers, and retailers), additional costs accrue. The greater the distance between consumers and their source of food, the more expensive that food is going to be.

Virtually every aspect of the American food industry is highly dependent on large and constant inputs of petrochemicals. Agriculture currently uses about 12 percent of all the energy consumed by the U.S. economy. Centralization of the food system creates a need for treating many foods with chemical additives to preserve freshness, taste, and color. No one is certain about what long-term health effects these chemicals may cause, but some researchers suggest that there are connections between the high incidence of cancer in our society and the vast amounts of chemical pesticides, herbicides, and fertilizers that have been introduced into the biosphere and into our homes.

Are You Aware of the Nature and Purpose of Food Additives?

An impressive array of chemicals and non-nutritive substances are added to fresh foods before you buy them at the grocer's as packaged products. Preservatives are used to slow down the process of deterioration; colors and flavors are added to please the consumer's aesthetic sensitivity; and some additives are nothing more (or less) than fillers to add inexpensive bulk or weight to the package. The history of food additives is as old as salt and spices, but recently a number of additives have been adjudged more damaging than beneficial. It is our philosophy that food should be produced in such a manner as to eliminate the need for most preservatives and keep the processing activities under our control, so we'll know just what is in our food. A book by Zenas Block *It's All on the Label: Understanding Food, Additives and Nutrition*, will enhance your knowledge of food additives and their implications.

Do You Waste Part of the Food You Now Buy?

A study of the garbage cans in Tucson, Arizona, revealed that 10 percent of the food purchased in each home ended up in the garbage. In a single year, a city with 300,000 inhabitants threw away *10 million dollars worth* of food![3] Whether by quantity or cost, if you now throw away *any* quantity of good food, rethink and change that activity before you invest time and money to obtain more.

FOOD-PRODUCING PLANTS AND ANIMALS

Your decision to produce food at home implies that you will be caring for a number of plant and animal species. The nutrients you will get from these food-producers must first be supplied *to* them during their own growth. Simply stated, the practice of agriculture means helping the life cycles of whatever plants and animals you want and hindering the life cycles of their enemies.

Each species has a life cycle and a range of living conditions that must be managed carefully to maintain a continuous supply of the food. Each species requires material inputs and produces material wastes that must be obtained and disposed of. Certain combinations of food species are particularly compatible in the sense that the waste products of one crop or animal can be used as the input nutrients for another. The goal is to create an ecosystem in which you, the human, nurture the food species to provide a continuous source of food and at the same time conserve the nutrients that recycle within and among the various parts.

The examples of food plants and animals that we'll use throughout this book have been chosen for their suitability to the temperate climate and related conditions typical of the Northeast United States and regions of similar climate. Remember that in other geographical locations a different balance of crops and procedures may be more suitable. Your task is to create from the many possible options a system that meets your personal needs.

Guidelines for Choosing Food Supplies
USE YOUR CLOSEST RESOURSES

Your closest resource for producing good, nutritious food is likely to be your own garden.

1. Use the space, soil, and sunlight around you.
2. Try to minimize transport of food and waste materials.

Several years ago, New Alchemy's gardeners measured the amount of time and energy required to grow a family-size vegetable garden. The results were surprising. Our crop yields, balanced against the on-site work (such as planting, cultivation, etc.), showed a satisfying ''profit'' of 370 percent. In other words, more than three times as much food energy was produced as was invested in the gardening work. However, when the energy cost of trucking organic nutrients to the garden was added in, the net energy return dropped to barely breaking even. The gasoline energy consumed in making about 20 trips for seaweed and manure with our truck was several times that of the energy expended through our physical work.

3. Produce food at home that substitutes for the most expensive food you now buy.

Specific high-cost foods to consider include fresh salad vegetables (particularly in the winter season) and protein. These lower-volume high-value foods are the best targets for home food production, so subsequent chapters will emphasize methods of year-round vegetable growing and home protein production.

When you first consider the idea of growing and preparing food at home, questions of time, money, and nutritional value may seem to be in conflict. These concerns often overlap: you may gain on one value at the expense of another.

For starters, let's look briefly at three questions.

How Much Time Do You Spend in Food Preparation?

Many of the methods discussed in this book do involve spending more time preparing the item for serving than you'd spend if the food were purchased "ready made." On the other hand, food grown at home is close at hand when you need it and doesn't require the time of a trip to shop. It may take less time to prepare a quick salad from a head of commercially grown lettuce than to pick your own salad greens, yet this means paying more money and sacrificing considerable nutritional value.

How Much Money Do You Spend on Food?

The money you now spend for food might be better invested in setting up home food-production areas aimed at providing a reliable, sustainable supply of higher-quality foods.

How Are Food Tasks Shared in Your Family?

- Who provides the money?
- Who selects the food and gets it home?
- Who prepares and cooks it?
- Who washes dishes?
- Who manages food wastes?

Involving more of the family, especially young children, in the basic tasks of food production can improve the sense of family interdependence. Producing food promotes personal self-reliance, feelings of self-worth, and gives you a feeling of participation in an important part of your life.

SUPPORT YOUR LARGER ECOSYSTEM

On Earth all living things are connected through the immediate and long-term effects of their activities. Innocent or informed, you as a food eater are irrefutably linked with how your food is grown and harvested. If your grain or meat comes from Iowa, you are a direct participant in a farming process that promotes extreme erosion of the soil there. If you eat bananas from Central America, you are a participant in the destruction of tropical rain forests and the use of deadly herbicides and pesticides that take place in those growing regions. This type of awareness gives us much to think about. We at New Alchemy choose to take as much control as possible over our food supply and become more consciously responsible for our ecological impact.

It is important to understand that though side effects and by-products of any food process are inevitable, they can be structured to *reinforce—* instead of destroy—ecological diversity and stability. For example, if you keep honeybees primarily to provide sweetness for your food, your bees will also assist the life cycles of many wild plants and increase the food yields of many crop plants within a radius of up to two miles. Or if you choose tree crops and food shrubs to provide you with fruit, fuelwood, or berries, the same trees and shrubs will simultaneously provide a number of local environmental benefits, including erosion control, modification of extreme summer and winter temperatures, and habitat for wildlife.

An overriding concern in today's economic and political climate is security of home and family. It is our belief that the best strategy to provide personal and social security is to create the kinds of sustainable, productive, and life-enhancing food processes presented in this book.

REFERENCES

1. ROBERTSON, LAUREL, CAROL FLINDERS, and GODFREY BRONWEN. *Laurel's Kitchen*. New York: Bantam Books and Nilgiri Press, 1976, p. 402.

2. LAPPÉ, FRANCIS MOORE. *Diet for a Small Planet*. New York: Ballantine Books, 1971, p. 362.

3. ROBERTSON, *et al.*, p. 40.

BIBLIOGRAPHY

BLOCK, ZENAS. *It's All on the Label: Understanding Food, Additives and Nutrition.* Boston: Little, Brown, 1981.

GUTHRIE, HELEN A. *Introductory Nutrition,* 2nd ed. New York: C.V. Mosby Co., 1971.

LAPPÉ, FRANCES MOORE. *Diet for a Small Planet,* revised edition. New York: Ballantine Books, 1971.

ROBERTSON, LAUREL, CAROL FLINDERS, AND GODFREY BRONWEN. *Laurel's Kitchen.* New York: Bantam Books and Nilgiri Press, 1976.

U.S. DEPARTMENT OF AGRICULTURE, AGRICULTURAL RESEARCH SERVICE. *Nutritive Value of American Foods in Common Units.* Ag. Handbook #456, Washington, D.C., G.P.O., 1975.

Chapter 2

Indoor Gardening

Michael Greene

A friend tells the story of his first exposure to a genuine indoor green thumb. "It was my first week at college and everyone was busy socializing and exploring the dorms for lively get-togethers. On one particular floor I encountered a familiar, savory aroma emanating from behind a semiclosed door. Allowing my gourmet olfactory judgment to overcome any shyness, I peered into the room and was delighted to find a major fall harvest operation in progress. The particular crop in question stood a stunning six feet in height and reached clear to the grow-light affixed to the closet ceiling. It was indeed a successful harvest of a summer-school bumper crop, and over the next few semesters this ambitious team of indoor farmers grossed nearly 500 dollars. Not bad for a four-square-foot garden!"

While we do not recommend that particular growing strategy or crop selection with its accordant legal restrictions, we do offer in the following chapter considerable food for thought (and belly) on the merits of indoor food production. We rural folk are often accused of utter, irresolvable insensitivity to the restrictions facing our urban friends when it comes to providing food. Despite the successes of our colleagues in the urban gardening movement at Boston Urban Gardeners (BUG) and in urban community-garden projects across the country, the majority of our apartment-bound or otherwise space-limited friends generally have felt left out of New Alchemy's consideration.

We're happy at last to answer that oft-voiced criticism with a bit more than a bibliography or guide to urban gardening efforts. Michael Greene, New Alchemy's genuine, honest-to-goodness city slicker, has compiled a detailed guide to the use of existing home or apartment space for its fullest food-growing advantage.

This chapter is not written just for city dwellers—it's for anyone who has a sunny window, enjoys sprouts, or tries to make the most of recycling kitchen wastes. And it's written by a true believer and practitioner. Michael's home is a perennial source of sprouts, worm castings, mushrooms, and other indoor delights.

THE EDITORS

FOR YEARS gardeners have gotten a jump on the growing season by planting seedlings indoors during late winter and transplanting them outside in the spring. This time-tested practice is a good one, but for those of you who have no "outdoors" to which you can transplant—or who would like to garden on a year-round basis—some additional gardening techniques have been developed. Through these procedures you can produce food in your own home at *any* season. This chapter describes a number of methods of bringing food production indoors. We'll divide our discussion into four main categories: Growing Sprouts, Raising Seedlings, Growing Vegetables Indoors, and Indoor Composting Through Worm Culture.

Growing Sprouts

Sprouts are the seedlings of various vegetables and grains. You can home-grow sprouts that will be ready to eat from three to eight days after they are planted. Anybody can do it: tenant or homeowner, city or country dweller, old or young, in any climate, during any month of the year. These unique vegetables are inexpensive, low in calories, highly nutritious, and tasty as well! You've probably eaten sprouts in salads; but if not, you're in for a pleasant surprise.

Most food crops reproduce by bearing seeds. Each seed contains the embryonic form of the plant—a true storehouse of proteins, carbohydrates, and fats. The seed remains dormant until growing conditions are favorable. It then becomes active and undergoes a number of rapid and remarkable changes. It is at this initial stage of development that the plant is highest in its nutritional content. The rapidly growing young plant converts the stored food into a more digestible form and begins producing vitamins. By sprouting seeds and eating the young vegetables, you can take advantage of the enhanced nutrients of this stage of the plant growth process.

In addition to being loaded with vitamins and proteins, these "live foods" are quite tasty. Sprouts have gained recent popularity, and you can now buy ready-made packages in many supermarkets and health-food stores. Sprouts make excellent additions to salads, sandwiches, and soups. Occasionally they are even served as a separate entree. Alfalfa, the most commonly eaten sprout, has a crisp, nutty-type flavor. Wheat sprouts are sweet, and radish sprouts add a touch of spice. With dozens of other seeds from which to choose, even the pickiest eaters (including young adolescents) will enjoy at least one or two kinds.

It's easy to create a sprout garden. You need no exotic equipment; recycled household containers serve nicely. Since the seeds take up little space, a small shelf in a cupboard or even the top surface of your refrigerator will do. The seeds germinate in darkness, so you need not worry about light. All that the seeds require to sprout are air, adequate moisture (provided by rinsing them a couple of times a day), and a warm temperature in the range of 65–85°F. With such simple requirements for success, sprouting is probably the easiest, most efficient, and most economical method of home food production.

JAR METHOD

There are many methods of sprouting. One of the simplest approaches is known as the *jar method*, so that's the one we'll examine first.

The Equipment

As you may gather from Fig. 1, any widemouthed jar can become a sprouting container. A canning or kitchen jar, or a recycled peanut-butter or mayonnaise container will do. Lids for the jars can be made from cheesecloth or another type of mesh material, such as nylon stockings. After you fit the material over the container, hold it in place with a rubber band, string, or jar ring. Use two or three layers of cheesecloth for small seeds. (Commercially produced plastic lids may be purchased at your local health-food store if you feel they are worth the investment.)

Many different kinds of seeds are suitable for sprouting. We recommend that you begin with alfalfa, clover, mung bean, radish, cabbage, lentil, wheat, buckwheat, or fenugreek. These seeds sprout easily, yield large quantities, and can be obtained at most health-food stores.

The Procedure

Measure out the proper amount of seeds according to Table 1, place them in the jar, and affix the lid.

Fig. 1 Materials for jar-method sprouting

Table 1 *Sprouting Seeds in a One-Quart Jar*

SEED	AMOUNT OF SEED[1]	DAYS UNTIL HARVEST[2]	COMMENTS[3]
Wheat	1 cup	2–3	Don't green. Very sweet in taste. Excellent raw, especially when combined with buckwheat. Good for baking (e.g., sprouted-wheat bread).
Buckwheat	1 cup	3	The seed coats add a crunchy texture to these pleasant tasting sprouts. Be sure to buy raw, unroasted whole seeds.
Lentils	½ cup	3–4	Chewy texture, pleasant bean-like tasts. Combines well with other sprouts, particularly mung beans.
Alfalfa	2½ tb	4–5	Allow it to green. Alfalfa is easy to sprout, has a high nutritional content, and a crisp, nutty flavor; sometimes called the "king of sprouts."
Cabbage	5 tb	4–5	Allow it to green. The sprouts smell and taste like the vegetable. Excellent when combined with clover or alfalfa.
Clover	2 tb	4–5	Allow it to green.
Fenugreek	3 tb	4–5	Greening greatly enhances the flavor of these sprouts, making them spicy instead of bitter. Adds a kick to soups and salads.
Mung beans	⅓ cup	4–5	Don't green or they'll become bitter. Mung beans are often used in oriental cooking. They will loose crispness after 3 or 4 days of storage in the refrigerator.
Radish	3 tb	4–5	Allow it to green. Sprouts have a spicy taste similar to the vegetable.

[1] The amount of seeds suggested here will produce about three-quarters to one full quart of sprouts. Adding more than this can cause the growing seedlings to block the opening of the jar, thus reducing air circulation and encouraging spoilage.

[2] In the colder months, sprouts may take an additional day before they are ready for harvest.

[3] All these seeds should be soaked for eight to twelve hours and then rinsed two or three times a day.

Clean the seeds by filling the jar with water and rinsing it out three or four times. Rinsing is a simple procedure; the cheesecloth lid will retain the seeds while it allows the water to drain. Rinsing removes any impurities on the seeds. After you have cleaned the seeds, fill the container with luke-warm water, place it in a warm area, and allow it to stand for about eight to twelve hours.

Fig. 2 Allow seeds to soak

After soaking the seeds for the prescribed time, drain out the water. Since this liquid will now contain some soluble nutrients, you should use it to water your houseplants or perhaps as a broth or base for homemade soup (see Fig. 3). Place the jar(s) in a tray or pan in a tilted-down position and store in an accessible and relatively dark area, such as a kitchen cabinet. The tilted position will permit excess water to drain. *Make sure the seeds do not totally cover the lid* and block air from entering the container; without proper drainage and air circulation, the seeds can rot. Figure 4 shows you how they should look.

Your sprouts should be rinsed two or three times a day. This is one of those simple chores that is easy to forget. Develop a habit of rinsing the seeds at breakfast, dinner, and possibly before bed.

Once sprouts have reached the desired length, they should be harvested or they will quickly lose their good taste and high nutritional content. If you don't eat them as soon as they are ready, fully drain out any excess water, place them in a sealed jar or plastic container, and store them in the refrigerator. They will keep for up to one week, although some flavor will be lost after a few days.

Before harvesting the plants, you may want to place them in a well-lit area for six to eight hours so that they can develop chlorophyll. (Avoid exposure to direct midday sun, however.) This greening process increases the nutritional content of the young plants. The taste of alfalfa, clover, rad-

Fig. 3 Drain the water

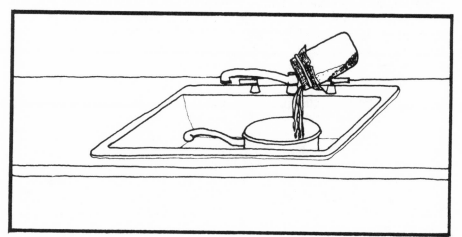

Fig. 4 Allow seeds to sprout

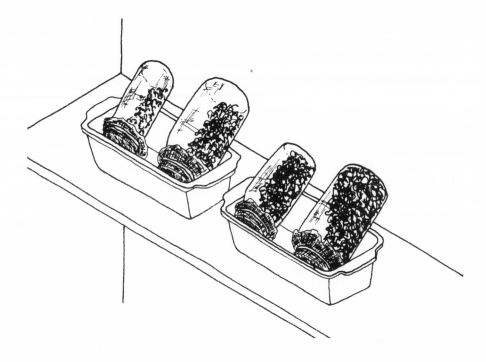

ish, cabbage, and fenugreek seems to improve through this process, although mung beans become more bitter. Taste the sprouts both before and after, and decide on your own preference. Table 1 tells you which sprouts are receptive to the greening process.

Seed hulls can be removed from some of the sprouts by emptying the seedlings into a bucket of water. The sprouts will tend to sink to the bottom, while the hulls will rise to the very top. With a strainer, remove the hulls from the top.

Additional Tips

For sprouting to be successful, you must have viable seeds. The types of seeds recommended in this book are rarely sold for purposes other than gardening or sprouting, so you should not run into trouble with poor germination. Probably the best place to obtain them is at your local health-food store. The advantage of purchasing at these establishments is that their seeds are "untreated." Seeds used for gardening are often coated with chemicals to protect against insects and diseases. These chemicals are poisonous and should not be consumed. Some seed companies (W.A. Burpee Co. is one) sell untreated seeds. If you are ordering by mail, be sure to specify that you want *untreated* seeds.

Once you get the hang of it, you may try sprouting other plants. Packages of grains and legumes (members of the bean and pea family) are sold in any supermarket. Since they are considered a food item, however, there are no regulations governing their germination percentage. Therefore it's best to stick to packages marketed solely for sprouting or labeled "seed quality."

Purchasing seeds in bulk can reduce their cost, although it is *not* economical to buy a large quantity and then have them lose viability due to improper storage. Seeds should be kept in a cool, dry area. Place them in containers with tight-fitting plastic lids to ensure that moisture is kept out. Be certain the seeds are dry before they're set aside for storage. Label the container with the name of the seed it holds as well as with the purchase date. When properly stored, most seeds will remain viable for a couple of years.

Potential Problems

If you have viable seeds, yet your attempts to sprout them are unsuccessful, it may be due to one of the following problems.

Incorrect Levels of Moisture or Air When jars contain excess moisture, the sprouts can rot, producing foul odors and foul tastes. Rotting can also result from inadequate air circulation. Be sure to drain the containers of water thoroughly and encourage proper air circulation. During hot summer months, you may find that the sprouts quickly dry out. In this case take steps to rinse them more often than you would in cooler weather.

Inadequate Temperatures Most seeds germinate well when temperatures range from 65–85°F. If your living quarters are consistently cooler than this during winter months, either the sprouts will grow slowly or the seeds will fail to germinate. Try to find a warm area (perhaps by the stove or boiler) where you can place the containers. Put a paper bag over the jars to block out light. If excess heat seems to be a problem in the summer, try to place the sprouts in a cooler part of your home.

TRAY METHOD

An alternative sprouting method that deserves special mention is that of growing certain sprouts in shallow trays of soil. Although this procedure is a little more complex and requires some extra equipment, an important benefit is that the young growing sprout will actively take minerals from the soil and increase the nutritional value of your yield. Sunflower and buckwheat seeds are commonly sprouted by the tray method. Like the seeds we discussed earlier, they usually can be obtained at health-food stores. If they're not stocked, however, check with your local agriculture/

garden shop. Large packages of sunflower seeds, often sold as birdfood, are cheap and free of chemical sprays. Hulled sunflower seeds usually have the capacity to germinate and may be used, but unhulled seeds sell for one-half to one-quarter the cost. Started in soil, these sprouts can't be surpassed for their taste as a crunchy snack or as an addition to salads.

The tray method of sprouting requires strong, reusable planting containers. Surprisingly enough, plastic cafeteria trays are perfect! The following instructions are designed for a 14-by-18-inch tray.

1. Prepare a soil mix composed of equal parts sifted compost (sift through a quarter-inch screen) and rich garden soil. Remove rocks, twigs, and other debris. If compost is not available, rich garden soil alone will do. Worm castings may be used in place of the compost-soil mixture.

2. Fill the tray to the rim with about 3⅓ quarts of the soil mix, which should be slightly moist but not soggy wet. Spend a couple of minutes running your hands through the mixture, breaking up clumps, removing small stones, worms, etc. Spread the soil evenly over the tray.

3. Press your fingers into the soil along the edge of the tray in order to create a half-inch-wide drainage ditch. Beginners often make this ditch wider than necessary, reducing available growing space for the sprouts. The half-inch trench really is sufficient.

4. Following the illustration in Fig. 5, use another tray (or flat board) to press the soil lightly and create a more compact surface. Do not apply too much pressure but just enough to make the soil a bit firmer and more evenly spread. Repair the drainage ditch if it gets pushed in.

5. Measure out the correct amount of seeds; 1¼ cup of dry buckwheat or 1⅔ cup of sunflower should be used for each 14-by-18-inch tray. Soak the seeds in a container of water, covered with a mesh-like material according to the directions given for the Jar Method in the preceding section. Drain the water after eight to twelve hours and let the jar stand tilted down for an additional six to ten hours. During this period the seeds will expand and begin their process of germination.

6. Now spread the seeds evenly over the tray. They should be placed very close together, actually touching one another. But don't carry it to the extreme; even though buckwheat and sunflower will grow in patches where seeds are double or triple layered, it's best to avoid such a high density. Also, try to keep seeds out of the drainage ditch.

7. Wet the seeds down with water. A quart sized plastic or glass container with *tiny* holes punched in the lid is an excellent homemade sprinkler. Water the seeds by passing over the tray two or three times with the sprinkler. *Remember:* The trays don't have drainage holes. If too much water is added, the seeds may rot. The drainage ditch

Fig. 5 Making the trench and pressing the soil

around the edges of the tray has been created as a precaution against this problem. Stop adding water *as soon as moisture begins seeping into the ditch*. If the soil is already moist before you begin sprinkling, you'll need to add only 10 to 16 ounces of water at a time.

8. After watering, put a lid on your sprout garden by placing a second tray upside down on top of the first one.

9. Within two days the young sprouts will be trying to push the plastic lid off! Remove this covering to expose the seedlings to light and add another 10 to 16 ounces of water to the tray. The sprouts should be watered twice a day, preferably in the afternoon and evening. The evening watering should be lighter, especially during the cooler months of the year. Be sure to water *very gently*, as a heavy sprinkle will knock the tender seedlings down into the soil, causing them to rot.

10. Place the trays by a sunny window. Turn them around once or twice a day (easily done when watering) to expose all of the young plants to the incoming light.

You can set up special grow-lights or fluorescent lamps near the window to supplement your natural light. If you leave these lamps on for three to five hours a day, the sprouts will receive light from all sides, making the turning of the trays unnecessary. This combination of natural and artificial lighting is not required unless (a) your windows do not receive direct sun, or (b) you build special indoor shelves for your sprout garden.

With shelves you can increase the available growing area, by utilizing vertical as well as horizontal space. Figure 6 shows a shelf garden used to

Fig. 6 Trays by window with supplementary light

produce a continuous supply of buckwheat, sunflower, and wheat-grass sprouts.

We use shelves that are four feet long and one and one-half feet wide. The exact size and ultimate height of your shelves will be determined by the dimensions of your window. Since sprouts don't need light during the first two days of growth, early sprouts can remain close together on the two lower shelves.

To maintain the continuous productivity of your sprout farm, time your planting on a weekly schedule.

Day 1—Soak enough seeds for three trays.

Day 2—Plant the seeds and place them on the bottom shelf.

Day 3—Soak enough seeds for three more trays. Move established trays to middle shelf.

Day 4—Plant the three new trays. Place these trays on the lower shelf.

Day 5—Soak seeds for three more trays. Move each planted tray up one shelf.

Day 6—Plant the three new trays. Place them on the lower shelf. All three shelves will now be filled.

Day 7—Harvest and remove the trays on the upper shelf. Grow a continuous supply of sprouts for your household by repeating the full process of soaking and planting every other day.

If temperatures in your home range from 65–85°F, and if you've followed the above instructions, every two days you'll be harvesting a miniature jungle. You'll be astounded by the productivity of this method of home food production. If you're growing more food than your household will eat, simply change your planting schedule to allow harvests on a three- to five-day basis.

Harvest sprouts by cutting them at the base of the stem and washing them thoroughly. Since the seedlings will be about six inches long, they'll be easier to eat if you cut them into small pieces (about two inches long) before they're added to salads, soups, or sandwiches.

After the harvest, empty the spent soil into your compost heap or worm bin. Composting allows you to use the same soil repeatedly, thereby reducing the cost and trouble of constantly replacing your supply of sifted soil. Getting your soil from a compost or worm bin will take about ten minutes per tray load. Toward the end of this chapter we'll talk in detail about culturing worms and composting.

Cleaning the sprouts also takes a bit of time. Since they have grown in soil (unlike those of the jar method), you must be sure to remove the attached debris. In addition, many of the sunflower seedlings will still have

Measure soil
temperature to
monitor seedling
growth.

pieces of the hull attached to their first leaves. If you are the type who thoroughly chews your food, this may not pose a problem—the hull will provide a crunchy addition to your meal. However, most people will find it worthwhile to clean off as many hulls as patience allows. This can be done in full during the harvesting/cleaning procedure, or a little at a time when you inspect and water the growing seedlings.

Perhaps the major drawback to this system of home food production is the initial cost of purchasing the planting containers. As we pointed out, plastic cafeteria trays are well suited for the job, and they can be obtained from restaurant suppliers. The 14-by-18-inch trays will cost about $3 apiece; 18-by-26-inch trays will run about $6. Twelve trays will be needed for the three-shelf method we've described (three planted trays on each shelf, three trays covering the seeds on the bottom). This will cost from $36 to $72. You might opt to buy only four or five at a time, experimenting with this technique of food production to see if you're interested in using it further. Another alternative is to use traditional wooden or plastic seed flats. While these containers are less expensive and easier to obtain, they're not nearly so durable or long-lasting as the cafeteria trays. Seed-flat trays usually come with drainage holes, so if you do use them, please remember to modify the watering instructions we stated earlier. Further expenses may include shelving materials and/or lighting fixtures, although shelves often can be built from recycled wood.

Growing Wheat Grass in Trays

The tray method is also a good way to grow wheat grass. Just follow the previous instructions, observing three minor differences:

- Use one cup of dry seeds (approximately 1½ cups after soaking) for a 14-by-18-inch tray.
- Although seeds should touch when spread on the tray, they should never be layered on top of one another.
- You need not be quite so gentle when watering this crop, because the seedlings will not fall into the soil as easily.

Wheat grass is different from most other sprouts; instead of eating the plant, you extract the juice for use as a drink. This liquid is rich in vitamins and chlorophyll and is reputed to have a wide variety of medicinal benefits. However, it has a very strong taste, so only three to four ounces of this strong tonic should be consumed in one sitting. For more information on using wheat grass, we recomend *Be Your Own Doctor*, by Dr. Ann Wigmore.

Raising Seedlings

Perhaps the most popular form of indoor food-plant gardening is growing vegetable seedlings to transplant into the outdoor garden. When you have actual plants, rather than seeds, ready to set out in the spring, you can reap earlier harvests. You'll also extend the length of your growing season and thereby allow certain warm-weather crops more time in which to mature.

At the New Alchemy Institute we grow a wide range of vegetables in seed flats. These include asparagus, broccoli, brussels sprouts, cabbage, Chinese greens, celeriac, celery, collards, eggplant, kale, kohlrabi, leeks, lettuce, mustard, onions, peppers, sorrel, spinach, and tomatoes. We also grow a wide variety of flowers and herbs. Cucumbers, squash, melons, pumpkins, and okra can also be started indoors, but special care is necessary to prevent damage to these seedlings when transplanting them.

To get good germination and grow healthy plants, you must provide proper growing conditions: This means good containers, rich soil, and sufficient levels of light and heat.

SETTING UP
Containers for Starting Plants

Seed flats are shallow containers with holes in the bottom for drainage. We build them with inexpensive 1×4s or furring strips. You can buy plastic flats or use makeshift flats: grocery store produce cartons, half-gallon milk cartons cut in half lengthwise, any kind of old flat pan with holes punched in the bottom. If you're going to do much gardening, however, the regular size and stability of wooden flats is well worth the effort. Don't make them so big that they're awkward to handle when they're full of wet dirt. Ours are about 12 by 18 inches. Take into consideration where you're going to put the flats before you decide on a size. For example, you'll be unhappy if your cold frame will accommodate the width of one and one-half flats instead of two. Seed flats need not be more than three-quarters of an inch deep, as the young plants will be placed in the ground before they've grown an extensive root system.

Soil Mixture

You'll need a light, rich soil mixture to supply the plants with adequate nutrients and encourage the development of strong root systems. Commercial potting mixtures are good but expensive, and it's easy to make your own blend. We use a combination of one-third sifted compost, one-third peat moss, and one-third vermiculite. Nancy Bubel, author of *The Seed-Starter's Handbook,* suggests the following mixtures:

- Equal parts compost, good soil, and sand or perlite or vermiculite.
- One part leaf-mold, two parts loamy soil, and one part sifted compost or rotted manure.
- Four parts good soil, two parts peat, two parts compost or leaf-mold, and two parts vermiculite—plus limestone.

When you prepare a homemade blend, remove pebbles, twigs, and clumps of soil by sifting the materials through a quarter- or half-inch screen. If your garden has a heavy clay soil, you're probably better off not to include it in your mixture, as it may hinder the flat's ability to absorb water.

Heat

Most seeds germinate best around 75°F, a warmer temperature than you would normally maintain in your house. The usual solution is to use an electric soil-heating cable under your seedling flats. We have a shallow wooden box with a heating cable (covered with sand) in the bottom and a lid to close at night to keep it warmer. You do get better germination when the flats are covered, so put a piece of clear plastic or glass over them if you

Fig. 7 Starting and
growing plants under
lights

don't have a box with a lid. A permanent setup is nice but not necessary—
you can keep your heating cable and flats on a shelf or table or floor. Temperatures don't have to be as high for seedling growth as they do for germination, although heat-loving crops (eggplant, peppers, tomatoes,
melons, etc.) appreciate continued warmth.

Light

Once the seeds have germinated, the seedlings will need good light.
While light coming through a window in late winter is sufficient to turn
sprouts green for eating, it isn't sufficient for normal growth of seedling
vegetables. You may have success using aluminum-foil reflectors in con-
junction with a south-facing window. We find we get better peppers, eggplant, and tomatoes under a grow-light near the furnance. You'll need a
double row of tubes to give adequate light to a flat that's 16 inches wide.
You can improvise ways to attach your lights above a shelf or table, or
build a permanent setup of several shelves with lights above each shelf.

The seedlings get more light up close to the tubes, so prop the flats up when the seedlings are tiny and then remove the prop when the plants come within two inches of the light. The recommendation for artificial light is 12–16 hours a day.

PLANTING

Line your flat with a single layer of newspaper, fill it with soil mixture, water well, and firm the soil. Scratch little straight lines to put the seed in—very shallow for tiny seeds, deeper for large ones. We usually make the rows about 1½ inches apart. Space the seeds evenly in the rows and push the soil over on them, firming gently. Normally we place the seeds about ½ inch apart, but small seeds may be planted closer than that. If you suspect they may not have good germination due to age or water damage or whatever, put them much closer together. Be sure to label each row that has a different variety in it. (You think you'll *remember*, but you won't!) Use a waterproof marker, soft pencil, or grease pencil. Plant things that have similar germination periods and similar seedling size in the same flat. You don't want to sow lettuce that will come up in two days, for example, next to parsley that may take two weeks; the lettuce seedlings will be ready for transplanting into a larger container before the parsley even germinates.

Seed flats can lose their moisture quickly, especially when they're placed on heating cables. Don't let them dry out! Seeds won't germinate if they become dehydrated. Even after emerging, the young plants are very sensitive to this condition since they have such a small root system and are confined to a shallow area. Check the soil a couple of times a day to make sure it stays in a moist (but not soppy-wet) condition. Water *regularly* and *thoroughly* with a sprinkling can. Be gentle, or you'll wash away the seeds or damage the young plants.

USING SEEDLINGS

When the seedlings have developed their first true leaves (actually the second set of leaves visible on the seedlings), they can either be (a) thinned out (and possibly eaten), (b) transplanted into a container that provides more room for further growth, (c) transplanted into a permanent container, or (d) transplanted into an outdoor garden.

Thinning Out

Thinning the flat is a simple procedure that gives the young plants more room to grow. You're just removing enough of the seedlings to leave the remainder with space to grow larger. If possible, cut the seedlings at the base instead of pulling them out, so you don't disturb the roots of the remaining plants. Psychologically, it's sometimes difficult to destroy any of that beautiful yield you waited for; but once you see how the survivors grow and thrive, you'll know that you did them (and yourself) a great favor.

Transplanting to Larger Quarters

Transplanting the seedlings into another flat with wider spacing also gives the young plants more room to grow. We like to transplant into plastic nursery cartons (boxes about 3 inches deep, 6 inches wide, and 9 inches long) with drainage holes in the bottom. Into a carton that size we transplant four tomato plants and six of most other things. Take care in removing the small seedlings from the flat. Water them well first, to loosen up the soil and facilitate separating the delicate roots without damaging them. (Again, be careful not to drench.) Take out a little clump of seedlings by digging under them with a finger or a table knife or flat stick. Gently pull the seedlings in the clump apart and set them individually in the new cartons, poking holes in the soil so the roots can fit in easily without bending. If the stems are at all leggy, set them in a little deeper than they were in the flats. Firm the dirt around each plant and water again. *Relabel!* At this point they no longer need the extra heat of the heating cable, but they still need good light.

At New Alchemy, we have cans filled with soil mixture for transplanting. We use the same mix for transplanting flats as we use in the original seed flats. (See p. 26). When plants are kept in small containers like this, they will probably need some extra feeding to keep on growing well. We fertilize them with a commercial preparation of fish emulsion that is rich in nutrients in a form quickly available to the plants. Once every two or three weeks is about the right schedule for feeding. We also use a foliar spray of seaweed extract—the plants absorb the nutrients through their leaves Table 2 provides a schedule of planting and transplanting common vegetables seedlings.

Individual or Permanent Containers

Sometimes we use deeper individual pots for special plants. If you're starting out this way, fill the pot with a good seed-flat mix and add three to five seeds. About two weeks after they have germinated, thin the seedlings by cutting them at their base. In the case of melons or cucumbers, which will be planted on hills, leave two plants in each pot. As we mentioned earlier, cucumbers, melons, squash, pumpkins, and okra don't take well to transplanting because disturbing their roots shocks the entire plant and inhibits its growth. However, these and other plants can be started indoors in biodegradable containers (pots that decompose when placed in the soil)

Table 2 *Double Transplanting for Spring
Gardens*

VEGETABLE	WHEN TO SOW	TIME TO GERMINATION
Broccoli	1st or 2nd week in March	3–4 days
Cabbage	1st or 2nd week in March	3–4 days
Cauliflower	1st or 2nd week in March	3–4 days
Collards	1st or 2nd week in March	3–4 days
Celery	last week in February	2–3 weeks
Chinese cabbage*	mid-March	3 days
Cucumber*	1st week in May	5–6 days
Eggplant	end of March	2 weeks
Kale	1st or 2nd week in March	3–4 days
Lettuce	mid-March	2–3 days
Melons*	1st week in May	5–6 days
Parsley	last week in February	3 weeks
Pepper	1st week in March	2 weeks
Tomatoes	mid-March	3–4 days

*Note: Plant these crops in peat pots; place two or three seeds in each pot. Once the first true leaves have appeared, select the strongest seedling in each pot and pinch off the others. These plants do not get transplanted—the whole pot goes into the

and later set into the garden soil *in* their containers. Peat pots, available at most plant shops, are commonly used for this purpose. Peat pots dry out very quickly, so be sure to supply adequate moisture.

For single plants *not* sensitive to transplanting, we often transplant to half-gallon milk cartons cut in half, or we get gallon ones from a local ice-cream shop. You can use plastic milk jugs with the tops cut off; tin cans with holes ice-picked in the bottom are quite good, too. You can even make individual pots from short cylinders of newspaper and place them in flats to hold them up.

Other special plants, such as herbs and some perennials, can be transplanted to individual pots to grow as houseplants or as outdoor container plants. Patios, porches, balconies, rooftops, and driveways can nurture a wide variety of nutritious edibles in any number of containers.

Transplanting Outdoors

Moving seedlings to the garden will expose them to many erratic environmental conditions while they are still delicate. Often at this stage vegetable seedlings are placed inside a cold frame or under a cloche to ''harden off'' before being put into the outdoor garden. A full discussion of cold

TIME FROM GERMINATION TO FIRST TRANSPLANT	TIME FROM 1ST TO 2ND TRANSPLANT	TOTAL TIME
10 days	2–3 weeks	5–6 weeks
10 days	2–3 weeks	5–6 weeks
10 days	2–3 weeks	5–6 weeks
10 days	2–3 weeks	5–6 weeks
2 weeks	5–6 weeks	9–11 weeks
plant in peat pots—no transplant		5–6 weeks
plant in peat pots—no transplant		5 weeks
2 weeks	6–7 weeks	10–11 weeks
10 days	2–3 weeks	5–6 weeks
10 days	3 weeks	5 weeks
plant in peat pots—no transplant		5–6 weeks
2 weeks	3–4 weeks	8–9 weeks
10–14 days	6–8 weeks (transplant into peat pots)	10–12 weeks
10–14 days	4 weeks (transplant into peat pots)	6 weeks

ground (it's biodegradable). Be sure to skim off the top edge of the pot, which shows above the soil line.

frames, cloches, and outdoor-season-extenders is found in Chapter 4, Outdoor Gardening.

Growing Vegetables Indoors

Growing food indoors need not be confined to raising sprouts and seedlings. Many common vegetables, including lettuce, chard, spinach, mustard, beets, and radishes, can be grown inside near a well-lit window or under artificial light. Others, such as tomatoes, peppers, and eggplant, can be started in large movable containers outdoors during the summer, then brought inside before frost and encouraged to continue their growth and ripening of fruit.

With indoor gardening, your main concerns will be to provide your crops with sufficient space, adequate light, and the correct temperature. Most vegetables do quite well within a range of 50–80°F.

LIGHT

Unless your home is shaded entirely by a neighboring building, there's a good chance that at least some of your windows receive a fair amount of

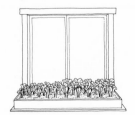

Seedling flat

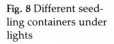

Fig. 8 Different seedling containers under lights

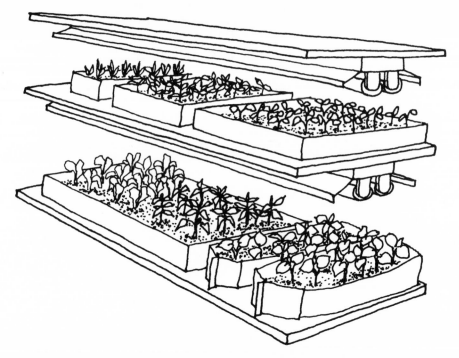

direct sunlight. The vegetables we'll discuss here require at least six hours of direct sunlight for good growth. Windows with a southern exposure are best, since they receive direct sun most of the day. An eastern or western exposure (with a slightly southern orientation) may be adequate. Deciduous trees may hinder indoor vegetable growth during the summer, but in the winter they'll allow plenty of light to enter the window. If the plants you grow near windows tend to lean toward the outside light, you can turn the containers every day or two to produce even growth, or you can add supplementary artificial light on the inside. Turning will be more difficult, of course, if your growing container is long.

Your windowsill garden will suffer if it is exposed to cold winter drafts. Weather-stripping will help your vegetables—and save money on your heating bills as well!

If your windows do not provide enough natural lighting, you can use fluorescent lamps or grow-lights. Artificially lit gardens can be located anywhere in your home, including kitchen cabinets, unused closet space, attics, basements, or even on a table top in your living room. A fluorescent fixture with two 4-foot, 40-watt tubes in a reflector will be sufficient for a 1½ × 4-foot growing area. Leafy and root-producing vegetables grow well under two cool white (or one cool white and one warm white) fluorescent tubes. Replace the tubes after 18 months of full use. Don't buy tubes marked "white" or "daylight," because they are not well-adapted for

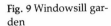

Fig. 9 Windowsill garden

plant growth. Grow-lights are available commercially. Although they may be a little better, they're also more expensive.

Design your indoor display so that you can adjust the height of the lamps to allow room for the growing vegetables. The lights should be six to fifteen inches above the top of the plants. Lamps should be turned on for a period of 12 to 18 hours a day. Since your plants will need some actual darkness as well, it's best to turn the lights on in the morning and off before you go to bed.

CONTAINERS AND SOIL

Although some vegetables can grow in shallow soil, you should stick with containers that are at least eight inches deep. This is particularly important for root crops such as carrots and beets. They won't produce well if their roots hit the bottom of the pot. Many types of boxes and buckets can serve as containers. Large clay or plastic pots eight inches or more in diameter (similar to those used for houseplants) or home-built wooden frames are probably your best bet.

Construct your boxes 1½ feet wide and 8–12 inches deep. Their lengths can vary to fit your available space. To prevent rotting, you should treat wooden boxes with a preservative. Unfortunately, many of the wood preservatives with which we're familiar contain toxic chemical compounds. (This includes some that *claim* they don't.) Two notable exceptions are copper nephthenate or zinc nephthenate. Or, you can build frames from redwood or cypress. Otherwise, reconcile yourself to the fact that you'll have to replace the containers after they've been used a few times.

When you build the frames, be sure to provide for adequate drainage. A ⅛- to ¼-inch hole every 6 inches will do. Drainage can also be achieved by using pieces of wood for the bottom and leaving slight gaps between the strips. Place trays or dishes under the frames to keep water from dripping onto the floor.

Since your plants will be growing in a small area, it is critical that you supply them with proper nutrients. Begin with good soil. Regular garden soil tends to become crusty and compacted in containers, so you will probably want to purchase—or make your own—special mix. Two excellent blends are:

> one-half sifted compost
> one-quarter peat moss
> one-quarter vermiculite
>   (sand can substitute for some of the
>   vermiculite; rotten manure
>   can replace the compost)

or

> one-third commercial potting mix
> one-third sifted compost
> one-third garden soil

One of the nice things about these mixes is that they're alive with various soil organisms (possibly even earthworms). Most soil microbes are beneficial to plants. However (there's always a catch), a few are harmful. Here at

New Alchemy we rarely have problems with pests in our soil mix. We have *never* sterilized our soil. If you want to sterilize your blend, you can place it in an oven set at 300°F for half an hour. Unfortunately, sterilization kills the beneficial soil microbes as well as those that are potentially harmful. We believe it's not worth the trade-off.

Even with the best soil mixture, most container-grown vegetables will benefit from an occasional addition of fertilizer. Organic fertilizers include seaweed extract, fish emulsion and rock minerals. Solid fertilizers can be applied after the plants have begun to grow or at the beginning when you add the soil mixture to the container. Liquid fertilizers can be fed every 1½ to 3 weeks when you routinely water the plants. Commercial products are quite strong, so be sure to follow the recommendations printed on the package. (You'll be sorry if you take the "more is better" approach.)

Water collected from soaking sprouts can be applied as a nutrient boost to indoor vegetables. You can also make liquid homegrown fertilizers by soaking compost or manure in a sealed bucket for about a week. Unfortunately, this "manure tea" has a foul odor (as does fish emulsion, a popular commercial fertilizer). These organic brews also tend to be low in phosphorous and potassium, two important plant nutrients particularly vital for root crops. You can balance them out by sprinkling a *very* thin layer of wood ash on top of the soil every few weeks. Wood ash is high in both potassium and phosphorous, but it can hinder seed germination; so never use it before the plants are a couple of inches tall.

SPECIFIC PLANTS

Mustard, lettuce, spinach, and Swiss chard all grow well under lights. Except for chard, these leafy plants are particularly sensitive to warm weather. They will "bolt" (send up a seed stalk) if temperatures are too high. Spinach will bolt when it's exposed to excessive amounts of light. If this starts to occur, harvest your plants immediately or they'll become inedible. Bolting can be avoided by growing these crops in the spring, fall, or winter, when household temperatures are likely to range between 55 and 68°F. Leave lights on no more than 14 hours a day.

Lettuce

Lettuce is perhaps the favorite indoor vegetable. With some modifications, lettuce-growing instructions can be applied to the various other greens we've discussed

The many different kinds of lettuce can be divided into four general categories: large head lettuce (varieties include Great Lakes or Iceberg); small head lettuce (e.g., Buttercrunch); loose-leaf (Oak Leaf and Salad Bowl, for example); and romaine (e.g., Paris White). All types may be grown indoors.

Loose-leaf has some advantages over other lettuces for indoors. It matures in about 40 to 50 days, a good 4 to 6 *weeks* before the others. You don't need large fully grown plants to begin harvesting. Pick the outer leaves continuously or plant seeds thickly and harvest some of the thinnings every few days. These two approaches may be combined to provide constant growing room for the plants. Remember, if you eat your thinnings and use your available space efficiently, you can grow a lot of food in a small area.

Other Greens and Root Crops

Spinach and mustard need 4- to 6-inch spacing for the final crop. They reach maturity in approximately 45 days. Swiss chard needs about 8 inches and reaches maturity in about 70 days. You can increase total yields in the container by adjusting the distance between the rows. Consider using the method of diamond spacing. Figure 10 shows how diamond spacing places plants in equilateral triangles instead of squares; this can decrease by about 10 percent the distance needed between rows and thereby increase the number of plants accommodated.

All these leafy crops can be grown in indoor window boxes. Certain root crops, including carrots, beets, and radishes, also grow well in these settings. Beets produce flavorful greens as well as roots. Radish greens are also edible (best if they're steamed with other vegetables). Final spacing for beets should be 3 to 4 inches; they take 50 to 60 days until maturity. Carrots require 70 to 80 days and should be spaced at 2 to 3 inches. Most varieties of radish grow to maturity in 20 to 30 days, spaced 1 to 2 inches apart.

BRINGING PLANTS INDOORS IN WINTER

One of the nicest things about indoor gardening is that it enables you to save many of your outdoor plants from the cold weather of fall and winter. Tomatoes, eggplants, and peppers grown in large containers (such as five-gallon buckets) can be brought indoors before the first frost to allow for full ripening of late fruit. Start plants especially for this purpose a month or so later than you do plants that ripen outdoors. Choose small or "patio" varieties of tomatoes. With proper timing, you can have fruit until Christmas, although ripening is much slower in the late fall. Make sure the plants have adequate natural or artificial lighting.

You may also consider bringing in some of your favorite herbs before the first frost. These plants, grouped in trays on kitchen windowsills or hung in baskets, are very attractive. The fragrance that herbs add to the winter home is alone worth the price of admission

The culinary herbs that grow easily indoors are thyme, sage, oregano, and parsley. Chives, mints, and lemon balm will be encouraged by regular watering and a slightly richer potting soil containing extra compost. Like

Fig. 10 Increasing yields with diamond spacing: above, diamond spacing, 38 plants; below, conventional spacing, 32 plants.

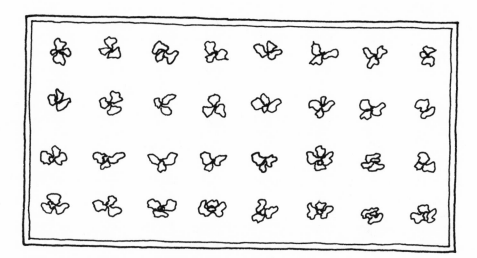

other houseplants, herbs thrive if occasionally put under the shower spray for a few minutes or if misted with a plant sprayer. If you dig these plants out of your garden, try not to damage the roots. Parsley has quite a long tap root; if it's broken, the plant may survive but it will tend to go to seed. Keep as much of the dirt around the roots as possible and place the plant in the indoor pot. Herbs generally transplant better if you cut back some of their leaves. Be sure to water frequently after transplanting.

Dill and basil are short-lived annuals that will do better if seeded directly in midseason in pots you will bring indoors in the fall.

You can harvest your herbs frequently, but don't cut off more than half the leaves at a time.

EVERYDAY CARING FOR YOUR PLANTS

Once you have planted and established your indoor garden, it will be time to do the everyday work: watering and insect control. These are the most difficult, because they demand your continuous attention. You have to be diligent in watering your indoor vegetables, because the containers can dry out quickly, especially in warm weather. Thorough, as-needed waterings are far more beneficial than frequent, light sprinklings.

You can't really tell if the container should be watered just by looking at the upper soil. Instead, stick your finger right in and feel whether or not the soil is moist. Since overwatering can suffocate the plant's roots and cause soil compaction, don't water unless it's necessary.

As we noted earlier, soil in newly seeded containers should be kept moist until the plants have germinated. Unfortunately, this very requirement can encourage a fatal condition called "damping-off." Damping-off is a fungal disease that attacks the tender stems of newly emerged seedlings, causing the plants to fall over and die. The disease is discouraged by adequate air circulation. Planting seeds under a very thin (⅛- to ¼-inch) covering of sand, vermiculite, or sphagnum moss instead of soil also helps to prevent this condition. If some seedlings fall over after emerging, remove the dead ones, reduce waterings, and encourage air circulation (perhaps by discreetly using a fan). Damping-off is also caused by contaminated soil. If most of your plants are affected, empty the container, scrub it out with ammonia and water, and use new soil. The old soil can be added to an indoor or outdoor compost heap.

By creating a healthy soil mixture and adding supplemental fertilizer, you should be able to avoid most nutrient deficiencies and diseases. Still, you might be bothered by insects. Many pests can be controlled simply by handpicking. If at all possible, avoid the use of poisons (even organic ones). After all, you'll end up eating the stuff! Several methods of safe biological control are described in Chapter 3, Solar Greenhouse Gardening.

Indoor Composting Through Worm Culture

Lately it seems as though the old proverb "waste not, want not" has been replaced by "no deposit, no return." The per-capita trash disposal of Americans averages an astounding six pounds per day. Much of this garbage is actually valuable material that can be reused. This is particularly true of kitchen wastes, which include leftover table scraps, spoiled food, fruit rinds, coffee grounds, vegetable peels, eggshells, etc. If you isolate these materials from the general trash, you can reuse the nutrients by composting the "garbage" into a rich, valuable plant fertilizer.

This transformation is quite sanitary and may even be done indoors. One of the most effective methods is to place the kitchen wastes in small boxes containing garden soil, an organic medium, and earthworms. The worms will consume the composting food, digest some of its nutrients, and mix the remains into the soil, thereby enriching it. Soil contains a wide variety of microorganisms that help break down wastes. The final mixture, known as *castings,* is prized for its beneficial effects on the growth of houseplants, flowers, and vegetables.

There are many species of earthworms. The red worm (*Lumbricus rubellus*), smaller than the commonly known night crawler, is most ideally suited for intensive culture. This is because the red worm is able to utilize a wide variety of foods, grows well in small areas, thrives in high population densities, and is a prolific breeder. Under favorable conditions, these worms will double in population every 60 to 150 days.

Worms are expensive critters; commercially, one pound—containing approximately 1300 worms of all sizes—costs between $3 and $10. Ideally, a home-composting unit for a family of five should contain about fifteen pounds of worms. This would cost between $45 and $150. To save money, buy about five pounds of initial stock and give them time to reproduce. Assuming the composting units (earthworm beds) are properly tended, and that the worms double in population every 150 days, you'll have the needed number in less than a year.

ESTABLISHING THE BEDS

Earthworm beds can be located in an inconspicuous but convenient space, such as a storeroom or basement. Their optimum size will depend upon the population density of worms in the bins and the amount of kitchen wastes produced by the household. A family of five will find that a well-stocked bin about 6 feet long and 3½ feet wide (21 square feet) is sufficient. While the exact length and width of the boxes can vary according to your setting, they should be at least 1½ feet deep. The boxes can be made of recycled containers, such as refrigerator liners, or they can be constructed from newly purchased materials. Wooden frames are excellent; however, the lumber should not be treated with lead-based paint or creosote, because these compounds are harmful to earthworms. You can treat wood with either zinc nephthenate or copper nephthenate, both of which are available at most lumber stores. Redwood, cedar, and other aromatic woods should be avoided, as their resinous saps will inhibit the worms. And don't use pine lumber, because it soaks up water and can decay when exposed to the moist bedding. Locust wood is a good bet.

Adequate drainage can be provided by drilling one or two ⅛-inch holes every square foot. These holes should be covered with a fine screen to prevent the worms from escaping. To ensure against rust, use nylon or other

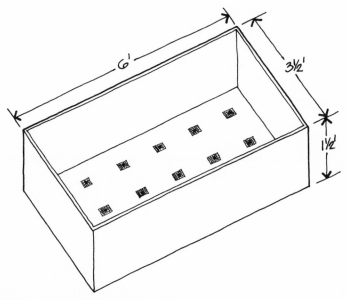

Fig. 11 Wooden worm bed with drainage holes and screening

nonmetallic materials for screening. Figure 11 gives you an idea of how your completed worm bed will look.

At least 10 days before you obtain your earthworms, fill the frames with a proper soil-like medium. A number of materials, including shredded cardboard or a sawdust/coffee-grounds mixture, can be used for this purpose. Among the best substances are horse manure (at least six months old), mature compost, or leaf mold. The bedding should be moist but not sopping wet and it should have a neutral pH. (We'll talk more about pH later.) Fill the frame with the bedding medium, water it, and wait at least ten days before stocking it with worms. This time lag will enable you to establish proper levels of moisture, pH, and temperature. If the manure is not aged and is still rapidly decomposing, it will heat up when placed in the box. Temperatures above 85°F will be unhealthy for the worms. Aerating the bed by thoroughly stirring the manure every three to four days will hasten the cooling process.

When you obtain your starting stock of worms, empty them on top of the prepared bedding and gently spread them out. Shine a bright light on the worms to drive them down into the bed and to discourage them from attempting to leave it. As a further precaution, make sure that the top level of the soil is at least three inches *below* the rim of the container. If you've purchased only five pounds of worms, use a wooden inner partition to restrict them to about one-half of the bed for the first six months. Red worms breed most prolifically when placed in high densities, so restricting their physical environment will help speed their rate of reproduction.

Special care is required to assist the worms in adapting to their new environment. Faithfully observe the following precautions throughout the first week.

- Leave a light shining on the bed.
- Lightly water once a day.
- Check pH levels every other day.
- Do *not* begin adding kitchen wastes.

MAINTAINING THE BEDS

Earthworms are relatively easy to please, but these intensive beds must be properly tended. Routine maintenance includes ensuring that the following conditions prevail at all times:

An adequate food supply.   Unless there is enough food, worms will neither grow nor reproduce.

Correct temperatures.   The temperature of the beds should remain between 60° and 80°F. When the level goes below 50°F, the worms' activities will be slowed. They will die if exposed to frost.

Correct amounts of air and moisture.   Earthworms like a moist environment, not too wet and not too dry. To test moisture, take a handful of material from the middle of the bed at a depth of four or five inches. Remove as many worms as possible and squeeze the sample. If water droplets are not released, it is too dry. When more than five to ten droplets drip out, it is too wet. Another way to tell if the bed is too dry is by looking at the worms. Dry soil will cling to their skin. If the soil has a proper amount of moisture, or if it is too wet, the worms can be removed without these attached particles. Moisture levels should be checked about once a week. When the bedding is dry, use a sprinkling can to distribute water evenly over the bed. If it is too moist, introduce air by gently turning the top six inches of soil with your hand or with a four- or five-pronged digging fork. Aerate the upper layer every two to three weeks, regardless of the moisture level, to prevent the bedding from compacting.

Proper pH.   By testing the bedding's pH, you can determine its degree of acidity. The pH scale ranges from 0–14; 7 is neutral; a lower number indicates an acidic state and a higher number indicates alkalinity. Red worms are most comfortable when the pH of their environment is close to neutral (between 6.8 and 7.2). The easiest way to test a bed's pH is to use litmus paper, which is available at most drugstores. When the paper is pressed into a ball of moistened soil, it will change color, taking various shades of red and blue. This color change reflects the pH of the sample. Color codes are available with the paper.

If the pH is too high (alkaline), the worms will become thin and sickly, and may die. High-alkaline conditions (pH 8 or more) can be remedied by thoroughly watering the bed and mixing in an acidic material such as used coffee grounds or peat moss. Acidic conditions, also fatal to the worms, can be remedied by applying agricultural limestone (do not use hydrated or quick-lime). A level teaspoon per square foot is usually sufficient to alleviate a mildly acidic state. The lime should be applied on top of the bed and lightly watered in. If the bed is highly acidic, with a pH of less than 6, mix one teaspoon of lime per square foot into the top six inches of bedding, then sprinkle an additional teaspoon on top and lightly water it in. Check the pH of the bed two or three days later to determine whether or not the acidic condition has been relieved. When a bed is acidic and already fairly wet, simply mix the limestone into the soil. Liming the beds should be a routine practice, since the rapid decomposition of organic matter tends to make the medium acidic. Test pH levels once a week.

FEEDING

Feeding the worms is a simple matter. Begin by keeping kitchen scraps separate from other household garbage. Five-gallon plastic buckets with handles and lids are well suited for this purpose. Used containers can be obtained inexpensively at most donut shops. A lidded bucket of kitchen wastes, emptied frequently and occasionally washed, will not smell bad. In fact this process actually is quite sanitary, as odorous substances are confined instead of being left in the general trash.

Worms will consume most of your food wastes, although meat and dairy scraps will take longer to decay than will vegetable matter. (Worms can't eat bones or shells.) Generally, the smaller the individual substances, the quicker they will be consumed. Shredding, grinding, or blending the materials is helpful though not necessary. Large materials, like whole spoiled fruit, should be broken or cut into small pieces.

Mix about one-third cup limestone into each five-gallon container of kitchen scraps. Coffee grounds and fruit rinds (particularly citrus) are more acidic than other wastes and will require a bit more lime. Here is a four-step method of applying feed to the worm beds.

1. Along the side of the bed, dig a trench 9 to 12 inches deep and 6 to 8 inches wide.
2. Fill the trench with the food, and mix in the limestone (about one-third cup for a five-gallon container). Stir in the limestone with a small hand trowel. Stoics can use their hands.
3. Take some of the soil that was displaced when you made the trench, and cover the food. A thin layer of soil (3 to 4 inches) will reduce the

odors of the decomposing wastes and thereby decrease potential problems with flies. Sprinkle some limestone on top and mix it into this soil layer.

4. So that food will be distributed to all areas, subsequent trenches should circle the outer perimeter of the bed. A five-gallon bucket will fill a trench about three feet long.

The worms will migrate toward the feed and will actively begin to consume it within one to three weeks. If your household produces a five-gallon container of wastes every five days, you will end up circling the entire bed in about one month's time. At this point, most of the feed in the original trench will have been consumed. You can then begin recircling the bed. If the quantities of food in the original trench have not yet decomposed, postpone adding scraps to that trench. Instead, begin a new feeding zone running down the middle of the bed. Make sure that you leave some space between the side and middle trenches. Decaying food in the upper portions of the bed will block air from entering the lower soil. The decomposing wastes also tend to heat up and at certain stages of decay emit unfavorable gases into the surrounding soil. With space between the trenches, worms can safely migrate in and out of these areas and air will still penetrate the soil. Each trench in Fig. 12 is approximately three feet long.

Because kitchen scraps are often quite wet, usually the feeding zones will not need to be watered. If you do have a lot of dry material in your waste bucket, add water before placing it in the bed. Feeding zones may be aerated every week to ten days by gently lifting a section a couple of inches up and allowing oxygen to penetrate. Do not turn the trenches as you would the rest of the bed. If you feel the area is too acidic, sprinkle in some lime.

Fig. 12 Placement and order of worm feeding

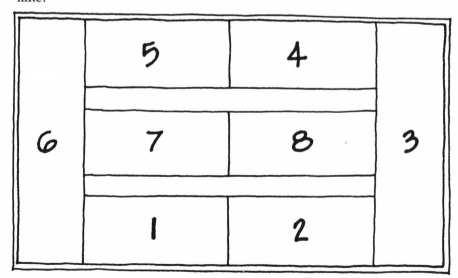

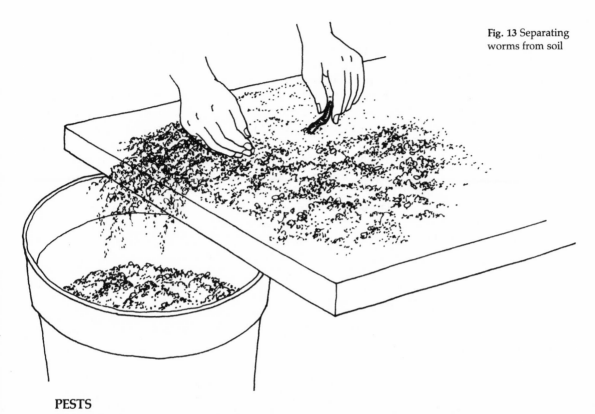

Fig. 13 Separating worms from soil

PESTS

A worm bed is a living ecosystem inhabited by a number of micro-scopic organisms. Large numbers of nematodes (small roundworms about one-quarter inch long) and small brown-and-white mites found in the bed help decompose the food. They are not bothersome to the homeowner, to the earthworms, or to the plants that are fertilized with the castings.

However, red mites are an earthworm pest. They are smaller than most plant mites, bright red in color, and resemble a very small red spider. If a bed becomes infested with these creatures, you can place melon rinds on the surface to act as a lure and then dispose of the infested rinds. Frequent trappings will provide some assistance in controlling red-mite populations. Maintaining a neutral pH in the bedding is the best way to discourage these unwelcome guests.

HARVESTING

In addition to its food-waste-disposal service, a composting worm bed produces two valuable assets: rich soil and continuous production of the worms themselves. The soil contains many of the nutrients originally present in the food wastes, which are a rich soil supplement. A mixture of one-half worm soil and one-half vermiculite will promote the health and vigor of seedlings started in flats. Houseplants will also thrive when grown in this mixture. In the garden, place a handful of the soil in holes dug for vegetable or flower transplants.

To harvest wormless soil, dig out a portion of the bed that is relatively dry and free from undecomposed food. Place a mound of soil on a board or table under a bright light. As the worms migrate down an inch or two to avoid the light, remove the upper layer of soil. Repeat this process every few minutes. By the time you get to the bottom of the mound, you'll have a batch of relatively worm-free soil (you'll undoubtedly miss a few) and a bunch of squiggly worms. Since the harvest process is rather slow, you might prefer doing more than one mound at a time.

When a large amount of soil is harvested, add fresh bedding material to replace the lost volume. Since this will supply additional feed to the worms, harvesting about one-third to one-half of the soil every six months will actually improve the productivity of the bed.

Both the worms and the castings are useful in the garden. Add a handful of worms, along with adequate organic fertilizers, to the soil around newly established bushes and trees. As they eat the organic matter, the worms slowly will make nutrients available to the young plants. Worm-compost soil usually is significantly richer than the surrounding soil in major plant elements such as nitrogen, phosphorus, and potassium. Worms also strengthen the drainage capacity of heavy soils.

If you are raising chickens or fish, worms will make an excellent supplemental feed. You'll also have a homegrown ready supply of fishing bait. Be neighborly and leave a few worms outside in bowls during the spring to help your local birds feed their youngsters. Charm your friends by giving them a batch of worms to start their own waste-disposal units.

You can also transfer large numbers of worms (to stock a new bed or feed chickens) simply by digging and moving a section of the feed trench, worms, soil, and all. This procedure is not recommended if clean worms are required, because it is difficult to separate the worms from decaying food.

INDOOR COMPOSTING OF SPROUT WASTES

Remember from our earlier discussion that sprouts can be grown in soil for an increase in minerals, and that there may be wastes from the sprouting process such as unsprouted seeds, seed hulls, soaking water, and roots of clipped sprouts. The nutrients in these sprout wastes can be recycled by indoor composting to produce rich soil for the tray method of sprouting. Worm bins used for this specific purpose can be simpler than the ones we've just described. A less elaborate version, such as that shown in Fig. 14, will be adequate. *Note:* The inner bucket must have holes for drainage. Place bricks in the lower bucket to allow room for water and to ensure that the two containers do not become stuck together.

After you've punched and screened holes in the bottom of the upper container, add two or three gallons of well-rotted compost and about 1000 worms. After each harvest of sprouts, empty the spent soil into this bucket. A 24-gallon container will hold about 25 trays of soil with some room to spare. Aerate and add moisture if necessary. Since sprout wastes are far less acidic than kitchen scraps, much less limestone will be needed to maintain a neutral pH within the bedding. The only other necessary maintenance chore is the occasional separation of the buckets to drain whatever water has collected in the lower one. Loaded with nutrients, this liquid should be used as a fertilizer for your houseplants or garden.

The speed with which the earthworms convert the sprout wastes into castings will depend largely on their population density. Even with high densities, you'll have to wait a few weeks after emptying the last tray for the full bucket to contain castings acceptable for reuse as a planting medium for sprouts. If necessary, you can harvest some of the lower soil before the upper regions have fully decomposed. Dedicated growers probably will find it worthwhile to maintain more than one worm bin in order to keep a continuous supply of soil on hand. Sift the mixture to remove worms and undecomposed matter (such as sunflower hulls) before replanting.

Fig. 14 Two 24-gallon drums, one placed within the other

BIBLIOGRAPHY

Bubel, Nancy. *The Seed-Starter's Handbook.* Emmaus, PA: Rodale Press, 1978.

Carter, Gary. *The Beansprout Book.* New York: Simon and Schuster, 1973.

Cross Whyte, Karen. *The Complete Sprouting Cookbook.* San Francisco: Troubador Press, 1973.

Farallones Institute. *The Integral Urban House.* San Francisco: Sierra Club Books, 1979.

Flanagan, Ted. *Growing Food and Flowers in Containers.* Charlotte, VT: Garden Way Publishing Co., 1973.

Gaddie, Ronald E., and Donald E. Douglas. *Earthworms for Ecology and Profit,* Vol. I and Vol. II. Ontario, CA: Bookworm Pub. Co., 1977.

Hunter, Margaret K., and Edgar H. Hunter. *The Indoor Garden.* New York: John Wiley and Sons, 1978.

Jordan, William H., Jr. *Windowsill Ecology.* Emmaus, PA: Rodale Press, 1977.

Newcomb, Duane. *The Apartment Farmer.* New York: Avon Publishing Co., 1977.

Olkowski, Helga, and William Olkowski. *The City People's Book of Raising Food.* Emmaus, PA: Rodale Press, 1979.

Ray, Richard M. (ed.) *Fundamentals of Gardening.* San Francisco: Ortho Books, 1976.

Wigmore, Ann. *Be Your Own Doctor.* New York: Hemisphere Press. (Available from Hippocrates Health Inst., 25 Exeter St. Boston, MA. 02116.)

Yepsen, Roger B., ed. *Home Food Systems.* Emmaus, PA: Rodale Press, 1981.

Chapter 3

Solar Greenhouse Gardening

Colleen Armstrong and Susan Ervin

In 1974, researchers at New Alchemy set out to design a year-round food-growing ecosystem for the cold-winter climate that we experience here in the Northeast. Our goal was to devise a system that would: not require heat from fossil-fuel; never use chemical fertilizers or synthetic pesticides; rely on biological resources and nutrient-cycling for healthy and productive plant growth. It was to be affordable, durable, and buildable, either as a freestanding structure or attached to the southern side of a conventional building. The New Alchemy bioshelter was born that year.

With mixed expertise and plenty of sweat, we built our first bioshelter, a freestanding, one-hundred-percent passive solar structure that satisfied our criteria and made year-round food production possible. Thermal storage replaced furnaces; rich compost replaced fertilizers; and beneficial insects in an integrated control program replaced pesticides. A living ecosystem was established, and the plans for building such structures were made widely available.

People often ask, ''Aren't all greenhouses solar heated?, Are bioshelters and solar greenhouses the same thing?, If not, what's the difference?'' The distinction between a bioshelter and a solar greenhouse is that a bioshelter is *multifunctional*. Our bioshelters enclose diverse, highly integrated ecosystems in which the by-products of one organism become the raw materials for another. For example, our fish ponds store solar heat and raise fish protein; futher, they supply to hydroponic and soil agriculture plenty of warm, fertile water enriched with fish wastes.

Whether you're talking bioshelters or solar greenhouses, today's business is booming—and justifiably so. Contractors here on Cape Cod can't keep up with local market demand, and green-house designs and materials are improving almost daily. A once-dying commercial glass industry is being revived by the solar-greenhouse boom. Homeowners of all ages are discovering that greenhouses—from compact little cold frames all the way up to attached bioshelters—provide a most rewarding supplement to the family income.

To determine whether or not you can take advantage of the solar-greenhouse concept, you must consider several things. This chapter is a good place to start your research. Colleen and Susan, as well as Kathi Ryan, have guided our greenhouse agriculture work individually and collectively for more than eight years. They're among a very small number of true enclosed-solar-garden-ing specialists in the country, if not the world. Colleen is the man-ager of the Cape Cod Ark, our largest commercial-scale bioshelter. She has studied, taught, and written about most aspects of solar greenhouse management, especially biological pest control.

They have divided the chapter into four sections, all of which focus on plant production. "Why a Solar Greenhouse?" is a brief overview of the different types and sizes of solar greenhouses and their contribution to home food production. "Smaller Green-houses" explores the use of mini-greenhouses: cold frames, hot-beds, and cloches. "Larger Greenhouses" offers an extensive dis-cussion of how to get the most benefit from a large solar greenhouse; here you'll examine climate considerations, agricul-tural management, special tips for individual crops, maximizing food production, harvesting, seedling production, and insect con-trol. Finally, the authors have prepared a Home Greenhouse Ques-tionnaire to help you reach your own best decision.

Other important greenhouse food systems, such as aquacul-ture and hydroponics, are discussed in detail in Chapter 5.

THE EDITORS

Why a Solar Greenhouse?

WHEN IT COMES to year-round food growing, a solar greenhouse is the ultimate in season extenders. Here in the Northeast where we depend largely on trucked-in foods during the long winter, solar greenhouses promise fresh, locally grown vegetables 12 months a year. Green salads made with lettuce and other fresh vegetables are most expensive in the winter, and a steady home supply is a valuable resource. In addition, fresh greenhouse vegetables provide a constant supply of vitamins and minerals.

Whereas conventional greenhouses rely on supplemental light and fossil fuel to provide the exact conditions needed for plant growth, solar greenhouses are designed to obtain their heat and light entirely for the sun. Energy enters the greenhouse in the form of sunlight, which is either directly utilized for plant growth or converted to heat and stored. The greenhouse is oriented toward the south to allow maximum exposure to the sun, and the glazing angle is such the light will pass throught efficiently even during the cold winter months.

Solar greenhouses come in a wide range of sizes. The simplest ones can be categorized as mini-greenhouses. These season extenders are not quite year-round structures, but they are low in cost and easy to construct. Gardeners have been using cold frames and cloches (see Fig. 1) for years in order to start seedlings in early spring and keep crops going in late fall.

Fig. 1 Cloche in winter

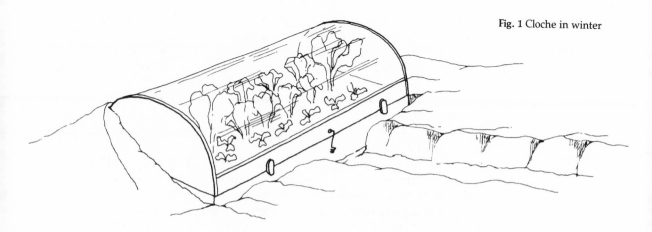

Fig. 2 Daytime warm-air circulation in an attached greenhouse

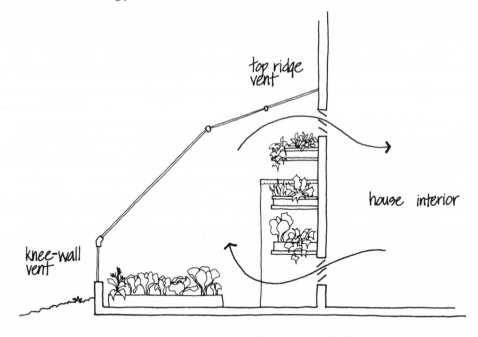

top ridge vent

house interior

knee-wall vent

Larger greenhouses may be freestanding or attached. A site is selected not only for optimal solar orientation, but also for protection from the wind. Most larger greenhouses are double-glazed to retain heat as well as admit sunlight. Thick walls absorb heat, and additional heat storage in the form of rock or water mass is included inside the house. Curtains can be used over the glazing to shield against nighttime cold.

Perhaps most popular is the attached greenhouse; this dual-purpose structure provides a solar heat source for the home as well as a place to grow food year 'round (see Fig. 2). An attached greenhouse is built *onto* a house, a school, a community building, a restaurant, a senior citizens' home, or just about any other type of building. Attached greenhouses can provide the building with additional humidity and oxygen, not to mention a unique extra living space. New solar homes approach 100-percent reliance on solar heat; a well-designed greenhouse built onto the southern side of an existing house can provide up to 50 percent of its heat.

If the design or siting of your house won't accommodate a solar greenhouse attached to the southern side, you can build a freestanding greenhouse that has the correct orientation. Often, freestanding greenhouses are snuggled back into an earth bank on the northern side; this provides good insulation and protection from wind (see Fig. 3). A freestanding greenhouse can afford a larger growing area than an attached, and may be suitable for a school or community project.

Exploring the design and functions of solar greenhouses has been one of New Alchemy's primary tasks. We call our greenhouses bioshelters, to

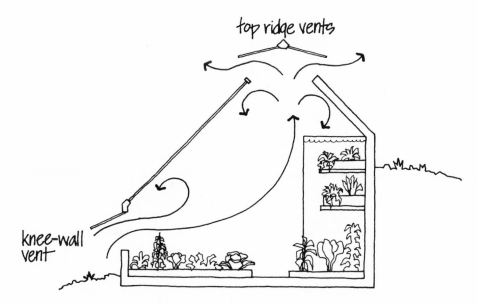

top ridge vents

knee-wall
vent

Fig. 3 Knee-wall vent
and top-ridge vent for
freestanding green-
house

indicate that they're not just buildings, but living ecosystems. The abundance of life is the most captivating aspect of a bioshelter. In *Tomorrow Is
Our Permanent Address* (pp. 143–144), Nancy Todd describes a winter visit
to our largest bioshelter, the Ark:

> For people who live in a climate in which they must cope with long
> months of hard, frozen ground, cold, snow, and ice, having access to a
> bioshelter can be as revitalizing as the proverbial old-fashioned spring tonic.
> Once, on a frigid day in February, we took friends to see the Cape Cod Ark
> for the first time with their children. The sun was bright, glancing off the icy
> snow, but the wind was biting. We slithered and skidded toward the Ark,
> clutching the children, the children clutching at us. The rutted ice had
> nowhere relented into puddles except right in front of the building, where
> the reflected sunlight in the solar courtyard had forced a slight glacial retreat.
>
> The feeling on opening the door of the Ark and stepping in was one that
> compares to the moment of stepping out of a plane newly arrived in the trop-
> ics, having flown out of winter. At once we were engulfed by moist, soft,
> warm air and the smells of plants and earth. All of us, even the children,
> paused for a moment and let it wash over us. The next impression was one of
> green; of the depth and vibrance of the green of the plants in contrast to the
> hard, bright, white-and-blue world that we had just closed the door on.
>
> We began to move about and explore, shedding clothes as we went.
> Down and wool had begun to feel prickly and cumbersome. The children
> dashed about, discovering frogs and flowers and a strawberry in blossom.
> We launched into an explanation of the building as our friends drifted about,
> enjoying first the flowers—nasturtiums, geraniums, alyssum, and the inevita-

ble New Alchemy marigolds—then the range of plants and herbs. Finally, we wended our way to the solar-algae ponds, where the children had glued their noses to the outsides of a tank, waiting for a fish to emerge through the gloom of the deep-green, algae-laden water.

It was, granted, one of those propitious, kindly days when the Ark was at its best, well past its solstice slump, with an eighty-degree temperature brought on by the intense sun. But even after many seasons, with the novelty long gone, we find it impossible to be blasé about being close to our bioshelters. The earthy smells and the greenness are wonderfully reassuring. The earth is, after all, only asleep. Winter is not absolute and eternal, however fierce and adamant it seems. And we have a distinct feeling of satisfaction—bordering at times, we're afraid, on smugness—that apart from the fossil fuels used once in manufacture, this climatic outpost of a garden is not based on an ongoing and illicit consumption of a nonrenewable resource. Nor is it robbing other people of their share of that resource. Nor—again except during its manufacture—is it a source of harm to our area of the Cape. And beyond the unquestioned economic and gustatory pleasure, there is an unqualified joy in knowing we can provide our family and occasionally our friends with fresh salad, herbs, and vegetables grown without poisons.

RESOURCES

Several excellent sources for solar-greenhouse design are: *The Solar Greenhouse Book,* by James C. McCullagh; *The Complete Greenhouse Book,* by Peter Clegg and Derry Watkins; and *The Food and Heat Producing Solar Greenhouse,* by Rick Fisher and William Yanda.

Also, you may find that in your community there is an experienced solar designer and builder who will know how to design well for local conditions.

Smaller Greenhouses

People tend to be dazzled by the idea of large greenhouses. We certainly can't deny that large greenhouses are excellent season extenders, but we must admit that they can also be expensive—at least in terms of initial investment. Here at New Alchemy we've found a lot of less costly ways to extend your season. Cold frames, hotbeds, and cloches are all good examples. In this section, you'll find out how to build, maintain, and use these ''miniature'' greenhouses.

COLD FRAMES

Cold frames are outdoor boxes with transparent lids that can be opened and shut. Many good plans for cold frames are available—nearly every gardening book suggests plans for at least one. The simplest method

"The feeling on opening the door of the Ark and stepping in was [like] stepping out of a plane newly arrived in the tropics . . . At once we were engulfed by moist, soft, warm air and the smells of plants and earth."

is to place your seedlings against the southern wall of your house and position a window over the seedlings and against the wall. This will provide some protection. You can make your own temporary cold frame by placing bales of straw or bags of leaves in a rectangle and arranging old window frames covered by a sheet of clear plastic over them. Heavy rain, though, will fill up the center of the sheet and cause the plastic to fall in on your prized seedlings. To avoid this, tilt your cover sheet from north to south; this allows rain to run off and admits more winter southern sunlight.

For a more durable, permanent cold frame, choose a spot (near the garden) that offers at least six hours of spring and summer direct-sun exposure. Level it off and build a rectangular frame about two feet high at the back and about a foot high in the front. It can be any length and width you like. These dimensions are determined by how much space you want and what you intend to use for the lid. Old window frames are good and cheap, sometimes even free. At New Alchemy, we find that the glass covers break too easily; we like to use fiberglass, which is lighter and easier to lift. A double-glazed box will retain more heat than a single-glazed one will. Even a sheet of plastic thrown over the frame will help. The lids should be hinged at the back and have a wooden bar or something to rest on when they're open, with door hooks to keep them from blowing down. They can also be propped open with sticks; but either way, you should tie a long, strong string between the edge of the lid and the front of the box frame to keep the lid from blowing over and ripping out the hinge screws or breaking the glass.

You can cover the cold frame at night with an old carpet or blankets, and pile leaf bags or bales of straw around the cold frame for insulation. For additional heat control, you can insulate the box with styrofoam panels.

If you'd like to make a more substantial and efficient cold frame, the folks at Rodale Research Institute have designed nice airtight cold frames with night shutters and styrofoam insulation all the way around—including beneath the planting bed. In these frames they have maintained temperatures and yields as high as those in their larger solar greenhouses. It's all described in the November 1980 edition of *Organic Gardening and Farming* magazine.

Siting Your Cold Frame

In siting a cold frame or hotbed for winter food production, it's important to remember accessibility. The easier to use, the better it will be. A winter growing box should be located close to the house, protected from strong winds, and oriented to the south. A cold frame that's used only in spring to harden off seedlings should be convenient to the garden.

Using Your Cold Frame

Before tender seedlings are transplanted outside, they must be hardened off (that is, toughened up) because sudden exposure to the vagaries of cold, wind, and sun will be too much of a shock. A cold frame is the best place to harden off seedlings.

Young plants should be moved out to the cold frame a week or ten days before you intend to set them in the garden. Be sure to loosen and enrich the soil in your cold frame before you plant anything. Many people cut squares of soil around the individual plants in cartons or flats a few days before transplanting, thus minimizing root damage on the day of the actual process. We have found that this makes little difference in our plants' survival rates. But you should try, just to see if it makes any difference for you. During the first few days, open the frame for only a couple of hours during the warmest part of the day. Throughout the next week, increase the exposure gradually until it's open all day and closed only at night. Finally, leave the frame open at night, too, unless it seems like it's going to be a cold one.

If you have a mixture of hardy and sensitive plants hardening off at the same time, you'll have to be more cautious. Watch out for strong winds while the plants are still tender. When it's gusty, close the frame, as wind can be every bit as damaging as cold. Later in the spring you don't have to be quite so gradual with the hardening off process. We still close the frame at night for the first few days, since greenhouse plants are always a little sensitive; but we have been known to leave the frame open all day if it's already warm outside. Venting is always necessary. Open the lid just part way if you don't want to overexpose tender plants very early in the spring. On sunny days be especially careful not to leave the coldframe open for too long while the plants are still sensitive.

Be sure to water plants in the cold frame often. They'll probably dry out much more rapidly than they did inside. Remember also that you're more likely to get a frost on a clear, full-moon night. It's better to keep plants a little longer in the cold frame than to set them out when they might get killed by frost.

HOTBEDS

A hotbed is a cold frame with something to heat it. Traditionally, rotting manure or some other organic material has been the heat source, though you can use a heating cable to make a germination box. You can grow seedlings in a hotbed in the very early spring, in preparation for hardening them off in a cold frame. A hotbed can also keep things growing longer in the late fall.

Manure Hotbed

To prepare a traditional manure hotbed, dig a pit a couple of feet deep and pack in about a foot and a half of fresh, hot manure. Wet the manure down and then cover with six inches of good soil for direct planting, or only a couple of inches if it's for seedling flats. Place a frame similar to a cold frame over the filled pit. You can put flats out to germinate in the hotbed immediately. You should probably wait about three days before you plant seedlings directly. Check the soil temperature to make sure you won't *cook* them. Venting the box can help control overheating.

"Slow-Stove" Wood-Chip Hotbed

In the last few years, as fuel costs have risen, research work has begun on the use of slowly composting wood chips in a greenhouse as a source of bottom heat for growing beds. As the wood is composted (with some additional nitrogen), the heat in the wood is released over several months (instead of several *days*, if the wood were burned), and beneficial by-products such as carbon dioxide and moisture are released into the greenhouse. At the end of the composting period, the remaining compost can be added to the soil.

CLOCHES

A cloche is a movable transparent cover placed over in-ground crops to protect them from the cold. Cloche means ''bell'' in French; the French traditionally used bell-shaped glass covers over individual plants. We build cloches out of fiberglass and wood. Fiberglass is rigid, so it doesn't require support as plastic films do, and it lasts longer. Each cloche is wide enough to cover about a 4- by 6-foot section of a raised bed. Fiberglass is stapled to a rectangular wooden frame, forming an arch about 2½ feet high. Fiberglass half-moons are stapled to each end. We don't fasten the top of the end pieces, so they flop open slightly, providing ventilation. The cloches would be warmer later in the fall if these end pieces were tightly closed, but then you'd have to ventilate them manually more often.

Another type of cloche to cover crops in the ground is a tent of bamboo or wire and polyethylene. Stick the ends of bamboo strips or sturdy wire into the ground to form a row of arches over the plants you want to cover. Lay a piece of plastic over the arch. Then arch a second set of bamboo strips over the first ones, sandwiching the plastic between the two. Cut the plastic wide enough to allow at least a six-inch edge to lie flat on the ground, and shovel dirt onto the edges of the plastic. Leave one end accessible for easy access to the crop; you can weight it with a board.

We plan the placement of cloches when we do the fall planting. Obviously, it's easy to cover things planted in a block just the size of the cloche, and this method wouldn't work if we planted in long skinny rows. Cover low-growing crops like lettuce, carrots, beets, and various greens. Extending the season for tomatoes or other large plants requires taller structures.

Cloches can be used in the spring for early crops. We get lettuce in early April from cloches, and tomatoes started under cloches bear fruit as much as a month earlier.

Larger Greenhouses
CLIMATE

A well-designed greenhouse will provide most of the conditions for plants to grow comfortably, but you must do your part, as well. You will need to understand and regulate the climate inside the greenhouse. Light, temperature, humidity, and carbon dioxide interact to create the greenhouse climate.

Light

Light varies according to season and place within the greenhouse. During the winter, the sun crosses the southern sky in a low arc. At this season light intensity is lowest, and hours of sunlight are fewest. Solar greenhouses are oriented due south to admit the greatest amount of solar radiation at this coldest and darkest time of year. The north wall and ceiling are opaque and insulated. This prevents light from entering on the north side, but greatly reduces heat loss from the building.

The portion of the greenhouse near the south wall and the central area will receive full, direct sun. The area closest to the north wall will receive the least light. Painting the north wall white will help reflect sunlight back onto the plants. In a large greenhouse, the north-wall area probably will not have enough light for good plant growth and should be used as work area and for heat storage. Partial shade areas with little direct light are sufficient only for shade-loving plants. For maximum production, choose plants on the basis of the light patterns within your greenhouse. Fruiting crops always prefer full, direct light. In the shady areas or in the low-light seasons of the year, grow shade-tolerant crops like chard, kale, lettuce, beet greens, endive, New Zealand spinach, leeks, Chinese greens, herbs, and turnip greens.

Temperature

Solar greenhouses should be designed to collect excess heat during the day and store it for later use. Adequate heat storage reduces wide day/night temperature variations. A greenhouse with no heat storage will get very hot and stuffy on a sunny day in the winter—but as soon as the sun fades a little, it will get cold. Water, thick cement walls, mud, or rocks can

Cross section of the
New Alchemy Cape
Cod Ark

1. Intake vent for rock storage: Warm air from the top of the greenhouse is drawn down by a ½-HP fan and blower into one corner of the rock storage.

2. Rock storage: A 2,000 cu. ft. bed of 3-to-5 inch diameter rocks traps and holds heat from warm air during the day. At night cold air coming through the rocks picks up stored heat from the rocks and helps maintain greenhouse temperature.

3. Outlet plenum: Air from rock storage is returned to the low part of the planted area through adjustable block vents in the concrete block plenum wall. Warm air helps prevent freezing on sunless days and at night; air motion breaks up stratified air, reducing problems such as mildew and other moisture-related difficulties.

4. Top of outlet plenum: Wood plank surface serves as a raised, warmed seedling and cutting propagation area.

5. Open pond: Four-foot-deep concrete pool serves as a low-temperature heat reservoir, a source of prewarmed irrigation water, an observation tank for fish-feeding experiments, and as an indoor habitat for frogs, turtles and other desirable aquatic and amphibious animals and microorganisms.

6. Solar ponds: Translucent plastic fish tanks five feet tall and five feet in diameter. Nine tanks on two levels for the intensive aquaculture of tilapia and other edible fish.

7. Loft: A suspended laboratory observation platform.

8. Hinged Kalwall vault skylight: Entire assembly lifts to exhaust hot air in warm weather. Curved outer membrane and flat inner membrane are nailed to a 2-by-4 perimeter frame and curved plywood supports running vertically every five feet.

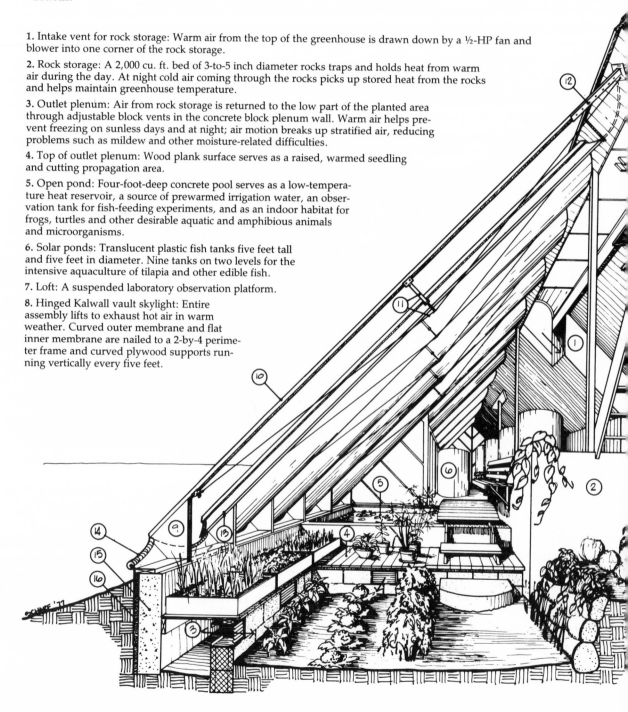

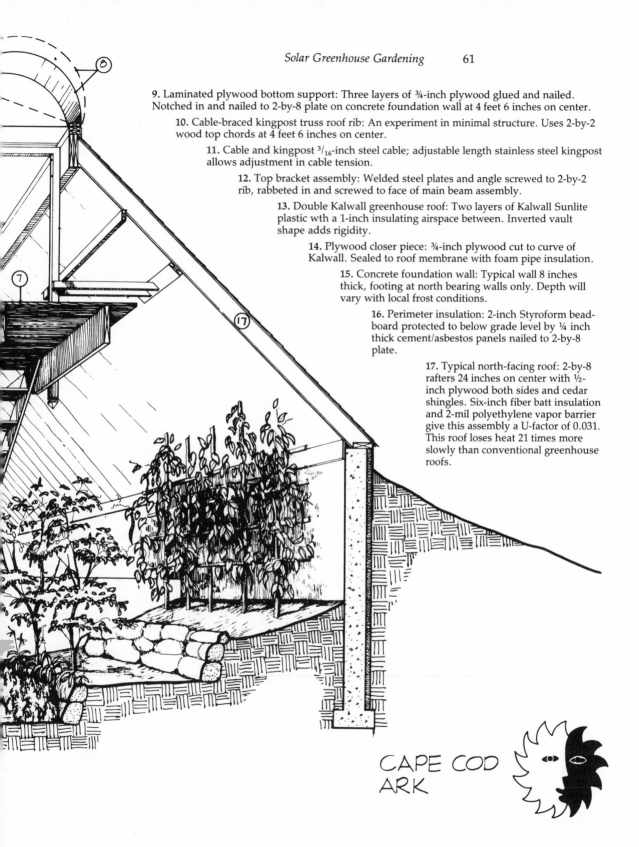

9. Laminated plywood bottom support: Three layers of ¾-inch plywood glued and nailed. Notched in and nailed to 2-by-8 plate on concrete foundation wall at 4 feet 6 inches on center.

10. Cable-braced kingpost truss roof rib: An experiment in minimal structure. Uses 2-by-2 wood top chords at 4 feet 6 inches on center.

11. Cable and kingpost ³/₁₆-inch steel cable; adjustable length stainless steel kingpost allows adjustment in cable tension.

12. Top bracket assembly: Welded steel plates and angle screwed to 2-by-2 rib, rabbeted in and screwed to face of main beam assembly.

13. Double Kalwall greenhouse roof: Two layers of Kalwall Sunlite plastic wth a 1-inch insulating airspace between. Inverted vault shape adds rigidity.

14. Plywood closer piece: ¾-inch plywood cut to curve of Kalwall. Sealed to roof membrane with foam pipe insulation.

15. Concrete foundation wall: Typical wall 8 inches thick, footing at north bearing walls only. Depth will vary with local frost conditions.

16. Perimeter insulation: 2-inch Styroform beadboard protected to below grade level by ¼ inch thick cement/asbestos panels nailed to 2-by-8 plate.

17. Typical north-facing roof: 2-by-8 rafters 24 inches on center with ½-inch plywood both sides and cedar shingles. Six-inch fiber batt insulation and 2-mil polyethylene vapor barrier give this assembly a U-factor of 0.031. This roof loses heat 21 times more slowly than conventional greenhouse roofs.

CAPE COD ARK

collect and store heat in a greenhouse. Many solar greenhouses rely on enclosed bins of rock for *thermal mass* (heat storage material). In the Cape Cod Ark, the water in our fish ponds is the main thermal mass. We've found that the dark-green solar-algae pond water is the most efficient heat storage medium. Water contained in these cylinders absorbs more heat than it would in a similar in-ground pond. (See Chapter 5 for further information on solar-algae ponds.)

The plant area nearest your thermal storage will be a little warmer than other areas in winter. Heat-loving plants will appreciate being close to this extra warmth.

Conventional greenhouses rely on supplemental heat, cooling, and light to regulate daily and seasonal temperature fluctuations. Most conventional greenhouse crops have been selected for an environment in which temperatures are controlled within a few degrees of the optimum for a specific crop. But solar greenhouses rely on fluctuating natural processes, and careful crop selection can make a big difference. Horticulturalists working in solar greenhouses must select crops that will grow, flower, and fruit within wider extreme conditions. Appendix A at the end of this chapter lists vegetable varieties best suited for success in solar greenhouses in the Northeast. In other regions different varieties may be preferred.

Warm-weather plants—like tomatoes, cucumbers, and peppers—will survive in a cool winter greenhouse, but their productivity will be very low. So will their resistance to pests and disease. To make the most of cold winter days, select leafy green vegetables. Fortunately, many of the same crops that tolerate low light intensity also tolerate low temperatures.

In winter, plant cold-tolerant crops near the door. The area closest to the entry door is a cold spot within the greenhouse. Try to minimize the amount of traffic through the outside doors. An enclosed entryway, or airlock, will decrease heat loss.

While thermal mass serves the function of keeping temperatures from dipping too low, proper ventilation keeps temperatures from soaring too high. Vents must be large enough, properly placed, and, of course, they must be *used*. It takes constant attention to remember to open the vents when the day gets warm and to close them when it starts to cool off.

Vents should be placed near the top of the greenhouse to allow rising hot air to escape. Knee-wall vents facilitate air circulation. For adequate ventilation, we think knee-wall vents and ridge vents should run the entire length of the greenhouse, as we illustrated earlier in Figs. 2 and 3. A rule of thumb is that the ventilation area should be equivalent to 15 percent to 30 percent of the floor area (see Fig. 4).

For partial venting, open the ridge vents. For more rapid and complete ventilation, open the knee-wall vents as well. As a rule, air temperatures at the level of the plants should not be allowed to go over 80°F. Be careful not

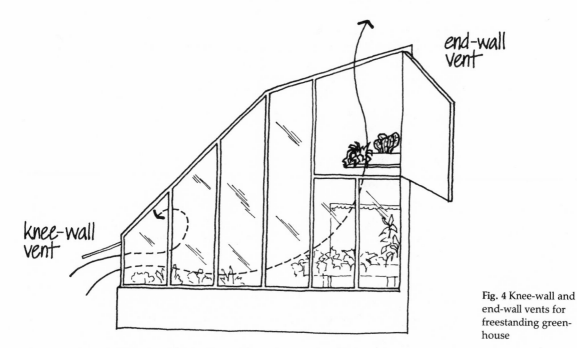

end-wall vent

knee-wall vent

Fig. 4 Knee-wall and end-wall vents for freestanding greenhouse

to let out too much precious heat in the winter. It's usually best not to use knee-wall vents in the winter, because the cold air entering at growing-bed level could shock or frost nearby plants.

Keep a logbook of greenhouse air and soil temperatures. You may not want to collect temperature data daily, but occasional readings will help you choose what to plant and when. It's interesting to follow the temperatures in your greenhouse: "Did you know it went down to two below last night and the greenhouse didn't go below 45?" or "Hey, you turkey, it's 98 degrees in here! Are you trying to steam the greens?" A maximum-minimum thermometer is good because it records the low and high of the day.

Humidity

Greenhouses tend to be quite humid. Plants transpire water, moisture evaporates from the soil, and all this moisture has nowhere to go. Often it condenses on the glazing material and decreases light transmission.

During the winter months, greenhouses are often closed tight and relative humidity is high—particularly on cloudy days. The air can be completely saturated with water, and relative humidity can approach 100 percent. The combination of low temperatures and high humidity in winter can cause disease and infection in plants. Some of the most common diseases are botrytis, leaf rot, stem rot, and cladiosporum. Fungal infections cause yellow, tan, or brown tissue in leaves or stems. The tissue will usually be soft and mushy. At a later stage of development, the reproductive spores will be visible as tiny gray dots on dead brown leaves. Although fungal diseases seldom occur, the best control is prevention. Select plants that have been bred to resist attack and that prefer the greenhouse environment. A good source for disease identification is your county agricultural agent and/or a Rodale Press publication entitled *Organic Plant Protection*. The easiest way to reduce humidity is through ventilation. Fans can be used to stir the air and reduce moisture, too. Most plants will prefer a relative humidity of 50–65 percent.

Carbon Dioxide

Photosynthesis is the process by which green plants convert the energy of sunlight into chemical energy. Water and carbon dioxide (CO_2) are necessary for photosynthesis to take place. During the day, as plants photosynthesize, they use up the CO_2 in the greenhouse atmosphere. Unless CO_2 is replenished by incoming air, by some biological process (such as composting), or by some other means, the rate of photosynthesis will be constrained.

Various biological processes release carbon dioxide into the atmosphere. If your greenhouse is alive with soil microorganisms, depletion of CO_2 will not be such a problem. Organic material in the soil releases CO_2 through decomposition. A small compost pile or a worm bed can be incorporated into the greenhouse to provide CO_2. Mulches, fish, insects, toads, and people are all significant contributors of CO_2 in a closed greenhouse environment.

AGRICULTURAL MANAGEMENT
Soils

Just as it does in the garden, the health of the soil will determine the health of the plants in the greenhouse. In the Cape Cod Ark at New Alchemy, we started with the original soil inside the greenhouse and "seeded" it with biologically diverse soils from fields, meadows, and forests of southern New England. To these soils we added compost, seaweeds for trace elements, and composted leaf litter. Our intent is to build soils that have the following characteristics:

- high fertility
- high organic-matter content
- good water retention
- optimal carbon dioxide production through bacterial activities
- shelter for diverse animal populations, including earthworms, pest predators, and parasites

The most practical measure of soil fertility is the amount of produce a given area actually yields. The soil is the basic source for plant nutrients. Outdoors, nutrients are tapped seasonally; in the greenhouse, the soil's nutrients are tapped 12 months of the year. We rotate crops to balance nutrient demand and consistently work to maintain soil fertility.

Many greenhouse gardeners grow their plants in containers. We definitely prefer gardening in deep soil beds. Each bed is replenished with good compost in September, after the summer season has drawn to a close. Compost revitalizes the many microorganisms that break down organic material into nutrients and minerals; it also recreates a good soil structure. In addition, we irrigate our beds with warm, nutrient-rich fish-pond water. The solar-algae ponds provide phosphate compounds and soluble supplies of nitrogen in the form of nitrate and ammonium.

Water

Transpiration and evaporation will be quite rapid throughout the warm seasons in the greenhouse. Daily watering may be necessary. During the winter, Don't water excessively or you'll contribute to high humidity. If you're using tap water, you may want to condition it before watering the plants. In winter, tap water is very cold(40–45°F) shocks plant roots and may damage foliage. An easy method of preheating is to store the water for the following day in a bucket or barrel where it will absorb heat and have a chance to dechlorinate. Two storage barrels will allow you to condition water for use on alternate days.

We use fertile water from the fish ponds as much as possible. Foliar sprays of fish emulsion and seaweed extract are good nutrient supplements, too, especially on seedlings.

A large watering can with a sprinkler is a practical watering device for most greenhouses. If your growing area is larger than 100 square feet, watering with a hose will save a lot of time. Water with the hose or spout *close* to the soil surface. Spraying water over the plants from waist height puts too much water on top of leaves. Be sure to soak the roots well. A skimpy surface watering won't do it. Water early in the day once or twice a week in the winter. Try to do this on sunny, clear days so plant tissue has a chance to dry off as quickly as possible. In the summer, water late in the day to decrease evaporation and to prevent burning of the plant leaves when sunlight strikes the water drops. When there are many cloudy days, the greenhouse will be moist enough to delay watering. Wait until it's necessary. Head lettuces will rot at the base if water collects inside heads.

VEGETABLES FOR SOLAR GREENHOUSES IN THE NORTHEAST

A wide assortment of vegetables can be raised through the seasons. (See Fig. 5 for the diversity of crops in a solar greenhouse.) Light intensity,

Fig. 5 Inside view of
the New Alchemy
Cape Cod Ark

air and soil temperatures, and productivity will determine the selection for each season.

We have found that Dutch lettuce and tomato varieties are superior in production to most American varieties. European greenhouse crop-breeding conditions seem to more closely approximate conditions in solar greenhouses than those of the more controlled and conventional U.S. greenhouses. Oriental-type turnips are best suited for greens production. In our Resource listing at the end of this section, a number of reliable seed suppliers are suggested.

Winter vegetables should be selected for their adaptability to cool soil and air temperatures. In our greenhouse, average soil temperatures at a two-inch depth during the coldest months have been as follows: November, 60°F; December, 59.5°F; January, 55°F; February, 59°F; March, 62°F. At this time of year, air temperatures fluctuate between 77°F on clear days and 50–60°F on cloudy days. With an average minimum air temperature of 49.2°F and an average maximum air temperature of 70.8°F, the climate is similar to a spring season in a temperate zone. These soil and air temperatures are quite sufficient for bountiful winter vegetable production. Lettuce, endive, celery, chard, beet greens, brassicas, spinach, parsley, and other herbs are all suitable crops (see Appendix A). In the dead of winter, eliminate the fruiting brassicas and celery from your planting plan.

SPECIAL TIPS FOR INDIVIDUAL CROPS
Celery

Celery is a relatively high-priced, popular vegetable on American markets. Although it is one of the most difficult plants to grow, we have had encouraging results in our greenhouses. Space it at one plant per square foot. It will occupy bedding space for 72 to 77 days, about one-half of its total growth time. Seeds should be started in flats approximately two months prior to transplanting time. We blanch our celery by placing boards on each side of the plants after they've been in the beds for two months, or one month before harvest. This makes for a juicier crop that's more delicate in flavor. Water frequently.

Tomatoes

In New England, many conventional greenhouse tomato growers have dropped production with the rising cost of fuel. Retail prices often exceed a dollar a pound on Cape Cod. Vine-ripened homegrown tomatoes invariably will be more flavorful as well as cheaper than shipped tomatoes.

Greenhouse tomatoes have a fall and spring season. The spring season is more productive. We have harvested 3.2 pounds of fruit per square foot in the spring and only 1.5 pounds per square foot in the fall. For spring crops, a mid-March planting gives mid-May fruit. For the fall crop, a late

Fig. 6 Double leading
tomatoes

Pruning to develop a second top.
A. First flowering truss
B. Axial sucker to be trained into
   second indeterminant stem
   (first leaf below flower truss)
C. Axial sucker(s) to be pruned

Tomato plants with double tops,
strung up to a trellis. Prune leaves
below ripening cluster.

July planting gives fruit by mid-October. Seeding should be done two months prior to your intended transplant date. Light-reflective material (e.g., aluminum foil) placed behind the plants will boost fall production.

Double leading of tomatoes is a European method in which selected suckers are pruned into second stems. This technique can double fruit yield without affecting fruit size. It is an excellent method for maximum space utilization and allows more light to reach the fruit for better ripening (see Fig. 6, Double Leading Tomatoes).

Our favorite variety of tomato for greenhouse production is Jumbo from Stokes Seeds, Inc. Their production and flavor are good. Harvest lasts about 2½ months, and we have picked as many as 13 pounds of fruit per Jumbo plant from spring production.

Lettuce

Lettuce can be planted quite densely: eight square inches per head provides plenty of space. Always use transplanted seedlings, so you can keep all your space in production. We suggest growing a combination of head lettuces and loose-leaf varieties. Loose-leaf lettuce can be picked a leaf at a

time over an extended time period. We'll give some tips on sequential picking in the following section, ''Maximizing Food Production.''

Kale, Turnip Greens, and Beet Greens

Bring healthy younger plants from the garden into the greenhouse in
late fall. They will continue to produce throughout the winter. After transplanting, trim them back so they don't lose water through their leaves; this
way they can adjust more quickly. Remove the plants whenever they start
to bolt. Production may slow down in late December and January but will
speed up again later. Parsley can be brought in from outside, too—but if
you damage the taproot, it will bolt. For best spring production, reseed
kale in the early winter and set out new seedlings when the fall ones start
to look like small palm trees.

Cauliflower and Broccoli

Spring production is better than fall. Seed in January, set out in March,
harvest in May. For fall production, seed in mid-July, transplant in late
August, harvest in November. The key to good production is selecting the
right variety. Cleopatra is a favorite broccoli for the fall crop. Allow plenty
of space: 18 inches between plants and 24 inches between rows.

MAXIMIZING FOOD PRODUCTION

Successional planting is even more important for the greenhouse than
it is for the garden. Maximizing production takes planning and attention.
By growing seedlings to good transplant size in flats before you put them
in the ground, you can keep your growing space plant-covered and as productive as possible. For example, you can maintain seedling tomatoes in
small individual pots on a shelf until they reach a foot in height, while
using ground space for a spinach crop. If you seed small quantities of lettuce frequently, you'll have a nice seedling to set out every time you harvest a mature head. A yearly planting schedule helps maximize efficiency.
Appendix B at the end of this chapter shows three alternative planting
schedules for one year and presents in tabular form the corresponding
retail prices per square foot.

Harvesting

Most plants dictate the particular time and manner in which they'll be
harvested. Some crops produce best when selectively picked over time.
We harvest from the same kale, parsley, chard, pak choi, mustard, beet
greens, turnip greens, and loose-leaf lettuce from the fall until the spring.

Don't pick from undersized plants or you may permanently stunt
them. As a general guideline, we recommend that plants have at least five
full-sized leaves before you start harvesting. Pick carefully so you don't

disturb the roots. Don't leave the shafts of leaves attached to the plant. (That's really easy to do with thick-stemmed crops such as chard and Chinese greens.) The remainders of these stems tend to rot and can spread fungi.

Picking single leaves can contribute to higher productivity by allowing more air to circulate around each plant and by reducing crowding, which causes older leaves to die from insufficient light.

Single-harvest cropping is popular among large-scale vegetable growers, folks with larger greenhouses, and in community greenhouses. Harvesting can alternate from bed to bed. For example, one plot has head lettuce that's close to maturity, a second plot has celery in mid-development, and a third has new cauliflower seedlings. The lettuce will be replaced with tomatoes, the celery with a new lettuce crop, and the cauliflower with a new celery crop.

Harvest frequently for maximum yields and prime quality. It's best to harvest vegetables, especially the leafy greens, in early morning or late afternoon. If harvested at midday, vegetables may wilt more quickly.

Seedling Production

In addition to in-ground vegetable production, your greenhouse can provide the space and conditions for growing seedlings for the outdoor garden and for the greenhouse itself. A box with heating coils and a lid provides optimal conditions for germination. Refer back to Chapter 2 for detailed information on seeding boxes, soil mixtures for seeding, transplanting techniques, and so on.

Even if it's small, the space allotted for seedling production is very important and worthwhile. In 1979, for example, the Cape Cod Ark produced over 3000 seedlings in 75 square feet.

A systematic seeding and transplanting schedule optimizes the use of the germination box and seedling space. When a flat has fully germinated, it is immediately replaced with a newly seeded one. As mature transplants are moved to the cold frame to harden off, a second set of younger seedlings is moved into that space. On Cape Cod, three seedling tomato plants commonly retail for a dollar, so growing your own seedlings will save you money.

INSECT CONTROL

Don't make the mistake of regarding all insects in the greenhouse as pests; the only troublemakers are the little creatures who compete with us for our food. Other insects are harmless and a certain few actually are beneficial.

A number of steps can be taken to prevent pest infestation in the greenhouse. As usual, good preventive methods top the list. Paying careful attention to your plants is the most important way to help control damage. Many insects live on the underside of leaves, where they are protected from high temperatures and have access to water and succulent plant tissue. Often a harmful number of pests can accumulate before they're noticed. A routine periodic check made by flipping the leaves over and searching for small insects will help you notice pest infestations before they get serious. Pay close attention to young seedlings; their soft tissue is particularly vulnerable to aphid attack. Insects seem attracted to sick, pale plants, so a well-balanced, fertile soil will go a long way toward protecting plants from pests.

Common pests are aphids, whiteflies, spider mites, thrips, mealy bugs, and pill bugs. A magnifying lens or field glass (with a 10× magnification) should be used to find immature or nymph stages of most pests; adult spider mites and thrips are small enough to demand such a lens also.

A number of reference books contain helpful material on insect identification. The amateur will learn quickly from identification keys, pictures, and descriptions of plant-damage symptoms. In particular, we recommend material prepared by Walls, Clegg and Watkins, Abraham and Abraham, and Jordan; you'll find their books listed in the Bibliography at the end of this chapter.

Insect Control Using Natural Enemies

There exists a diverse community of insects who will help, rather than harm, your greenhouse plants. Doors and vents will provide entrance to the local beneficial-insect population, and you can do several things to encourage these creatures to move in and take up residence in the greenhouse. To attract them, border your vegetable beds with flowers that offer sweet nectar and rich pollen.

This approach is doubly gratifying, because growing flowers is one of the real pleasures of year-round gardening. Nasturtiums can be trained to climb ropes to the top of the greenhouse. Marigolds are summertime favorites. Among those that will bloom all winter are pansies and violas, alyssum, borage, ornamental sages, lobelia, miniature snapdragons, geraniums, and sweet peas. Carrot, dill, parsnip, mint, basil, and pennyroyal flowers are also good attractants of beneficial insects.

By planting perennial ''biological islands,'' one can further stabilize the insect ecology of the greenhouse. Most agricultural enviroments are intrinsically unstable because crops are planted, removed, and altered from season to season, and regulatory mechanisms can be disturbed in the process. For example, ladybug beetles can be introduced to control aphids on tomato plants. Once the crop is removed, the predators' food, the aphids, is gone as well. If there is a permanent island of diverse plantings, some of the ladybugs can harbor there until the next resurgence of aphids.

Use perennial plants to help control insects.

In these islands you can include permanent perennial plants, flowers, and herbs that provide continuing habitats for pollinators, predators, and parasites of insect pests—all this in addition to their beauty! Our geranium collection is an essential part of our whitefly control effort.

Sometimes you may need to purchase specific biological control agents from a commercial insectary. (See our Resource list, Commercial Insectaries.) Ladybugs, praying manti, green lacewings, and trichogramma wasps are the easiest to obtain.

Order the insects when you foresee a rise in the pest population that might be damaging to crop yield. For example, we know that our whitefly populations will soar in late spring, so we order the parasitic wasp, *Encarsia formosa* (Gahan). Before the insects reach a dangerous population density, become acquainted with the life cycles of both friend and foe. This will help you determine where and how to release the beneficial insects and enable you to recognize pest and predator at different stages of their lives. An excellent book to help you learn about insect life cyles is *Windowsill Ecology*, by William Jordan.

Sometimes ladybugs don't want to stay in their adopted home. Since they are daytime insects, introducing them at dusk will encourage them to rest that night and wake up adjusted to their new environment the next morning. Fall and winter releases tend to be successful because the vents are closed and the wanderers are forced to stay inside the building. By spring, when aphid populations are increasing, second- and third-generation ladybugs have grown accustomed to the greenhouse. Any escapees will help the surrounding outdoor garden!

Aphids

Aphids are probably the most common greenhouse pest. They are controlled by a number of predators and parasites. Generally less than ⅛-inch long, aphids appear in large colonies on young plants. *Myzus persicae* (Sulzer), the green peach aphid, is the most common offender in greenhouses, and *Aphidoletes aphidimyza* (Rondoni) is a hungry predator of the green peach aphid. The adult of *A. aphidimyza* is a dull fly, but the larval stage is bright orange and easily recognizable. The ⅒-inch orange maggot snags both adult and nymph aphids. Populations of *A. aphidimyza* increase in springtime as temperatures rise.

Syrphid flies are beautiful insects that resemble tiny bumblebees. The syrphid larvae feed on aphids plus some mealybugs and leafhoppers. The maggots measure between ⅟₁₆ and ⅓ inch, with a transparent skin and an eyeless pointed body. They suck out the vital contents of the aphid, leaving a shell that looks like a flake of dust on the undersides of plant leaves. Below 65°F, it takes two months or more for the syrphid fly to complete its life cycle. Warm weather speeds the process up to one month.

Just like the larvae of syrphid flies and gall midges, immature ladybugs will dine on aphids at a fast rate. Young insects have insatiable appetites because they are developing quickly. An immature ladybug beetle eats 400 aphids throughout the course of its development. The soft-bodied larvae look entirely different from the adults. They are greyish-blue with orange stripes, alligator-shaped, and grow to half an inch long.

Several local parasites can help your native predators control aphids. The most common of these parasites are chalcid and braconid wasps, who sting their host and then lay one or more eggs in the aphid's body. As the young parasitic wasp develops, the aphid dies, leaving its corpse intact. These "mummies" are slightly swollen and metallic yellow, bronze, or black, depending on the species. The mummy is usually the easiest life stage of a parasitic wasp to recognize, as the wasps themselves are so small, ranging from ⅟₃₂ to ⅟₁₆ inch. Braconids and chalcids both have found their own ways into our greenhouses.

Finally, there is a fungus that infects aphids. It thrives in cool, humid conditions, so it's a good control in fall and winter. Aphids infected with

Entomophthora aphidio (Hoffman) have a creamy color and velvet texture. The fungi break down the cellular structures, the aphid dies, and the reproductive hyphae of the fungi push out through the shell. Once the fungus enters the greenhouse, the spores will spread all over.

Whiteflies

The whitefly *Trialeurodes vaporarium* (Westwood) is another very common pest. *Encarsia formosa* (Gahan) is a parasite specific to the whitefly. Like many parasitic wasps, *E. formosa* needs warm temperatures for an effective rate of parasitism. This parasite has been an effective control of whiteflies in our greenhouses for several years. (See the Commercial Insectaries listing for specific sources of *Encarsia*.)

We also trap whiteflies. They are attracted to the color yellow, so we paint poles a yellow-orange and coat them with a sticky substance called Tanglefoot®. They're placed horizontally over the growing tips of cucumbers and tomatoes to trap whiteflies as they emerge from their eggs on the undersides of leaves.

Nasturtiums will attract both aphids and whiteflies. Usually, the pests will stay in the nasturtiums instead of moving on to the surrounding crop plants. One way to reduce a pest population drastically is to remove the infested nasturtium plant. If you have beneficial insects preying on pests in nasturtiums, check the leaves for predators and parasites before discarding the plant.

RESOURCES

Compost Resource

Biothermal Energy Center, P.O. Box 3112, Portland ME 04104. This research group can provide details on using compost for hotbed and greenhouse heating.

Seed Companies for Greenhouse Culture: U.S.A.

Johnny's Selected Seeds, Albion, ME 04910.

Stokes Seeds, Inc., 737 Main St., Box 548, Buffalo, NY 14240.

The Graham Center Seed Directory. A gardener's and farmer's guide to sources of traditional, old-timey vegetable, fruit, and nut varieties. For each copy, send $1.00 to: Seed Directory, Frank Porter Graham Center, Route 3, Box 95, Wadesboro, NC 28170.

Dr. Yoo Farm, P.O. Box 290, College Park, MD 20740. Oriental vegetable seeds.

Tsang and Ma International, P.O. Box 294, Belmont, CA 94002. Oriental vegetable seeds.

George W. Park Seed Co., Inc., South Carolina Highway 254, North Greenwood, SC 29647.

Epicure Seeds, Box 23568, Rochester, NY 14692.

Herbst Seedsmen, Inc., 1000 North Main Street, Brewster, NY 10509. Perennial flowers, annuals, vegetables.

Sluis & Groot of America, Inc., 124 Griffin Street, Salinas, CA 93901. Dutch seeds.

Redwood City Seed Company, P.O. Box 361, Redwood City, CA 94064. Unusual seeds.

Kilgore Seed Co., 1400 W. First Street, Sanford, FL 32771.

Kitazawa Seed Co., 356 W. Taylor Street, San Jose, CA 95110. Oriental vegetable seeds.

Seed Companies for Greenhouse Culture: Holland

Royal Sluis, Postbox 22, 1600 AA Enkhuizen, Holland.

Bruinsma Selectiebedrijven BV, Middelbroekweg 67, Netherlands. U.S. representative: A.W. Gerhart, 6346 Avon Belden Road, North Ridgeville, OH 44039.

Enza Zaden, Postbox 7, 1600 AA, Enkhuizen, Holland.

Rijk Zwaan, Zaadteelt en Zaadhandel, B.V. De Lier, Holland. (Wholesale orders only.)

Commercial Insectaries

Associates Insectary, P.O. Box 969, Santa Paula, CA 93060, (805) 525-7015. *Cryptolaemus montrouzieri*, mealybug predator.

Beneficial Insects Co., P.O. Box 232, Brownsville, CA 95919, (916) 675-2251. Ladybugs.

Better Yields Insects, 13310 Riverside Dr., Tecumseh, Ontario, Canada N8N 1B2, (519) 735-0002. *Encarsia formosa*, greenhouse whitefly parasite, and predatory mites. *Note:* Importation permits are necessary. Ask for Form 526. Write to Technical Permit, Technical Service Staff, PP&Q APHIS USDA, Federal Center, Hyattsville, MD 20782.

Bio-Control Co., 13451 Highway 174, P.O. Box 247, Cedar Ridge, CA 95924, (916) 272-1997/272-2529. Ladybugs.

Bio Insect Control, 1710 S. Broadway, Plainview, TX 79072, (806) 293-5861. Microbials, *Encarsia formosa, Cryptolaemus montrouzieri*, predatory mites, and more.

Biotactics, Inc. Sales, 7765 Lakeside Dr., Riverside, CA 92509, (714) 685-7681. Predatory mites.

California Green Lacewings, P.O. Box 2495, Merced, CA, 95340 (209) 722-4985/357-0750.

Fountain's Sierra Bug Co., P.O. Box 114, Rough & Ready, CA 95975, (916) 273-0513. Ladybugs.

King's Natural Pest Control, P.O. Box 52, Spring City, PA 19475, (215) 948-9261. Ladybugs.

Natural Pest Controls, 9397 Premier Way, Sacramento, CA 95826, (916) 362-2660. Scale parasite, *Encarsia formosa*, *Cryptolaemus montrouzieri*, predatory mites.

Peaceful Valley Farms, 11173 Peaceful Valley Rd., Nevada City, CA 95959, (916) 265-3339. Everything.

Rincon-Vitova Insectaries, Inc., P.O. Box 95, Oakview, CA 93022, (805) 643-5407. Everything.

Necessary Trading Co., P.O. Box 305, New Castle, VA 24127. Traps, microbials, ladybugs, predatory mites, *C. montrouzieri*, *E. formosa*.

Unique Nursery, 4640 Attawa Ave., P.O. Box 22245, Sacramento, CA 95822, (916) 451-9929. Ladybugs and lacewings (aphid predators).

Home Greenhouse Questionnaire

Greenhouse agriculture is one of the most appealing forms of home food production. The following list of questions will help you decide whether or not using a solar greenhouse suits your skills and circumstances. It will help you identify site details to consider before you construct one and give you some management ideas for its operation.

1. *Do you have a garden?*

A greenhouse can substitute (partially) for an outdoor garden space if you have none, or it can enhance the productivity of the garden you have.

2. *Could you benefit from an extended growing season?*

Cloches, cold frames, and hotbeds are all low-cost, simple-to-build structures that extend the growing season. They are good places to start seedlings and to harden off older plants before you transplant them into the outdoor garden.

3. *Does someone in your family have the skills to build a cold frame?*

4. *Is there a site around your home suitable for a cold frame?*

Cold frames should always be located on well-drained land that is free from depressions or danger of flooding in case of heavy rains. They should be protected on the north side by buildings, trees, fences, or hedges—anything that will provide shelter from the wind. They may even be placed below ground, so long as there is adequate drainage. Other site considerations include a southern exposure and convenience for tending.

5. *Would you like your greenhouse to provide heat for your house as well as produce food?*

This book is concerned mainly with greenhouses used for vegetable production. For more information on space heating with attached solar greenhouses, we recommend *The Passive Solar Energy Book* by Mazria (Rodale) and *Passive Solar Energy* by Anderson and Wells (Brick House Pub.).

6. *Will it be a season extender, or will you use it year 'round?*

Spring seedlings and fall salad greens are normally grown in cold frames and cloches. Some special vegetables can be grown during the summer in a larger solar greenhouse, whereas other crops are more suited to mid-winter. *The Bountiful Solar Greenhouse,* by Shane Smith, is a comprehensive book on year-round vegetable production in greenhouses.

SOLAR CONSIDERATIONS

7. *What is the most effective orientation of a greenhouse for you?*

This is determined partially by what types of plants you wish to grow, and partially by the exposure of your house. The exposure of your house depends on the positions of the sun during the season(s) you will use the greenhouse.

Ideally, a greenhouse should face true south. True south is different from ''south'' on the compass, and can be found by observing the directions of shadows at solar noon (when the sun is at its midpoint in the sky). For the time of solar noon, check your local newspaper for the times of sunrise and sunset, and determine the time of the sun's half-way point. The shadows at this time lie *exactly* north-south.

The bad news is that most homes were not built with solar orientation in mind. The good news: an orientation of 30° east or west of true south is usually acceptable for adequate greenhouse performance.

8. *Are the sides of your home that fall within 30° of true south partially shaded?*

In addition to its orientation, a home's solar potential is affected by the amount of shading it receives. It is important for the area to be shade-free during the prime solar hours of 9:00 a.m. to 3:00 p.m. You can estimate the hours of shadow that will fall on your site by using any of several solar-sighting methods described in various reference books at the end of this chapter.

If you are taking your measurements during the warmer season, remember that since most deciduous trees drop their leaves in the early to mid fall, their shadow may not pose a serious winter problem. Cutting or pruning may be required if a tree drops its leaves late in the season or if it has a dense array of branches above the "shadow point."

9. *Can you remove most shade-producing obstructions?*

A neighboring building may present a permanent problem.

SITE CONSIDERATIONS

In addition to solar orientation, a number of other site concerns will determine the feasibility of adding a greenhouse to your home.

10. *Which rooms face the southern side?*

A room that is used a lot during the day (e.g., the kitchen) is the best place for an attached greenhouse. However, if a lesser-used room faces south (e.g., a bedroom), fans and vents can be used to distribute heat throughout the house.

11. *Do any utility lines run through the area of the proposed greenhouse?*

Water, gas, electric, and telephone lines may interfere with the proposed site. If so, you'll have to either design the greenhouse to avoid the lines or divert the lines themselves. Diverting utility lines will increase the cost of construction.

12. *Will the addition of a greenhouse interfere with your home's drainage capabilities?*

13. *Will you require special permits for construction?*

Although a building permit is required in many areas for any structure, often no special permit is needed for a greenhouse. Check with your local building inspector.

14. *Will you have to alter your landscape dramatically in order to construct the greenhouse?*

Buildings, large rocks, trees, and perennial plants may not be worth moving or may be impossible to get around, or your home may not be properly oriented for an attached greenhouse. At this point, you may decide to put up a freestanding greenhouse. A freestanding greenhouse offers the advantage of easy orientation for maximum sunlight; but, of course, it means building a full structure instead of just an addition to an existing one.

DESIGN CONSIDERATIONS

The actual proportions of your greenhouse (including the slope angle of the glazed surface, its height, and width) depend on how large a growing area you want and how much money you want to spend. No matter what you decide, the greenhouse must be designed to provide adequate heat storage and ventilation. The surface area of ventilation openings should be roughly equal to 15 to 30 percent of the floor area of the greenhouse.

To maximize the length of time heat is retained in your greenhouse, it is important to consider both heat-storage materials (water or masonry) and the heat-loss rate back through the glazing. (*Note:* "glazing" means the glass or plastic windows of your greenhouse.) A passive solar greenhouse needs at least two gallons (¼ cubic foot) of water or ½ cubic foot of rock or concrete per square foot of glazing. Pay close attention to your glazing's insulation value. This will greatly affect its ability to keep your greenhouse warm at night and export solar heat to your house during the day.

15. *What is the best glazing material for you?*

In the Northeast, we recommend that your greenhouse glazing be at least two layers. The outside layer should be tough (for instance, glass or 0.04-inch fiberglass); the inside layer can be cheaper film with better light transmission (for instance, Sears Butyrate® film, DuPont Tedlar®, 3M High Trans® film, etc.). A third layer adds even more insulation value. Another approach is to use movable insulating night curtains or panels. (See Langdon's *Movable Insulation* (Rodale), Shurcliff's *Thermal Shutters and Shades* (Brick House Pub.) or *The Passive Solar Energy Book.*)

16. *Should you use a night curtain?*

For best performance, we recommend that solar greenhouses in the Northeast be triple glazed, or double glazed with a night curtain. Other regions of the country should follow locally successful examples.

17. *Is there an experienced contractor who can advise you or help you build the greenhouse?*

The best place to start is by asking a neighbor who already *has* a greenhouse. Also, you can look under "Solar Energy" or "Building Contractors" in the Yellow Pages, or check the classifieds.

COSTS AND SCAVENGING

Contractors will charge from $4000 to $9000 to build a mid-sized attached greenhouse with approximately 150 square feet of floor space.

You can reduce the cost significantly by doing some or all of the work yourself and by using recycled materials for construction.

18. *Are there any glass suppliers in your area?*

Often these businesses are willing either to give away or to sell at low cost damaged (or cosmetic-second) glass, which you can use for glazing.

19. *Are you eligible for state and federal tax credits?*

Although this may change, current federal policy (until 1985) allows a tax credit of 40 percent of the cost of a solar project, up to $4000. Also, many states offer additional tax benefits. These credits apply only to solar structures that have energy-saving potential. (Thus they *don't* apply to the construction of freestanding greenhouses.) Be sure to explore the current tax-credit provisions so you'll know exactly what you're entitled to claim.

BIBLIOGRAPHY

ABRAHAM, GEORGE, and KATY ABRAHAM. *Organic Gardening Under Glass.* Emmaus, PA: Rodale Press, 1978.

BUBEL, NANCY. *Seed-Starter's Handbook. Emmaus, PA: Rodale Press, 1978.*

CAMPBELL, STU. *Let It Rot!* Charlotte, VT: Garden Way, 1975.

CHAPEL, PAIGE (ed.). *The City Greenhouse Book: A Planning Guide for Neighborhood Projects.* U.S. Dept. of Housing and Urban Development, 1980.

CLEGG, PETER, AND DERRY WATKINS. *The Complete Greenhouse Book.* Charlotte, VT: Garden Way, 1978.

CROCKETT, JAMES UNDERWOOD. *Crockett's Victory Garden.* Boston: Little, Brown & Co., 1977.

DEKORNE, JAMES B. *Survival Greenhouse— An Ecosystem Approach to Home Food Production.* NM: Walden Foundation, 1975.

FISHER, RICK, AND WILLIAM YANDA. *The Food and Heat Producing Solar Greenhouse.* Santa Fe, NM: John Muir, 1976.

HARTMAN, H.T., and DALE E. KESTER. *Plant Propagation: Principles and Practice.* Englewood Cliffs, NJ: Prentice-Hall, 1975.

JORDAN, WILLIAM H., JR. *Windowsill Ecology.* Emmaus, PA: Rodale Press, 1977.

KILBORN, JEAN. "Vegetables in Shade," *Horticulture* LVIII(2), April 1980.

KLEIN, MIRIAM. *Horticultural Management of Solar Greenhouses in the Northeast.* Newport, VT: The Memphremagog Group, 1980. (Write to P.O. Box 456, Newport, VT 05885.)

MASTALEREZ, JOHN W. *The Greenhouse Environment: The Effect of Environmental Factors on Flower Crops.* New York: John Wiley & Sons, 1977. (Cut flowers and ornamental production.)

McCULLAGH, JAMES C. *The Solar Greenhouse Book.* Emmaus, PA: Rodale Press, 1978.

NEW ALCHEMY INSTITUTE. *New Alchemy Quarterly,* Winter 1980. East Falmouth, MA: New Alchemy Institute, 1980. (Reprinted 1983)

PIERCE, JOHN H. *Greenhouse Grow How.* Seattle WA: Plants Alive Books, 1977. (Write to 5509 1st Ave. So., Seattle, WA 98108.)

RUTTEL, JACK. "Grow Your Own Midwinter Sun Salads," *Organic Gardening and Farming,* November 1980, pp. 58–68.

SMITH, SHANE. *The Bountiful Solar Greenhouse.* Santa Fe, NM: John Muir Press, 1982.

TODD, JOHN, and NANCY JACK TODD. *Tomorrow is Our Permanent Address.* New York: Harper and Row, 1980.

WALLS, IAN G. *The Complete Book of Greenhouse Gardening.* New York: Quadrangle/The New York Times, 1973. (Commercial orientation.)

WITTWER, S. H., AND S. HONMA. *Greenhouse Tomatoes—Guidelines for Successful Production.* East Lansing, MI: Michigan State University Press, 1969.

WOLF, RAY (ed). *Solar Growing Frame.* Emmaus, PA: Rodale Plans, Rodale Press, 1980

YEPSEN, ROGER B. (ed.). *Organic Plant Protection.* Emmaus, PA: Rodale Press, 1976.

APPENDIX A
Vegetable Varieties Suitable for Solar Greenhouses in the Northeast

FALL (September—November)

Vegetable	Name of Variety	Seed Co.	Light Condition
Beet	Ruby Queen	Stokes	Direct
	Early Wonder Tall Top	Johnny's	Direct
Broccoli	Cleopatra	Stokes	Direct
Cauliflower	Opaal*	Rijk Zwann	Direct
Celery	Utah 52–70 Improved	Johnny's	Direct
Chard, red	Rhubarb	Stokes	Direct, partial
Chard, Swiss	Fordhook Giant	Stokes	Direct, partial
Endive	Full Heart Batavian	Johnny's	Direct, partial
Kale	Harvester LD	Johnny's	Direct, partial
	Gr. Curled Dwarf Scotch	Stokes	Direct, partial
Lettuce, Bibb	Ravel*	Rijk Zwaan	Direct, partial
Lettuce, head	Reskia*	Rijk Zwaan	Direct
	Zwaresse*	Rijk Zwaan	Direct
Leek	Elephant	Stokes	Direct
Parsley	Champion Moss Curled	Stokes	Direct, partial
	Plain Dark Green Italian	Stokes	Direct, partial

SPRING (March—May)

Vegetable	Name of Variety	Seed Co.	Light Condition
Broccoli	De Cicco	Johnny's	Direct
Cauliflower	Opaal*	Rijk Zwaan	Direct
Celery	Utah 52–70 Improved	Johnny's	Direct
Chard, red	Rhubarb	Stokes	Partial, shade
Chard, Swiss	Fordhook Giant	Stokes	Partial, shade
Chinese cab-bagge	Springtime	Stokes	Partial
Kale	Harvester LD	Johnny's	Direct, partial, shade
	Gr. Curled Dwarf Scotch	Stokes	Direct, partial, shade
Lettuce, Bibb	Ravel*	Rijk Zwaan	Direct, partial
	Ostirata	Stokes	Direct, partial

SPRING (March—May)

Vegetable	Name of Variety	Seed Co.	Light Condition
Lettuce, head	Zwaresse*	Rijk Zwaan	Direct
Lettuce, loose-leaf	Grand Rapids Tip-Burn Resistant	Stokes	Direct, partial
Parsley	Champion Moss Curled	Stokes	Direct, partial, shade
	Plain Dark Green Italian	Stokes	Direct, partial, shade
Spinach	Malabar	——	Direct
Tomato	Lito*	Rijk Zwaan	Direct
	Sweet 100	Stokes	Direct

WINTER (November—February)

Vegetable	Name of Variety	Seed Co.	Light Condition
Beet greens	Green Top Bunching	Stokes	Direct
Bok choi	White Cabbage	Tsang & Ma	Direct
Chard, red	Rhubarb	Stokes	Direct, partial
Chard, swiss	Fordhood Giant	Stokes	Direct, partial
Chinese cabbage	Chinese Pac choi	Johnny's	Direct, partial
	Matsusitima	Johnny's	Direct, partial
	Yellow Bud Radish	Tsang & Ma	Direct
Chinese kale	Chinese Kale	Tsang & Ma	Direct
Endive	Full-Heart Batavian	Johnny's	Direct, partial
	Green Curled	Stokes	Direct, partial
Lettuce, Bibb	Ravel	Rijk Zwaan	Direct
Lettuce, loose-leaf	Grand Rapids Tip-Burn Resistant	Stokes	Direct
Mustard	Broad Leaf	Tsang & Ma	Direct
Pak choi	Flowering White Cabbage	Tsang & Ma	Direct
Parsley	Champison Moss Curled	Stokes	Direct, partial
Spinach	New Zealand	Stokes	Direct, partial
Turnip green	Tokyo Cross F$_1$	Stokes	Direct
	Shogoin	Stokes	Direct

Source: *New Alchemy Quarterly,* Winter, 1980, p. 4.
*Also suitable for spring and fall growth in smaller greenhouses.

APPENDIX B
Maximizing Food Production

Maximizing food production in any size greenhouse takes planning and consideration for optimal growing seasons. Most of our vegetable and flower seeds are germinated in flats, transplanted into small boxes, then set into the soil beds. Growing seedlings to transplant size will save time and precious space. As one crop is maturing, a second can be started. A yearly planting schedule helps you adjust timetables for seed orders, seeding, and harvesting. Table B.1 shows three alternative planting schemes for one year. Table B.2 presents the corresponding retail price revenue per square foot for each schedule.

Table B.1 *Alternative Annual Planting Schedules*

Vegetable	Seeding	Harvest	Revenue (/ft²/yr)
SCHEDULE A			
Celery	mid July	late December	$ .69
Lettuce	mid November	late March	1.50
Lettuce*	mid June	late September	1.50
Tomato	mid January	late September	1.96
			$5.65/ft²/yr
SCHEDULE B			
Cauliflower	mid March	early June	$ .60
Celery	mid October	late April	.69
Lettuce	early August	late November	1.50
Tomato	mid June	late January	1.96
			$4.75/ft²/yr
SCHEDULE C			
Cauliflower	early September	late December	$ .60
Lettuce	mid November	late March	1.50
Lettuce*	mid July	late September	1.50
Tomato	mid December	late September	1.96
			$5.56/ft²/yr

*Lettuce grown under mature tomatoes.

Table B.2 *Retail Price Revenue for Vegetable Varieties**

Vegetable	Retail Price	Produce/ft²	Revenue (/ft²/yr)
Cauliflower	1.49/head	0.4 head/ft²	$ .60/ft²/yr
Celery	.69/bunch	1.0 bunch	.69
Lettuce	.79/head	1.9 head	1.50
Tomato	.49/lb	4.0 lb	1.96

*Based on December 1981 prices.

Chapter 4

Outdoor Gardening

Susan Ervin

Today the United States is experiencing a home-gardening boom. According to the 1982-83 *Gardens for All* Gallup National Gardening survey, 44 million American households grew food in 1982. (That's 53 percent!) Thirty-eight million grew their own backyard gardens or participated in community projects, and another six million grew food on porches, rooftops, and window sills.[1]

Our 12-plus years of gardening research here at New Alchemy Institute has taught us not to take for granted the enormous food-growing potential of small spaces such as backyards or vacant lots. We've found that intensive gardening accomplished through spare-time labor is surprisingly productive, yielding between two and six times the volume of crops per acre as conventional agriculture, yet consuming a mere *one* percent of the energy and less than half the amount of water. (Actually, the water figure can run as low as 25 percent of that required by conventional farming methods.)

At New Alchemy we practice what is commonly known as *organic* gardening. That means we don't use chemical fertilizers, pesticides, or herbicides. Instead, we supply the necessary nutrients by enriching the soil with kitchen scraps, grass clippings, seaweed, and so on. We control insect pests and weeds through good management. But most important, we try to make the overall impact of our gardening a *positive* one: We strive to improve rather than to deplete the soil; we conserve water and fossil fuels; we make use of materials like garbage and leaves that are often mistakenly regarded as trash; and instead of indiscriminately spraying poisons, we create conditions that help the crops themselves deal with pests.*

Because outdoor gardening is so popular and so possible for so many of you, we are dedicating a substantial section of our book to a discussion of this noble art. Considering the abundance of gardening texts that crowd today's bookstore shelves, you may wonder how we can find enough new material to fill these pages. The answer is that we've compiled the results of 12 years' actual hands-on experience and carefully documented research: weighing produce, testing soil samples, measuring seaweed piles, counting cabbage worms . . . the list goes on.

Susan Ervin, one of our premier gardeners, is the ideal author for this chronicle. For more than eight years, Susan has been battling bean beetles and squishing squash borers at New Alchemy, and she has gardened extensively in Costa Rica and North Carolina, as well. Under her watchful guidance, our outdoor gardens are a wondrous sight to behold and a true inspiration for our thousands of visitors. But Susan has done more than make our gardens thrive; she's helped us all to discover that gardening is a joyful activity which requires no unusual talents or advanced technical expertise. In the following pages, it's likely that she'll convince you, too.

This chapter offers some of the basic principles of a healthy small-scale agriculture along with the inspiration you need to get started on your own. Susan will guide you through the whole season, from the time you select the best garden site and choose what to grow, right up 'til the day you harvest the last of your late-winter carrots from beneath the snow.

THE EDITORS

---

* Rather than dwell further on the drawbacks of conventional farming practices, we'll recommend several books that address the problems in depth: *The Unsettling of America,* by Wendell Berry; *Organic Agriculture: Economic and Ecological Comparisons with Conventional Methods,* by Robert Oelhaf; *Topsoil and Civilization,* by Vernon Gill Carter; and *New Roots for Agriculture,* by Wes Jackson. Further information on these sources appears in the Bibliography at the end of this chapter.

CHOOSING A GOOD SITE is the first step toward a successful garden. Perhaps you won't find the ''perfect'' spot, but probably you'll be able to locate an acceptable one. Explore the land around your home to see which part or parts can be converted to garden space. To determine the feasibility of any particular site, check the following points.

Is the site level?

Sloped land is particularly vulnerable to water erosion. Techniques such as terracing (see Fig. 1), building a series of raised beds on the contours of the slope, cover cropping, and mulching will be particularly useful in these situations. A southern orientation is ideal. East- or west-facing slopes usually are acceptable. A northern exposure receives the least amount of direct sunlight and will greatly limit your range of growable vegetables.

Fig. 1 Terrace gardening

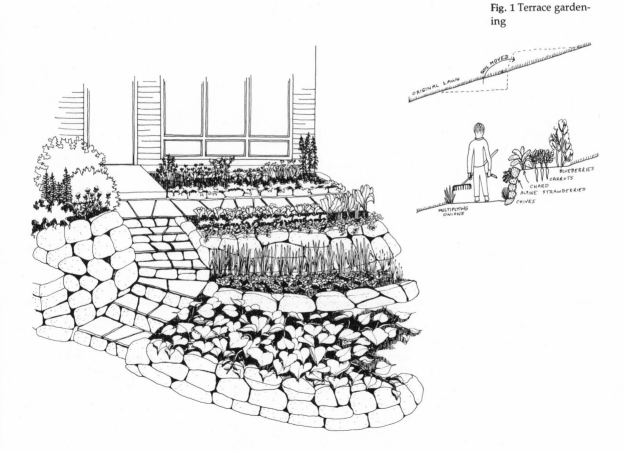

Will the garden get enough sun?

Lighting will be affected by shade from nearby buildings and trees. If you're examining the site in winter months, remember that the sun will be much higher in the sky during the growing season. You should take into account also the fact that deciduous trees will cast a more dense shadow throughout the summer months when they're in leaf than the bare tree of winter.

Your garden should receive full sun throughout most of the day. Six hours of full sun is the *minimum* light for growing the full range of garden vegetables. Your site should be 15 to 20 feet away from the trunk of the nearest tree and 3 to 5 feet from the nearest shrub to avoid root competition for nutrients.

Avoid low spots that have poor drainage or invite cold air to settle. Look for good, deep soil. In time, you can build soil anywhere, but it's certainly preferable to start with good soil. You'll want to pick a spot that's easy to clear, if possible. It's much easier to dig out weeds and grass than it is to clear brush and trees.

Another consideration in selecting your garden site is its accessibility. If a garden is close to the house, you'll be more likely to keep an eye on it. You'll also be likely to use it more. You could plant a small salad garden near the house for your daily needs and position a bigger garden a little further away. In permaculture planning (see Chapter 7), garden sites are always placed as close to the door of the house as possible and often along major pathways as well.

You'll need access to water, so plan on either running hoses from an outside faucet or laying plastic pipe to the garden site. In freezing climates, these will have to be shut off in winter. A fish pond is an excellent water source. (See the discussion of irrigation in Chapter 5.)

You may have to compromise in selecting your site. At New Alchemy, our garden site had the best soil on the property and was in grass instead of weeds, trees, or brush, but it's in a fairly low spot that frosts early. Plants on higher ground at the farm live a couple of weeks longer.

Even if you don't have room for a spacious garden, you can still grow food. Try replacing the traditional ornamentals with food plants grown close to the house. A vegetable garden can be remarkably beautiful, especially if you include flowers and herbs.

In a sunny bed near the house, plant tomatoes, eggplant, and peppers mixed with marigolds; border them with parsley and low-growing flowers like portulaca and lobelia. On the shadier side of the house, try lettuce, dwarf kale, and rhubarb chard mixed in with impatiens and begonias, and bordered by chives and alyssum. A variety of peppers could go along your

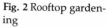

Fig. 2 Rooftop gardening

front walkway—round red cherry peppers, long red cayenne, yellow banana and Hungarian wax peppers, plus some green bells. Pole beans, peas, and cucumbers can be grown on a fence or trellis. Numerous dwarf plants can be grown in small spaces.

Chapter 2 explored the possibilities of container gardening, the indoor growing of food plants in window boxes and other containers. You can grow food in containers outside, as well, if your space is very limited. And if you don't have any open land at all, consider the roof over your head. Many structures have flat-roofed porches or additions, and inner-city dwellings have spacious rooftop areas that might accommodate an ambitious community garden. See Fig. 2 for an example of intensive rooftop gardening in containers.

The Soil

Soil building and maintenance is the heart of good gardening. Most food plants grow best in a rich fertile soil, and, as we will see later, healthy soil is the basis of pest control in organic agriculture.

Soil is composed of organic and inorganic materials. The inorganic part is rock that has been broken up over the ages by weathering. The organic part is made up of the remains of things that have lived—plant and animal residues, some completely decomposed, others still close to their original state. The breakdown of organic matter depends on the activity of microorganisms in the soil: fungi, bacteria, insects, and earthworms. These microorganisms utilize decomposing organic matter as food and return it to the soil as humus. This dark, crumbly material slowly continues to decay, providing needed nutrients for plant growth. The rate of activity of the microorganisms depends on the temperature of the soil, the moisture, the presence of adequate oxygen, and the type of organic material present.

To assess the quality of soil in a potential garden site, just dig up a sample and examine it.

Is it dark in color? Does it have a rich earthy smell, like soil in a forest? Are there earthworms in it?

If the answer to all three questions is yes, then your soil is probably fertile.

What kind of soil do you have?

It's a good idea for the neophyte gardener to take a soil sample and have it tested. Do-it-yourself soil-testing kits are available, but often it's better to have tests performed by the professionals at your county agricultural aid office or a university extension service. Call them; they'll tell you how to obtain and send the soil. The test report will describe the condition of your soil. Here on Cape Cod, for instance, most soils are sandy, low in organic matter, high in acidity, and have several nutrient deficiencies.

What is the soil pH?

Acidity-alkalinity is measured on a pH scale of 0 to 14, 0 being the most acid and 14 the most basic. This information will be included in your soil report. Unlimed soils at the New Alchemy farm have a pH of about 5.0. The desired pH for most garden crops is between 6.5 and 6.8.

What is now growing on your potential garden site?

Often, the existing vegetation is a good clue to the quality of your soil. For example, our natives—bayberry, cranberry, blueberry, sweet fern, oak, and pine—are all acid-loving plants, which indicates the acidity of Cape Cod soils. Table 1 shows the pH preferences of common plants.

Plants need a broad range of nutrients. Some elements, called *macronutrients*, are needed in large quantities; others, called *micronutrients*, are needed in much smaller amounts. However, they are all necessary for plant growth. Table 2 lists essential nutrients and their sources. Most nutrients will be supplied in adequate amounts by the use of a variety of organic materials.

Nitrogen, phosphorus, and potassium are all considered major elements for plant growth and are necessary in very large amounts. Anything organic (that is, anything that has been alive or comes from something living) contains nitrogen and many other nutrients. Some organic materials are much higher in nitrogen than others. Among the best sources are fresh green plants (especially legumes), animal manures, fish wastes, animal parts (blood and bone), and coffee grounds. Nitrogen and other nutrients are made available to plants as these substances decompose.

Natural rock minerals are a good source of potassium and phosphorus as well as of a number of micronutrients. Ground rock phosphate, a fine powder, is rich in phosphorus. Greensand, a mineral deposit from ancient sea beds, is a good source of potassium and also of trace minerals. Granite dust is another good source of potassium. Wood ashes contain both potassium and phosphorus, but they are better suited for maintenance than for initial compensation for nutrient deficiencies.

We feel that rock powders are superior to chemical fertilizers because the rock powders release their nutrients into the soil slowly. The chemical-fertilizer forms of potassium, phosphorus, and lime have been processed so that they are highly soluble. Nutrients are made readily available to plants, but they leach away very quickly. Because of these rapid losses, they must be reapplied each year and the price is ever-increasing. Rapidly released nutrients sometimes burn plants and destroy soil microorganisms. When leached out of the soil, these chemicals are a source of water pollution.

Lawrence Hills, a prominent British organic-gardening researcher, says, ''Plants can tell the difference between organic and inorganic fertilizers because the organic ones—especially the ground mineral rocks—are available slowly under exactly the same conditions of water, light, and warmth that plants naturally require. Provided the demands keep in step with the deliveries, a shop can manage on a very small stock.''[2]

Table 1 *pH Preference of Common Plants**

Quite acid (pH 4.0 to 6.0)		
Azalea	Heather	Pecan
Bayberry	Huckleberry	Potato, Irish
Blackberry	Lupine	Radish
Blueberry	Lily	Raspberry
Chrysanthemum	Lily of the valley	Rhododendron
Cranberry	Marigold	Spruce
Fescue	Mountain laurel	Sweet potato
Flax	Oak	Watermelon
Heath	Peanut	Yew

Slightly acid (pH 6.0 to 6.5)		
Apple	Gooseberry	Rape
Barley	Grape	Rice
Beans, lima	Kale	Rye
Bent grass	Lespedeza	Salsify
Bluegrass	Millet	Snap bean
Buckwheat	Mustard	Soybean
Cherry	Oats	Squash
Collards	Pansy	Strawberry
Corn	Parsley	Sudan grass
Cotton	Parsnip	Timothy
Cowpeas	Pea	Tomato
Eggplant	Peach	Turnip
Endive	Pear	Vetch
Gardenia	Pepper	Wheat
Gloxinia	Pumpkin	

Neutral to alkaline (pH 7.0 to 7.5)		
Alfalfa	Cantaloupe	Leek
Alyssum	Carrot	Lettuce
Asparagus	Cauliflower	Okra
Beet	Celery	Onion
Broccoli	Clover	Quince
Brussels sprouts	Cucumber	Spinach
Cabbage	Iris	Swiss chard

* Reprinted from *How to Grow Vegetables and Fruits by the Organic Method* by J.I. Rodale © 1970 by Rodale Press, Inc. *Permission granted by Rodale Press Inc., Emmaus, PA 18049.*

In most situations, the addition of organic matter will not in itself ensure adequate levels of certain critical elements, such as phosphorus and potassium. You can add these nutrients by applying rock powders or chemical fertilizers to the garden soil.

Table 2 *Essential Nutrient Elements* and Their Sources†*

Essential elements used in relatively large amounts		Essential elements used in relatively small amounts	
MOSTLY FROM			
AIR AND WATER	SOIL SOLIDS	SOIL	SOLIDS
Carbon	Nitrogen	Iron	Copper
Hydrogen	Phosphorus	Manganese	Zinc
Oxygen	Potassium	Boron	Chlorine
	Calcium	Molybdenum	Cobalt
	Magnesium		
	Sulfur		

*Unlike the 17 listed here, certain other minor elements (sodium, fluorine, iodine, silicon, strontium, and barium) do not seem to be universally essential, although the soluble compounds of some may increase crop growth.

†This chart reprinted with permission of MacMillan Publishing Company from *The Nature and Properties of Soil*, 8th Ed. by Nyle C. Brady. Copyright © 1974 by MacMillan Publishing Company.

If your local agricultural supply store doesn't stock rock minerals, they can probably order them for you. Organic farming groups such as Natural Organic Farmers Association (NOFA) of Antrim, New Hampshire, and Eaton Valley Agricultural Service of Derby Line, Vermont, place bulk orders.

Standard application for rock fertilizers is 10 pounds per 100 square feet every three or four years. It's better to apply them heavily every few years than lightly every year, since breakdown is slow. (It also saves labor.) Fall application is best, but if you've missed that, spring will do.

To summarize: Apply the following rock fertilizers every third or fourth fall at 10 pounds per 100 square feet:

• Ground rock phosphate (source of phosphorus)

• Greensand or granite dust (source of potassium and trace minerals)

• Ground limestone (source of calcium and alkalizer for acid soils)

A thorough discussion of soils requires a book of its own, and four excellent texts deserve special recommendation: *The Nature and Properties of Soil*, by Nyle C. Brady; *Soil*, by Gene Logsdon; *Soil Fertility*, by Jerome Belanger; and *Fertility Without Fertilizers*, by Lawrence D. Hills. (See Bibliography at end of chapter for further information.)

Soil Preparation

Now we'll examine several methods of preparing new garden plots and take a look at basic annual soil preparation practices.

There are different ways to establish a new garden. Your choice will depend on the size and condition of your garden-plot-to-be, the tools at your disposal, the amount of effort you're willing or able to expend, and the amount of time you have. You can use a rototiller, you can dig by hand, or you can decide not to turn the soil at all.

If you're creating a brand new garden, there's a good chance you'll be starting with an area that is in sod, either a part of your existing lawn or a grassy field. If not, probably you'll have to clear brush, bushes, and trees (this includes getting the roots out) before you can follow the steps below. In a lawn or field, your initial task will be to kill the sod. Start in the fall, if it's at all possible; you'll be way behind if you wait until spring. You can either use a rototiller to dig up the plot or dig it by hand.

USING A ROTOTILLER

To prepare the plot with a rototiller, mark off the boundaries of the plot and chop or mow it as low as possible. Then, beginning with a shallow setting and progressing to a deep one, till the whole area several times. A tiller doesn't really turn the soil under—it loosens up the soil and mixes it. Rear-powered tillers are more manageable than front-powered ones and are not at all strenuous to use. Rental centers always have tillers, and you can probably finish most of what you need to do in half a day.

Grasses are very tenacious, so it will be worthwhile to *remove* as many grass clumps as patience will allow. Otherwise you'll have a hard time during the summer trying to keep grass left in the garden from taking it over. Certain common grasses (like couch or twitch) can make a new plant from every little bit of broken root left in the soil. You can till, wait a week to let the grass roots dry out, and till again for an extra shot at the problem grasses.

After clearing out the grass clumps, spread leaves, manure, seaweed, straw, and the appropriate rock powders and till them all in. Thick layers of organic material get all tangled around the blades and do not mix in well, so do a thin layer at a time. Of course, compost is even better than these coarse materials.

Next, you'll want to hand-dig a straight edge around the garden, cutting the roots of the grass and weeds bordering it and leaving a slight trench to keep them from crawling back into the plot so quickly. You'll need to hand-dig the corners where the tiller has missed, if you're making a square or rectangular plot.

Finally, you can either seed a cover crop of winter rye or put on a good thick mulch (sée sections on Cover Crops and Mulching). If you are doing this soil preparation in the spring, you may want to use a black plastic mulch the first year to hold down determined grasses. We have successfully used old black plastic leaf bags held in place with seaweed and manure to eliminate any weeds or grass in a first-year plot.

HAND DIGGING

Although it's harder work, you can prepare your soil the same way with just a shovel and a spading fork. Again, begin by mowing. If the plot is covered with coarse, tenacious grasses, you'll want to dig out the roots. In any case, use a sharp shovel to dig and chop down to the depth of one foot. If there is only a shallow layer of topsoil and the subsoil is hard and poor, shovel the topsoil aside, loosen the subsoil, and then replace the topsoil. Preserving the topsoil like this is more work, but the effort will be worth it if you have a very poor subsoil. Just loosen and mix the soil; don't turn it over. A spading fork—like a small pitchfork but with broader, flat, dull tines—is good for breaking up clods and clumps. Again, the more weeds and grass you remove, the better off you'll be. They can be composted and thus not wasted, but they should *not* be left to reroot and reseed in the garden. Don't count on having a light, fluffy plot after one spading; the texture of a good garden soil results more from the presence of lots of organic material than from cultivation. Proceed with the edging, manuring, cover cropping, and mulching as you would for a tilled plot.

INTENSIVE BEDS

A special method of soil preparation is the building of intensive, or raised, beds. This procedure is based on an old European method. A block of soil is dug, loosened, and mixed with compost. The gardener walks only on pathways next to the bed instead of on the bed itself. These raised beds are an excellent way of loosening the soil and preventing further compaction, as well as of concentrating nutrients where you need them.

Each bed is a raised soil area three to five feet wide—a comfortable distance to reach across from either side. Raised beds can be any length you like. To build beds for the first time, you will "double-dig" the soil. This means that soil one shovel's depth is moved aside, a second shovel's depth is dug and loosened, and the topsoil is replaced.

Although your work will be much easier if you thoroughly till the area you're going to make into beds, tilling is not required for a proper raised bed. After you've tilled or at least cleared the area, lay out the dimensions of the first bed. Mark off a five-foot-wide strip, preferably running north to south, of whatever length is appropriate to your garden. Use strings tied between sticks to mark straight lines along the length of the bed. Starting at one end, dig a narrow strip across the width of the bed, moving one shovel's depth (eight inches or so) of soil aside or putting it into a wheelbarrow. You'll use this soil later. Then dig and loosen a second shovel's depth. Then move back and dig out another strip of topsoil, right next to the strip you first dug, and put this topsoil on top of the subsoil you left exposed on the first strip. Add compost or rotten manure and mix it in. Then loosen up the second strip a second shovel's depth. Move back, dig out a third strip of topsoil, and put it on the subsoil of the second strip, adding and mixing in compost. Loosen the third strip of subsoil, and so on, until you've reached the end of the bed. You'll have a strip of exposed subsoil at the end, onto which you'll place the topsoil that you put aside when you dug the first strip. Always stand on the undug portion of the bed while you're digging, not on the newly dug, uncompacted part. Figure 3 illustrates this digging-and-loosening process.

Next, dig a foot-wide pathway six to twelve inches deep alongside the bed, throwing the topsoil you dig out on top of the bed. Don't dig so deep that you're digging out poor subsoil and throwing it onto the fertile bed surface. Make the sides of the ditch sloping, not perpendicular, to prevent erosion. It's good to mix in lots of compost with this top layer. If you have only a little bit of compost, save it for this top layer instead of mixing it with the deeper soil. Rake the top and edges smooth. Don't let the bed hump up in the middle; in fact, make it slightly concave to prevent erosion.

A raised bed is an excellent way to prepare and improve the soil and will give you a pretty good first-season garden. Building a raised bed isn't nearly as complicated as it sounds. Look again at Fig. 3 for reassurance.

During the summer, fill the pathway or ditch alongside the bed with organic material—weeds, vegetable trimmings, spent plants, and thin layers of manure, leaves, seaweed, grass, and straw—as if you were building a small compost pile. This is *sheet composting*: thin sheets of organic material composting in place. It's handy to have a place to throw the weeds and vegetable material. These materials act as a mulch on the sides of the bed. They'll prevent excess moisture loss, and you'll be making compost right in the garden where you'll need it!

You may not want to put your whole garden into intensive beds. They're very good for mixed garden vegetables but a lot of work for things that need more space—corn, for example, or vine squash, pole beans, cucumbers, melons, and potatoes. If you have a light soil, or if you don't want to do so much digging, you can make adequate beds by loosening only one shovel-depth down. We emphasize the word *adequate*; these beds won't be quite as good as ones you loosen deeply.

A caution for whatever soil-preparation method you're using: *Don't work the soil when it's wet.* A clay soil can harden into brick-like lumps, a familiar occurrence to Southerners (like your author, who grew up in red-

Fig. 3 Digging intensive beds

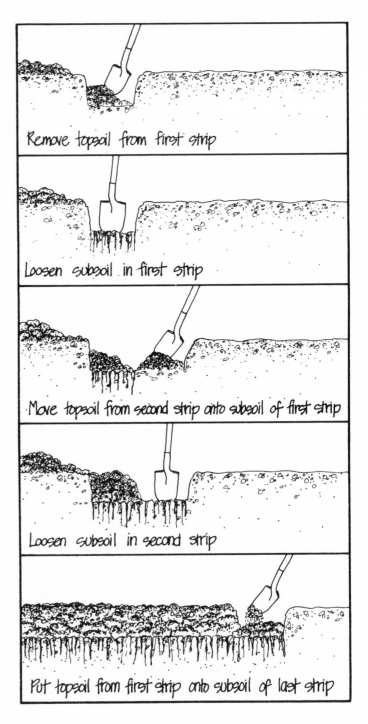

Remove topsoil from first strip

Loosen subsoil in first strip

Move topsoil from second strip onto subsoil of first strip

Loosen subsoil in second strip

Put topsoil from first strip onto subsoil of last strip

clay country). Even a sandy soil will compact if it's handled when wet. This is especially true of a soil low in organic matter, as a new garden no doubt will be.

NO-DIGGING METHOD

One interesting method of preparing a new garden requires no tillage. Our experience with it is limited, but the method appears to be promising. Bill Mollison of Australia describes it in his book *Permaculture Two.*[3] Without cutting or clearing grasses and weeds, he spreads a thin layer of high-nitrogen material such as blood or bone meal, or chicken or pig manure. Then comes a layer of coarse vegetable material—straw, seaweed, leaves, or weeds mixed with organic garbage. Then he "tiles" the whole area one strip at a time with a sheet mulch; this mulch can be thick paper, cardboard, old clothes, rugs, wood shavings, or whatever. Then he wets it down. (To discourage weeds, it's important that the mulch covers the lower layers completely.) Mollison then adds several inches of rich mulch, such as grass or straw with manure, and finally covers it all with a six-inch layer of seaweed, leaves, woodchips, or whatever weed-seed-free material he can get. It's best to do this plot preparation in the fall.

At planting time, holes are made through the layers of mulch, and plants are set in the holes. Next, some extra soil or compost is piled around them; then loose mulch is pulled back around the plants. Mollison finds that root crops don't do well the first year, because the soil is still compacted. The method works better for transplanted seedlings than for small seeds sown directly. He continues to bury kitchen garbage under the top layers of mulch, and each growing season he adds a fresh mulch layer along with some blood and bone meal.

There are a few problems associated with using this method here in the Northeast. The soil will stay cool under the thick mulch and fail to provide the best conditions for fruiting crops in our cool climate. Cool soil temperatures are not optimum for germination, either. Wireworms are often a problem in sod, and they may hang in longer in a plot like this than in a cultivated one, since cultivation exposes and kills them. Still, Mollison's method is an interesting alternative for those of you in gentler climates.

UPKEEP
Annual Soil Preparation

After the first growing season, soil preparation takes on a regular pattern. For the most part, you'll apply the same techniques you used to establish the new garden. You'll continue to compost, to cover crop, to mulch, to sheet compost, and to manure. In addition, you should start planning for crop rotations and possible fallowing.

OVERVIEW OF WAYS TO START A NEW GARDEN

Here is a condensed version of the several ways to start a new garden.

Fall Preparation with Tillage and Cover Crop
Till or hand dig in fall, removing grass clumps and weeds.

Spread compost, manure, straw, leaves, or seaweed; till in.

Seed with winter rye by mid-September.

Till in the rye in early spring, wait a week, till again.

Plant your garden, using as much compost as you can.

Spring Preparation with Tillage and Mulch
Till or hand dig in spring, removing grass clumps and weeds.

Dig in leaves, manure, seaweed, straw, or—preferably—compost.

Cover thickly with an organic mulch or (on strong sod) black plastic.

Move back the mulch to plant. The plastic mulch should be laid as you plant.

Make more compost and add it during the growing season.

Fall or Spring Preparation, Mollison No-Till Method
Without tilling or digging, sprinkle a thin layer of high-nitrogen material on the new plot in fall or spring (fall is preferable).

In the fall, every part of the garden should be covered in some way to prevent soil erosion and to add organic material. Take all dead plants to the compost area before cover cropping or mulching. Annual cover cropping carries many benefits: on-site nutrient provision, good winter-erosion prevention, and plenty of fresh green material to turn in the spring. Winter rye is the usual choice in the Northeast.

Thick mulch is an alternative to cover cropping. Even though you have mulched most of the garden during the summer, add another good layer of mulch and manure if you're not going to cover crop. Fall is the best time to apply manure. For us, the fall mulch is usually freshly fallen leaves covered with manure, whereas the summer's mulch is seaweed. Now that our soil is very fertile, we seldom cover crop. Mulching is sufficient to maintain fertility, and it requires less tillage.

Fall Preparation of Raised Beds

In the fall, we rotate our raised beds. We noted earlier that during the summer the ditch/pathways are filled with organic material, forming a

Cover with straw, leaves, weeds, kitchen scraps, etc.

"Tile" with paper, cardboard, cloth. Wet it down. Add a second layer of good organic material.

Cover with a thick layer of organic material that's free of weed seeds.

In spring, make holes through the mulch, plant, fill in with compost, replace mulch.

Replenish mulch each season. Bury kitchen garbage under it.

Combination Method
Till, removing as much sod as possible, and mix in manure, leaves, compost, etc., in fall or spring.

Proceed with the Mollison-mulch method, above.

Delayed Gratification Method (full-year cover cropping)
Till, weed, manure, and seed soybeans or buckwheat in spring.

Till in this cover crop in midsummer.

Reseed to buckwheat and till in late summer.

Seed winter rye in September to be knocked down and tilled in spring.

Plant garden in second spring.

(This procedure can also be followed in a selected *part* of your existing garden each year in order to maintain fertility.)

sheet compost. In the fall, we dig a new pathway down the middle of the bed, throwing the dirt on top of the old pathway, which is now filled with organic material. All the beds thus move over a path's width from where they were before, and the newly composted area is part of the next season's growing bed. Within a period of four years the entire area will be sheet composted. The double digging, as we described earlier, occurs only in the first year. Keep track of where your paths have been and in what direction they're moving, so you won't end up just alternating path and bed. Don't wait until the ground freezes and then try to dig your new pathways. One New Alchemist ended up using a pick axe to dig a pathway just before Christmas. Figure 4 provides a graphic diagram of the annual raised-bed cycle.

Sheet composting in pathways and rotating beds are the methods we use to manage our raised beds, but other possibilities exist. Organic material from the ditch can be dug out and spread over the bed surface in spring, leaving the bed in the same place. Or the sheet composting can be eliminated altogether. In this case, you'll mulch the sides of the beds to

Fig. 4 Annual raised
bed cycle

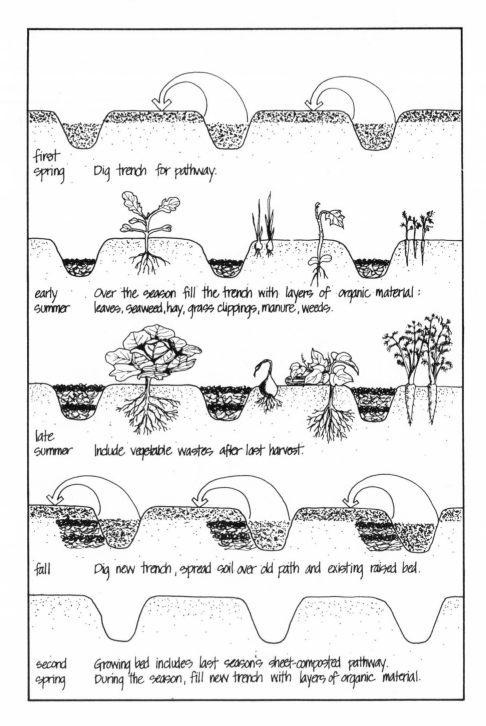

first
spring   Dig trench for pathway.

early   Over the season fill the trench with layers of organic material:
summer   leaves, seaweed, hay, grass clippings, manure, weeds.

late
summer   Include vegetable wastes after last harvest.

fall   Dig new trench, spread soil over old path and existing raised bed.

second   Growing bed includes last season's sheet-composted pathway.
spring   During the season, fill new trench with layers of organic material.

prevent excessive moisture loss, make compost in boxes or piles, and apply it in the usual way.

The better care you give your garden in the fall, the better start you'll get in the spring when there's so much to be done. Clean up well. All dead plants should go either in a compost pile or in the ditches of the raised beds. Clear dead vines off the trellises and poles. Remove impermanent poles and trellises, stakes, tags, and markers. Fall is the time to apply rock minerals if you need them. You'll feel good if your garden is put to bed snugly before the snow falls.

In the spring, you'll till cover-cropped areas, as we'll describe a little later in the discussion of green manures and cover crops. Till in mulch material, too, unless you want to establish a permanent mulch.

Soil-Building Techniques

Fertile soil is much more than an inert mass consisting of x amount of this element and y amount of that. Healthy, fertile soil contains a rich, active community of microorganisms; it has a good tilth, and it holds water well. All this is made possible by the presence of organic material. Organic soil management concentrates on the building of humus, the more-or-less stable substance resulting from decomposition of the soil's organic matter.

In this section, we'll discuss various methods of incorporating organic materials into your soil to build and maintain its fertility.

COMPOSTING

Composting is an excellent method of soil building, especially for small-scale agriculture. Compost itself is a mixture of organic materials piled together and allowed to decompose. A good compost pile is built strategically to create the ideal conditions for decomposition. As decomposition takes place, a compost pile may get as hot as 160°F. The heat comes from bacteria working on the organic materials. Actually, compost has been described as a bacterial bonfire, *not* just an inactive heap of dead stuff.

The primary purpose of composting is to convert organic materials into a product that contains concentrated nutrients. The bacteria in the compost heap absorb the nitrogen and slowly digest the carbonaceous materials, reducing the bulk of the pile and leaving a higher-quality concentrated fertilizer. The bacteria need nitrogen to work properly, so a heap made up solely of dry plants, straw, sawdust, and leaves (which are low in nitrogen and high in carbon) will not heat up and decompose quickly. A pile of dry leaves will take several years to break down, but a properly constructed compost heap can be ready in a matter of weeks.

What you need to make successful compost is a mixture of materials with the proper balance of carbon and nitrogen.

Do you have access to any of the following organic materials?

High-carbon	High-nitrogen
dry leaves	manure
sawdust	fresh grass clippings
straw	blood meal
seaweed	cottonseed meal
	coffee grounds
	weeds (chopped up)
	kitchen scraps

See Appendix A for the nutrient content of these and other common organic materials. The different materials should be applied in thin layers rather than all at once. Start with a thin layer of carbonaceous material (approximately six inches deep), then add approximately four inches of high-nitrogen material. Then, if you have access to manure, add a light, two-inch covering. Wet it all down and go on with the layering. We like to compare making a compost pile with making a casserole: The high-carbon materials are like the pasta, or rice, or whatever—that is, the bulk. The high-nitrogen materials are like the rich sauce. And the animal manure, like the cheese, pulls it all together.

In addition to the type of materials you use, four factors greatly influence the rate of decomposition: (1) the amount of moisture, (2) the air temperature, (3) the aeration, and (4) the size of particles. The pile should be damp but not soggy. Piles made in the summer will go faster than fall piles, but building compost is worthwhile whenever you have the raw materials. Turning a pile provides air to the microorganisms and thus speeds up decomposition. Reducing the size of particles exposes more surface area to the microbes and hastens decay, so you'll get compost faster if everything is chopped up before it's put into the pile. Turning the pile and chopping the materials require more work, of course. You're trading work for time. If you have pretty good garden soil already, you can afford to let the pile take its time. If you're trying to get going with a new garden that has poor soil, you'll probably want to get compost quickly.

QUICK COMPOST

So—to build a quick-composting pile, you'll need to collect all your materials and build the whole pile at once. The minimum size that will heat up is about 4 feet × 4 feet × 4 feet. You can make the compost in a free-standing heap or in a box. A box holds the heat in, which speeds up decomposition; it's also tidier, if you're concerned about that. Chop up all your materials with a shredder-grinder or a machete, or run over them with a lawn mower. We prefer to use a machete, as it doesn't burn up gasoline or make loud noises.

Layer the materials as described above. Avoid materials that are especially slow to decompose, such as sawdust or wood chips. If you use leaves or seaweed, be sure to chop or shred them well. Eelgrass, the most common plant that washes up on our local beaches, usually survives a short-term pile intact unless it's layered very thinly. For obvious reasons, weeds for composting should be collected before they go to seed. Fresh grass clippings are excellent, as is kitchen garbage or waste produce from the grocery store. If you use food garbage, it's best not to include meat scraps or bones. Coffee grounds are available in bulk from restaurants and are a good source of nitrogen. Use the best-quality animal manure you can get, leaving the horse manure that's three-quarters sawdust for a long-term compost pile, or for fall application to the fields. Manure with straw bedding will decompose faster than manure with sawdust.

After a couple of days, the pile should begin to heat up. It's interesting to have a long-stemmed thermometer stuck into the pile so you can see how hot it is, but sticking your hand in to feel it is good enough. When it's really hot, turn the pile with a pitchfork. If you have a freestanding pile, just fork all the stuff over into a new pile. If you build a box, it should be bottomless so you can lift it off the compost, move it over, and pitch the stuff back into it. Or you could have two boxes, and move the compost from one to the other. Turn the pile again in three or four days and keep on doing that until the pile doesn't heat up anymore. Add water if the pile begins to feel dry, but don't make it soggy.

If the pile fails to heat up or stops heating up before things are well broken down, you probably need more nitrogen. Urine diluted with water might get things going, or try manure or comfrey tea. Chopped wet green material, kitchen garbage, fresh grass clippings, or comfrey leaves will recharge the pile, too.

The compost should be ready to use in four to six weeks if you've used the right materials and turned the pile diligently. The finished pile will not be as fine as real humus, but it will be dark and crumbly and rich, even if there are still pieces of material that have not fully decomposed. The finished compost pile will be only one-third to one-half the size of the original pile.

LONG-TERM COMPOSTING

After about eight years of soil building at New Alchemy, our soil is excellent and we can afford to wait longer for finished compost. We make big piles without chopping the materials, and we turn the piles only once.

We don't complete a big pile in just one day, but we do try to get the whole thing done in a week or so. Materials are layered in the same way we layer them for a short-term pile, but we don't bother to chop or shred anything. Slower-rotting materials, like manure with lots of sawdust in it, can be included.

The pile should be about five feet wide, five feet high, and five feet (or more) in length. Make the pile flat on top so it will collect rain water, and cover the finished pile with a layer of straw to hold in moisture. During a dry summer, watering the pile occasionally will hasten decomposition. Late summer is a good time to build such a pile, when you're pulling spent plants out of the garden. We turn ours once in late fall and perhaps again in early spring, so the outside dry material gets moved to the center. Don't expect these piles to heat up very much. By early next summer, the pile will be pretty well broken down and the compost will be an adequate nutrient supplement, although it won't be of the highest quality. It will be lower in nitrogen than short-term compost, also coarser, and it may have living weed seeds.

NOTES ON MANURE

Animal manure is a major source of nutrients and organic matter in organic agriculture. It can be spread directly over your field or, better, used in compost.

Here on the Cape, where few livestock are raised, little manure is available. Human beings and equestrian horses are the only large animals. We are forced to settle for manure from riding stables, and it usually contains a lot of sawdust. In other areas, cow, chicken, and pig manure may be available, and all are better than horse manure. (Raising your own chickens is one way to get high-quality manure.)

As we stated earlier, use the best manure you can find for quick compost piles, and reserve the lower-quality stuff for direct application to the garden or for long-term piles.

Never put fresh manure directly on the field during the growing season. It's too high in nitrates and can burn your crops. Also, uncomposted manure can introduce various bacterial diseases. One year all our pumpkins collapsed in the field, rotten from the inside. We had applied fresh manure atop a thick mulch, thinking it would be okay by the time it leached through the mulch. It didn't burn the plants, but we're convinced that it caused the internal rot. If you're going to apply manure directly, you can do it in fall—or at least several weeks before planting—and till it in.

BACKYARD COMPOST

If your garden will be small and you don't have the materials, time, and/or energy to make a compost pile like the ones we've described, you can make small amounts of compost with your kitchen garbage. Even apartment dwellers can make compost in a garbage can. It feels good to make use of your garbage instead of sending it away to the dump.

Separate kitchen wastes from trash and keep them in a pail with a lid. If you empty the pail frequently, there will be no problem with odor. You can also empty the cat litter box into your compost bin.

A chicken-wire cylinder is a good container for backyard composting. To make one, coil chicken wire into a cylinder, overlapping the edges six inches or so for strength. Bend the nasty pointy wire ends around to fasten it together. Fold or crush in the bottom so it will stand up. Chicken wire usually comes in five-foot-wide strips; when you've got the bottom turned in, the cylinder will be about four feet tall. Place the cylinder where you want it and shovel in some dirt to hold it in place. A wooden bin is good, too, as we noted in our discussion of short-term compost.

When your organic garbage pail fills up, dump it in the cylinder or bin and cover lightly with soil or leaf mold or—best of all—manure. If you've placed only vegetable matter in your garbage and you have no rat problems, covering may not be necessary. Stop adding new garbage at least a month before you want to use the compost. We usually end one pile and start another in early winter; this gives the most recent additions ample time to decompose before late spring. When you complete a pile, turn the cylinder over, remove all the stuff, re-pile it, and let it finish decomposing. You may want to add a high-nitrogen substance (blood meal, manure, comfrey tea, or diluted urine) to effect more complete decomposition and thus produce higher-quality fertilizer.[4] While the completed compost pile waits for spring, you can start a new one in your compost bin.

Apartment dwellers can make compost in a garbage can on the porch, in the yard, or in the cellar. To make compost in a garbage can, put dirt in the bottom of the can, add your household garbage as it accumulates, and sprinkle with blood meal, bone meal, or diluted urine. A thin layer of dirt is okay, too, but won't give you as high a quality compost. See Chapter 2 for instructions on starting an earthworm compost system.

Keep the lid on the can to avoid odors. When the can is full or when you know you're going to need compost, stop adding fresh material, mix up the contents thoroughly, and wait until decomposition is complete.

Be ingenious in collecting compost materials. In the city, you could make a good compost just from shredded newspaper and wet coffee grounds. You can get mountains of spoiled produce from grocery stores. Tons of leaves are burned or hauled away every fall. Keep your eyes open!

USE OF COMPOST

If you have a new garden with poor soil, we suggest that in the spring you cover the whole thing with two inches of good compost and dig it in. If you don't have enough compost to do that, you can put a shovelful in the bottom of each hole you dig for a single plant. A layer of compost can be put in the bottom of the shallow trench you dig to start large seeds like beans, cucumbers, and corn. For fine seeds, such as carrots and lettuce, spread a thin layer of compost and seed directly into it. Make more compost during the summer and give your produce a side dressing around the plants' bases or along rows. You can't burn plants with compost, no matter how much you use. A few crops (such as sweet potatoes, peppers, and tomatoes) don't produce as well if they have too much nitrogen, but having too little compost is more likely to be a problem, especially in a new garden. So be generous.

Compost provides the needed nutrients in a form that is available to plants right away. And as it decomposes further, it continues to make nutrients available over long periods of time.

GREEN MANURES AND COVER CROPS

A *green manure* is a crop planted expressly to produce organic material that will be turned into the soil. A *cover crop* is a green manure that is planted in the garden in the fall to protect the soil over the winter and capture a few extra months of solar radiation. Green manuring is an excellent method of soil improvement because the nutrients are produced on-site rather than transferred from another ecosystem. The main drawback is the extra tillage required to plow green manures in, although ultimately it probably requires less labor than composting.

Plants such as alfalfa and clover are often deep-rooted; as green manures, they bring up nutrients from deep down in the soil. Others, like rye grass, form a shallow yet extensive web of roots. Winter rye will produce 400 to 800 pounds of root growth per year in a half-acre plot. The roots open channels in the soil for aeration and water movement.

Many green-manure plants are nitrogen-fixing. Bacteria in nodules on the roots of legumes convert atmospheric nitrogen into a form usable by plants. These plants will grow without depleting the nitrogen in the soil or will grow in nitrogen-poor soils. When dug back in, the nitrogen-fixing plants add their nitrogen to the soil. They can add 50 to 200 pounds of nitrogen per acre per year. Common legumes for green manure are clover, trefoil, peas, beans, vetch, and lespedeza.

Buckwheat and winter rye are the two cover crops we use most commonly in our region. Buckwheat is an annual plant that is very frost-sensitive, so it can be grown only during the summer months. It grows well on poor soils and is a good first crop on unimproved soils. Because buckwheat is very shallow-rooted, it's not the best cover crop for steeply sloped land. To build up the soil in a new garden plot, till well and then seed quite thickly, since buckwheat plants are rather spindly. It will flower and go to

seed about six weeks after planting; for maximum green-manure production, you should till it under when about one-fifth of the crop is in flower
and then reseed. If you start in May, probably you can get three crops in
one season, though we'd recommend seeding winter rye for the third
crop.

This intensive cover cropping ties up the garden space for a whole
growing season, but it will get you off to an excellent start the second year.

A local vegetable farmer and orchardist gave us a good idea for using
buckwheat. When a crop is finished in the summer, he pulls out the plants,
loosens up the soil, and scatters buckwheat. That way he doesn't have
bare, unproductive soil during the growing season, and the buckwheat is
turned under for green manure. You can plant buckwheat in a very small
space—where a row of beans has finished, or where a few early cabbages
have been harvested, or a tomato plant has died. Bees like buckwheat a lot,
so you're providing food for them at the same time you're feeding your
soil. It's a waste to plant buckwheat later than mid-August, since the first
light frost will kill it.

Winter rye or annual rye is not killed by frost. We can sow it as late as
the end of September here on the Cape and it will still grow, although mid-
September is better. It often takes several tillings to kill winter rye
completely. The best method is to chop or mow it quite early in the
spring—as soon as the snow is gone in northern areas. A week later, till it
in. If it re-sprouts, a second tilling may be necessary. It's preferable to complete the tilling process several weeks before planting; this allows the fresh
green material some time to decompose.

Every few years, you can cover crop a section of your garden for a full
season, taking it out of production and restoring fertility. This is called *fallowing*.

MULCHING

A mulch is a material put directly on the garden surface to conserve
moisture, inhibit weed growth, moderate temperature, and—if the mulch
is of an organic material—to add organic matter as it decomposes.

Mulching in the garden mimics the cycles of decay in nature. Each year
leaves fall to the ground, annual weeds and grasses die back, and all decay
and become a part of the soil. The effect of mulches on soil moisture and
temperature will be discussed later in this chapter; here we're concerned
with mulching as a method of soil building.

Our favorite mulches are leaf mold and seaweed. You can use whatever seaweed is available, although green seaweed (such as *Ascophyllum*) is
the best. We were initially concerned that soil nitrogen might be lost during mulch decomposition, but we've found that a seaweed mulch actually
increases both nitrogen and potassium.[5]

Collecting seaweed mulch on the shores of Cape Cod.

The main advantage of leaf mold (well-decomposed leaves with a high humus content) is the fact that leaves are so plentiful. The New Alchemy farm is close to the town dump, and we have signs there directing people to bring their leaves to us. Several local lawn services bring their leaves and grass clippings, too. Instead of sending your leaves to the dump, save them for your garden, and collect them from neighbors who don't use them.

Freshly fallen leaves are so light they'll blow away immediately. If you plan to put leaves on your garden in the fall, keep a supply of manure or seaweed on hand to weight them down. Or let the leaves rot over the winter and use them as a summer mulch. They decompose really well if you wet them down inside plastic leaf bags and seal the bags tightly. Otherwise, it takes a rather large quantity of leaves to break down well in a loose heap.

Another material you might be able to use as mulch is spoiled hay from riding stables or dairy farms. Spoiled hay and straw are both good and cheap (or free) in agricultural areas, but they're not common here on Cape Cod. Grass clippings are good around small plants. And there's still another alternative: you can grow your own mulch. Just take an area out of normal crop production and cover crop it with alfalfa, clover, buckwheat, or whatever. Cut the cover crop for mulch material in midsummer, leaving time for it to grow up again. This alternative is nice because it means you're importing fewer materials from outside.

Using Mulch

You should mulch between rows and around plants when they're big enough to avoid being smothered. Heat-loving crops such as tomatoes, peppers, eggplant, and melons shouldn't be mulched until they've blossomed, since mulch keeps the soil temperature down in the spring. You should mulch thickly for weed control—at least six inches and preferably more. If you don't plan to cover crop, add an additional layer of mulch in the fall to protect your soil from winter erosion.

PERMANENT MULCHES

A permanent mulch is a mulch that stays in place year after year. It is not tilled in and is renewed annually to maintain adequate thickness. In nature, organic matter falls to the ground, accumulates, and decomposes; a permanent mulch is a way of simulating this process and maintaining the nutrient supply in a good soil. After a few years of soil building (or right away, if you begin with a good piece of ground), a permanent mulch can save you a lot of labor along with the fuel you'd otherwise use in tilling. We've encountered a few problems—or at least special circumstances— when planting in an established mulch. In spring the soil under the mulch doesn't heat up quickly, so more seeds may rot or germination may be slower. The solution to that is to open up your rows or planting spots early, when the ground without mulch is starting to thaw. Move the mulch back, exposing the soil to the sun. Also, we have had more slug damage to young plants set in a permanent mulch. Rows should be cleared at least a foot wide. If you open up wide rows so the mulch isn't near the seedlings, you'll probably have fewer slug and other pest problems. We have found that after several years under mulch, a plot benefits from tillage; it's good to loosen up the soil again.

LIVING MULCHES

A living mulch is an established cover crop, often a legume, into which a food crop is planted. This method hasn't received much attention until lately; but with rising fuel and fertilizer costs, even conventional commercial farmers are beginning to see the promise it holds. Dead mulches obviously have to come from somewhere; either they're grown on the farm, harvested, and applied, or they're transported in from outside. To the home gardener, a single trip to the seashore to collect a load of seaweed or the purchase of three bales of straw may not be too much work or too much expense. But the number of truckloads of material we have to haul in for our half-acre garden here gets to be questionable in terms of fuel usage. A living mulch grows on-site and provides nutrients to crops growing in the same field. The cover crop and the food crop are grown at the same time, unlike a traditional fallowing wherein the field is taken out of production and cover cropped to restore fertility. Living mulch can also preserve moisture, reduce soil compaction from machinery, and eliminate root damage from cultivation.

A lot of research remains to be done with living mulches. We don't yet know under what conditions the living mulch will compete with the crop for nutrients and water and when it will help the crop. We don't know which plants make the best living mulches or which crops respond well. We don't know whether and how often the mulch cover should be mowed or whether planting strips should be tilled into the mulch. Our first efforts with living mulch showed severe water competition between crops and mulch.

If you want to try using a living mulch, White Dutch clover seems to do pretty well in the Northeast. What you want is a low-growing perennial plant that will make a dense cover to control weeds and that will over-winter well. Both corn and tomatoes have grown better in living mulch than they did in a clean-cultivated field. Soybeans also have shown positive responses to living mulches. Most likely you'll be hearing a lot about living mulches in the next few years. This method is by no means tried-and-true. As we noted above, our early results have been disappointing. But the concept is certainly worth pursuing.

An excellent book for inspiration and ideas is *The One-Straw Revolution*, by Masanobu Fukuoka. He describes permanent mulches, living mulches, double cropping, and other methods for a natural sustainable agriculture as well as the philosophical and spiritual basis for his no-till farming method.

Planning Your Garden

Winter is the time to start planning your garden. Your fall work is behind you, and the busy days of spring seem far away. Cold winter nights are the perfect time for looking at seed catalogs, deciding what to grow, and planning the next season.

First, it's advisable to start small. It's better to have a small garden in well-prepared soil, properly edged, properly fertilized, properly planted and tended, and used intensively, than to have a big, overgrown, untidy, infertile, frustrating one. If you have only a tiny space or a shortage of time or strength, you can have just a little salad garden—lettuce, herbs, spinach, a few cherry tomatoes in the sunniest spot, and some kale and Chinese cabbage in the fall. A 5-by-5-foot plot will provide a lot of salad greens. Trellises, poles, or ''teepees'' (poles tied together in a tripod) save space when you're growing cucumbers, pole beans, peas, or tomatoes.

Advancing in size, you can grow a garden large enough to provide a full range of vegetables all summer long or a bigger one to supply your winter food, too. A 25-by-30-foot plot should be about right for a summer garden for a family of four. With good management, you'll definitely have some excess for winter preserving.

WHAT TO GROW

It would seem obvious that you shouldn't grow things you don't really like to eat, but new gardeners often fail to realize that. Around here, people have a tendency to plant mountains of Chinese cabbage because it looks so nice early in the spring, but they're not really very interested in eating all of it. Some crops are notoriously high yielders, and most new gardeners find this promise too much to resist. Zucchini is the classic example.

So ask yourself a few important questions: Which vegetables are going to take up a lot of space? What is expensive or hard to find? What tastes best when it's really fresh?

Corn, potatoes, and squash all require lots of space; but whereas potatoes and squash are pretty cheap in the marketplace, sweet corn is not cheap and is delicious fresh-picked. Vine-ripened tomatoes are the only ones worth eating, but green beans and green peppers don't vary enormously so long as they're still crisp. Southern-grown melons may even be better than those you manage to grow in the Northeast, while, on the other hand, shipped iceberg lettuce bears no resemblance whatsoever to fresh garden lettuce. Fresh vegetables that you can't count on finding in your local market include kohlrabi, spaghetti squash, dill, Chinese greens, sorrel, rhubarb chard, wax beans, lima beans, okra, celeriac, mustard greens, hot peppers, stuffing peppers, herbs, and good lettuce. And don't forget the flowers!

Your site itself may dictate what you can grow. If your site is shaded, you may be limited to vegetables that grow well with a minimum of direct light, such as those listed below.

lettuce	onions
dill	beets
brussels sprouts	spinach
cabbage	Chinese greens
chard	kale

SUCCESSIONAL PLANTING

Whatever size garden you have, a very important aspect of its management is successional planting. Successional planting means keeping all your garden space in use throughout the growing season by following one crop with another. It's necessary to plan ahead and to time things properly. Plan on planting a crop for fall harvest in the same place you grew an early-spring crop. Or have new seedlings ready to set for late crops as soon as an early crop is finished. There are lots of possibilities. Here are a few examples:

Early cabbage followed by late lettuce

Early lettuce followed by beets or carrots for fall use and winter storage

Early bush beans followed by broccoli, cauliflower, or kale seedlings

Earliest corn followed by bush beans

Peas followed by cucumbers

Spinach followed by okra started in peat pots

Radishes followed by dill

Early beets followed by Chinese cabbage

The important thing is to keep your growing space in use—any of the late crops can follow any of the early crops. Successive small sowings of lettuce, radishes, beans, and others will provide more top-quality produce for a longer period than single larger sowings.

Select appropriate varieties for midsummer crops that mature in fall. In one catalog, for example, green beans range in time to production from 40 days to 65 days, so if you're seeding a large bean crop after an early summer crop, pick a quick-maturing bush bean. Certain broccoli and Chinese cabbage varieties are bred for early-spring planting, others for fall production. Some lettuces get off to an early start in the spring, others withstand midsummer heat and dryness well; some are more frost resistant. If you're planting root crops for winter storage, some varieties store better than others, retaining their color and flavor longer.

Another way to maximize production is called *catch cropping*. That means slipping in a quick crop while a slower one is maturing. You could plant lettuce, spinach, or radishes around your small tomato, eggplant, okra or pepper plants and have the early crop out of the way before the later crop needs the space. Early bush beans can be grown under late corn.

See Appendix B for a planting table for the Northeast. The information comes from J.I. Rodale's *How to Grow Vegetables and Fruits by the Organic Method*. In Rodale's book you'll find planting charts for other climatic zones of the United States.

Fig. 5 Plan for a small garden with north fence. Tall vine plants, such as tomatoes and beans, rise on the north end, and with these slow-growing vines are planted quick-maturing radishes, lettuces, and green onions. (The fence on which the vines grow can be made of chicken wire or any other convenient material.) Separate areas for carrots, beets, onions, and lettuce are divided into sections, to be planted one or two weeks apart. Adapted from *The Postage Stamp Garden Book* by Duane Newcomb. Copyright © 1975 by Duane G. Newcomb. Reprinted by permission of J.P. Tarcher, Inc., and Houghton Mifflin Company.

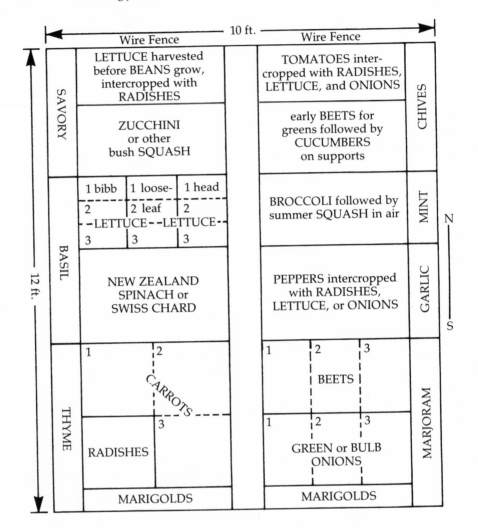

Interplanting of crops facilitates effective space and nutrient use, too. You can grow bush beans on the ridges along potato rows. Alternate rows of squash and corn; the squash spreads out between the corn rows. Some people grow pole beans in with their corn and let the beans climb up the cornstalks. (We've never perfected our timing on this one. Our corn tends to shade out our beans.) Shallow-rooted crops and deep-rooted crops can grow very close together without competing; we like to grow carrots and lettuce side by side. Crops that don't mind shade can be grown close to large shade-producing plants; for example, Swiss chard will thrive next to big tomatoes, but carrots will be shaded out.

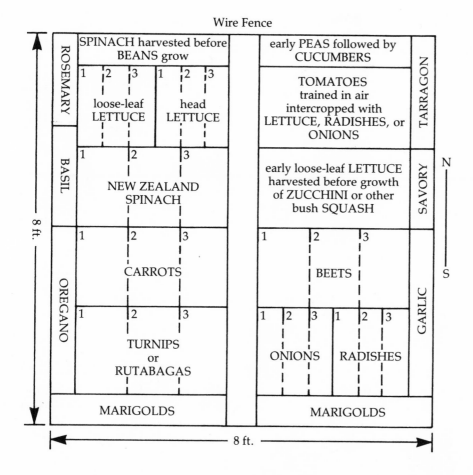

Wire Fence

| ROSEMARY | SPINACH harvested before BEANS grow | early PEAS followed by CUCUMBERS | TARRAGON |
| | 1 2 3   1 2 3 | |

Fig. 6 Plan for a small garden emphasizing early-spring vegetables. Cool weather plants, such as spinach and peas in this plan, can be planted early in spring and harvested before warm weather plants such as beans and cucumbers take over the same space. Marigolds and herbs here form the border. Adapted from *The Postage Stamp Garden Book* by Duane Newcomb. Copyright © 1975 by Duane G. Newcomb. Reprinted by permission of J.P. Tarcher, Inc., and Houghton Mifflin Company.

Figures 5, 6, and 7 show various designs for small gardens. These illustrations are reprinted from *The Postage Stamp Garden Book*, by Duane Newcomb.

PLANTING SCHEMES

It's a good idea to group together the crops that will be harvested last. Chard, Chinese greens, beets, leeks, carrots, lettuce under cloches (see Chapter 2 for a discussion of cloches) parsley, brussels sprouts, kale, and celeriac will be harvestable up until December in southern New England; these crops can interfere with your fall soil preparation if they're scattered all over the garden. You can start all your earliest crops in one section of the garden and replace them with the fall crops, giving the rest of the area over to full-season crops.

Fig. 7 Plans for a small garden with curved plots. This small bed has curving plantings much like irregular, natural-looking flower beds. Groups of vegetables are arranged in waving patterns, and niches here and there are filled with herbs. Adapted from *The Postage Stamp Garden Book* by Duane Newcomb. Copyright © 1975 by Duane G. Newcomb. Reprinted by permission of J.P. Tarcher, Inc., and Houghton Mifflin Company.

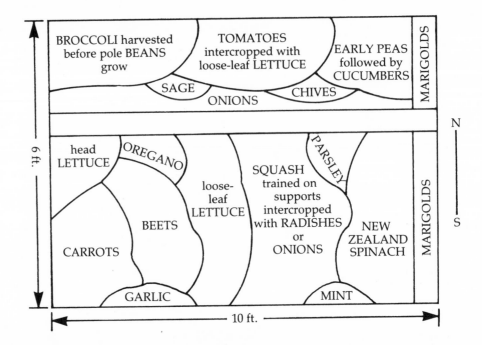

Rows or beds should run north–south to avoid shading. (One summer, a friend threatened to sue us for interfering with his solar rights because our very successful sunflowers were shading his whole plot.) If part of the garden is in partial shade, put shade-tolerant crops there. Lettuce, chard, kale, Chinese greens, dill, parsley and other herbs, beets, sorrel, and onions will do fine in a spot that's in shade part of the day. The cabbage family is somewhat shade-tolerant, too.

The seeding instructions on seed packages and in many garden books call for more space between plants and rows than our intensive approach requires. This broad spacing is for machine cultivation or reckless hoeing. Our intensive planting requires a fertile soil and careful tending. In raised beds, we leave just as much space between plants as each mature plant will fill. And if they're slow-growing plants, that space will be filled in temporarily with a catch crop. We sow direct-seeded crops thickly and plan on thinning if necessary. But you must use good judgment here; if you overcrowd plants, your results will be disappointing.

For row planting, we try to leave enough space between rows to move through carefully but not enough to stroll. Squash vines spread amazingly; it's practically impossible to leave space to walk between rows so just plan on tiptoeing in the squash patch. You can plant things that don't need tending between rows of things that do; for example, potatoes between double rows of bush beans. We like double rows or bands of crops rather

than single rows that waste so much space. Last summer we had dry beans, corn, and winter squash growing in one field. Double rows of corn were flanked with double rows of beans; in the center of a five-foot strip, a single row of vine squash was set; then we set another double-bean/double-corn strip.

Companion Planting

Companion planting is planting together certain crops that enhance one another's growth or protect one another from pests. Most of our companion planting is of the common sense variety—a deep-rooted crop next to a shallow-rooted one, a plant that can tolerate partial shade beneath a sun-loving one, nitrogen-fixing legumes interplanted with heavy feeders. Many people do their companion planting on the basis of who likes who. In most cases it's not known why certain crops respond well to one another, and often what seems to be true in your site is not true in your neighbor's. Because plants do exude chemicals from their roots, it does make sense that some combinations would do better together than others. A table of suggested companion plantings appears as Appendix C at the end of this chapter.

We interplant lots of flowers and herbs among our vegetables. The flowers and herbs attract beneficial insects and probably their odors mask the odors of the crop plants, confusing the pests a bit. Two good books on the subject are *Companion Planting*, by Louise Riotte, and *Companion Plants and How to Use Them*, by Helen Philbrick and Richard Greg.

Perennials

Perennial vegetables live and produce year after year. They should be placed to one side of your garden or else given a plot to themselves; otherwise they'll interfere with annual cultivation. Perennials usually take special handling during the first year or two; but once established, they require very little attention. Common successful perennials for a vegetable garden in the Northeast are asparagus, rhubarb, bunching onions, chives, sorrel and Jerusalem artichokes.

Many common herbs, including thyme, sage, rosemary, and oregano, are perennial. In addition to culinary herbs, you can grow many good tea herbs—lemon balm, mints, bergamot—and many medicinal herbs. A small herb garden is very beautiful as well as useful. Good books about herbs include *The Rodale Herb Book; A Modern Herbal*, by M. Grieve; and *Herb Gardening At Its Best*, by Sal Gilbertie.

Suggestions for Different Crops

In this section, we'll provide some special suggestions for individual crops. Try to find a regional seed source—that is, a seed company that sells

seeds adapted to and grown in your region. Agricultural supply stores and garden centers often stock varieties that are popular and successful locally. Some of our favorite seed sources for the Northeast are:

Johnny's Selected Seeds
Albion, ME 04910

Stokes Seeds, Inc.
Box 548
Buffalo, NY 14240

R.H. Shumway Seedsmen
628 Center St.
Box 777
Rockford, IL 61105

Vermont Bean Seed Co.
Garden Lane, VT 05732

Nichols Garden Nursery
1190 North Pacific Hwy.
Albany, OR 97321

Herbst Seedsmen
1000 North Main St.
Brewster, NY 10509

You might consider joining forces with friends or neighbors to buy seeds. This way you can share packets and enjoy a greater number of varieties. Some seeds save well from one year to the next; others don't. Table 3 lists the approximate age at which seeds of good initial viability stored under cool, dry conditions still give a satisfactory stand of vigorous seedlings.

In the following descriptions, the dates assume conditions similar to those here on Cape Cod. Our last frost is generally in mid-May. Therefore frost-sensitive plants can't go out until the third week in May. Adjust your seeding dates accordingly, depending on your own last-frost date. Most crops can be started in the greenhouse eight to ten weeks before that time.

Asparagus Perennial Start the seed in flats, transplant in mid-spring, or buy locally grown root stock. One method of culture is to dig deep trenches (a foot or more), fill in one-third of the way with rotted manure or compost, and set the young plants or root stock. Add ground limestone or mulch the surface with broken-up clam shells. Space seedlings six inches apart; space root stock a foot apart. As the plants grow, fill in the trench with more manure or compost. Many people grow fine asparagus beds without digging the deep trenches. They just set the plants in the regular way in rich soil. You'll want to let the plants put all their energy into growth and the development of a strong root system, so don't plan to harvest until the third year if you started with seeds, or the second if you used rootstock. To harvest, cut or break the shoots early in spring, taking any shoots thicker than your index finger and leaving the smaller ones. Get them while the flower heads are tight. Each year, give the asparagus a side dressing of compost or well-rotted manure and mulch it well to protect it in winter.

Basil A favorite culinary herb. Start seeds in flats in March. Water carefully; seedlings have a tendency to get leggy in the greenhouse and die

SEED	YEARS	SEED	YEARS	
Asparagus	3	Lettuce	5	**Table 3** *Seed Viability*
Beans	3	Martynia	1–2	
Beets	4	Muskmelon	5	
Broccoli	5	Mustard	4	
Brussels sprouts	5	New Zealand spinach	5	
Cabbage	5	Okra	2	
Cardoon	5	Onions	1–2	
Carrots	3	Parsley	2	
Cauliflower	5	Parsnips	1–2	
Celeriac	5	Peas	3	
Celery	5	Peppers	4	
Chard, Swiss	4	Pumpkin	4	
Chervil	3	Radish	5	
Chicory	5	Roselle	3	
Chinese cabbage	5	Rutabaga	5	
Ciboule	1–2	Salsify	2	
Collards	5	Scorzonera	2	
Corn	1–2	Sea kale	1–2	
Corn-salad	5	Sorrel	4	
Cucumbers	5	Southern pea	3	
Dandelion	2	Spinach	5	
Eggplant	5	Squash	5	
Endive	5	Tomatoes	4	
Fennel	4	Turnips	5	
Kale	5	Watercress	5	
Kohlrabi	5	Watermelon	5	
Leeks	3			

*Reprinted from *The Seed-Starter's Handbook* © 1978 by Nancy Bubel. Permission granted by Rodale Press, Inc., Emmaus, PA 18049.

from overwatering. Try Dark Opal basil: it has beautiful deep-purple leaves and pink flowers and is just as flavorful as the regular green basil. Basil is frost sensitive. Keep the flower heads pinched back for larger leaf growth.

Beans Inoculate all bean seeds with legume inoculant, a package form of the nitrogen-fixing bacteria found on the root nodules of legumes. By introducing the bacteria, you make sure it's there for the beans to use. It's available in gardening stores or through catalogs. Beans should be seeded directly and will not survive transplanting. Seed double rows to save space.

Green Beans   Bush beans can mature in as short a time as 45 days. Seed your first crop early, when the danger of frost damage has passed. Purple Pod beans can be planted earlier than other varieties because they don't tend to rot in cold soil. Don't seed all your beans at once. They yield best and give the nicest beans when they first start to bear, but they slow down after a while, especially if you're plagued with Mexican bean beetles. Replant a couple of times during the summer and keep them thoroughly harvested to lengthen their production season. If you let the beans get oversized, the plants will stop producing. Pole beans grow up to eight feet tall and need to be trellised or strung up some way (see Fig. 8). They produce over a longer period of time than bush beans do. We like the flat-podded varieties; Romano is very tender and "buttery" even at a large size. One very favorite green bean is the Mountaineer Half Runner or White Half Runner; it's sort of midway between a bush and pole bean, but it doesn't have to be strung up.

Wax Beans   Wax beans are yellow snap beans. We don't think they're as flavorful as green beans, with the exception of a flat-podded yellow pole bean that a friend in North Carolina grows. We call them "Polanski's Polish Pole Beans." Not widely available! But if you find a flat yellow pole bean with large brown seeds, plant it.

Dry Beans   Dry beans are one of our favorite crops because they come in so many pretty colors and patterns, they're a good source of protein, and they're easy to store. They take very little work, since the harvest is all done at once—and what's more they need no irrigation. Among the best-producing and hardiest varieties here are Dark Red Kidney or Charlevoix, Light Red Kidney, Maine Yellow Eye, and Jacob's Cattle. There are two rare old New-England varieties we've grown that do just as well, too, but are not generally available: Brown Beauty, a beautiful yellowish-brown bean, and Black Beauty, a long shiny black one, a much better yielder for us than the common Black Turtle. It's larger, too, for easier shelling. They're available, along with a couple hundred others we'd love to try, from Kent Wheely of Seed Savers Exchange, Princeton, MO 64673. This is a tiny operation run on love, so please include $2.00 for the catalog. The Vermont Bean Seed Co. in Garden Lane, Vermont also has an excellent selection.

Fig. 8 Bean trellis

We usually interplant dry beans with our sweet corn. All varieties of beans are ready here in September—early or late, depending on when we plant. It's best to let the crop dry in the field before harvesting, or you'll need access to a warm dry attic somewhere to dry them all. Normally, autumn is dry enough here to let them field dry, but one year we got constant rain for a couple of weeks *just* when the beans were ready to come in, and the whole crop sprouted in the field. Two days of rain won't hurt, if they're followed by good sun. Plants piled up wet will sprout or rot in no time.

Lima Beans   Home-grown baby lima beans are wonderful! The Southerners among us say that rather defensively, as the Northerners often remember lima beans from their childhoods as awful fat things in cans. We have more luck with baby bush limas than with pole limas, which sometimes are at the peak of production about the time it frosts. Plant in late May when the soil is warm. They're better frozen than dried.

Sprouting Beans   We grow Azuki and mung beans quite well here, and they're not bothered very much by the Mexican bean beetle.

Soybeans   Your author doesn't grow many soybeans because she doesn't like them. Certainly they're an excellent source of protein. For those of you who like soybeans and want to grow enough to make tofu and tempeh, Johnny's Selected Seeds has a number of good varieties for this climate. Most commercial catalogs have only a couple of standard varieties. There are certain varieties especially selected for eating green as shell beans. Soybeans are an excellent green-manure crop; after harvesting the beans green for shelling, turn in the rest of the plant, getting both fertilizer and a harvestable crop.

Beets   Beets can be seeded in early April, several weeks before the last frost. They don't like transplanting; direct-seeded beets will probably catch up with beets transplanted at the same time. Often beets don't germinate well, so plant rather thickly and then thin them if necessary. Thin before the roots get all tangled up or you'll damage them. Or pinch off the extras; beet thinnings are good to eat. Most beets are sweetest when they're fairly small—tennis-ball size. You can feel around the beet with your fingers to see if it's big enough. Lutz Greenleaf is an excellent one to try. It has prolific all-green foliage that stays tender month after month, and the beets have a good flavor even when they're huge. Some beets keep better than others—the very early varieties aren't keepers. For a fall crop, July 4 is about the latest you can plant here for full growth. Beets love seaweed mulch; their yield is doubled[6] and the foliage doesn't get the red spots it gets in unmulched soil.

Broccoli Start broccoli in flats in March and have transplants ready to go out in late April (or early May, if it's a cold spring). If they've been properly hardened off, a light frost won't hurt them—but a heavy frost will. Seed again in June for the fall crops, which should be set out in early July.

Brussels Sprouts Don't bother planting early brussels spouts—they'll taste bitter and sulfurous. Seed in June and set in early July for the fall harvest. They're sweeter after the frost.

Cabbage Start earliest varieties in flats early in March and have transplants ready to go out in late April or early May. Like broccoli, it takes a hard frost to damage cabbage. Seed mid-season varieties in late March, and fall-storage cabbages in May. Savoy cabbage is a favorite—beautiful and tender. The flat, dense Dutch types are good for the fall crop and should be set out in early July. Red cabbages seem to be more resistant to cabbage worms. Rotate all cabbage-family plants.

Chinese Greens Includes Chinese cabbage, Pak Choi, Shirona Greens, Tai Sai, and others. Can be seeded directly or transplanted, although transplant damage can cause poor head formation. They're very cold-tolerant, producing very early in the spring or standing through most of the autumn. If you want the Chinese cabbage to form good heads, don't harvest the leaves during the growing season.

Carrots Carrots do very well in sandy soils. First seeding can be done in mid-April. If the soil isn't kept moist after seeding, you'll get poor germination. Newly hatched carrots are tiny and delicate and can be destroyed easily by over-zealous hoeing. Thin properly, or they won't have room to grow. The Chantenays seem to be the most deeply colored and best flavored in our soil. July 4 is our cut-off date for full-sized fall carrots. If you mulch them thickly, carrots can be left in the ground all winter and dug up as you want them. They'll rot by spring.

Cauliflower Seeding instructions are the same as for cabbage for early and late crops. When you grow standard varieties, tie the leaves together to protect the heads from the sun, or they'll turn yellow-brown instead of snowy white. There are now some self-blanching varieties that don't require tying.

Celeriac Celeriac is a celery relative that forms big fleshy roots; it's very popular in Europe. The stalks are tough and fibrous. It's easier to grow than celery and doesn't require any special care. Seed early in flats; transplant early, as plants are frost resistant. Let them grow until late fall for biggest roots.

Celery Seed in early March in flats. Set out after danger of frost has passed. Without adequate water, celery will be tough and bitter. Blanching helps, too. In the greenhouse, we lay boards up against the plants. Outdoors, dirt can be hilled around them. Celery requires a fertile soil.

Collards A large-leafed member of the cabbage family, used for greens, and grown just like other members of the family. Collards do well in hot weather.

Corn Corn is a heavy feeder, so it should be rotated. We like to interplant with beans. For good pollination, which means full ears, you need at least four rows of the same variety together. You can plant in blocks instead of long rows. Seed earliest corn when the soil is about 60°F—or according to folk wisdom, when the oak leaves are the size of squirrels' ears. That's usually within the first half of May on Cape Cod. Seed mid-season and late varieties, too, for a full summer of sweet corn. Here, mid-June is the latest time to seed corn. We have a lot of trouble with quail eating the corn as it sprouts. We once attempted to imitate the Guatemalan Indian method of running strips back and forth to form a loose netting across the whole field, but soon gave up. Opting for the lazy route, we piled old sunflower stalks and brush on the rows—and it worked! Actually, you don't have to use enough to prevent the birds from getting in; they don't like landing on it. Single overlapping stalks right on the row are sufficient. Corn is the crop most likely to suffer from nitrogen deficiency, so you may need to side-dress it with compost, manure, or a nitrogen-rich mulch. We love the mixed yellow and white types, but we plant several varieties to mature at different times. Before picking an ear, feel the kernels through the husk. They should feel fat and juicy if it's ready. Don't peel back the husk and peek.

Cucumbers Seed in mid- to late May, up through early July. The seed will rot if you seed in early spring when the ground is cold. We sometimes seed cucumbers in peat pots to replace late peas, attempting to make use of the same permanent poles with wires for both climbing plants. They may produce more if allowed to sprawl. Cucumbers are susceptible to various bacterial wilts, especially in times of drought, so don't let them get too dry.

Pick frequently; if the fruits mature, the plants stop producing. If a cucumber does hide from you until it gets to be big and yellow, remove it anyway to keep the plant going.

Dill Dill can be started indoors and transplanted, but it does much better with a thick direct seeding very early in the spring and up into August for a fall crop. Dill tolerates partial shade. Some people like the taste of the fresh ''weed'' better than the seed. Successional sowings allow you to have fresh dill all summer, heads for pickling, and seed for winter use.

Eggplant Eggplant, which is difficult for our gardener friends in other regions, grows well here. Seed in flats early in March and don't overwater. Seedlings are susceptible to damping-off and rotting. Don't plant outside until the soil is really warm—the third week of May is the earliest for us. The plants need full sun and shouldn't be mulched until they've blossomed. You can get a small Oriental-type eggplant that produces much more quickly, but somehow we always find it disappointing. If you're going to grow an eggplant, it ought to be a big, full, lush, deep-purple glossy eggplant. Don't leave a full-sized fruit on the plant too long. If the skin gets dull, it will be tough and the seeds will be large and dark.

Jerusalem artichoke

Jerusalem Artichoke   *Perennial.* Jerusalem artichokes aren't related to globe artichokes; they're actually a kind of sunflower. Start them from pieces of tubers. They spread very assertively, so put them only where they can't take over. The tubers can be dug out so long as the ground isn't frozen too hard, and dug again when it thaws in the spring. They may produce 15 tons per acre. Pretty flowers, too. We planted them at the back of the garden next to the woods and *think* they helped close off rabbit routes.

Kale   Another cabbage-family plant grown for greens. It out-produces almost anything and can be picked until December here. The flavor is sweeter after frost. Plants set in the spring will keep producing, but an early-summer seeding makes a tenderer fall crop. We prefer the dwarf curled varieties.

Kohlrabi   Another cabbage-family member, grown for the peculiar looking swellings on the stems. Early and late seeding can be done the same as for the rest of the family. The tiny seedlings are often badly bothered by flea beetles in the spring. Kohlrabi is best when the swollen stem is no more than three inches across, sweet and tender. Big ones are pure wood.

Leeks   Leeks are underrated. An excellent fall crop, usable until early December here. We set seedlings out about six inches apart in June, or even up until the beginning of July. King Richard is a good variety. Mulch thickly to protect from frost and facilitate easy pulling.

Lettuce   The first lettuce can be seeded before danger of frost is past. We tried seeding lettuce in December last year, since volunteer lettuce from dropped seeds is always very early and hardy. Germination was very poor, but the few that came up *were* early and hardy as we expected. Sow lettuce frequently, up through late July. We always have a surfeit of lettuce in late June and then hit a slack time, more from poor planning that from the heat. When there's so much of it growing, it's hard to remember to plant more. Plant both loose-leaf and head varieties. You can pick single leaves from the loose-leaf plants, but leave the heads alone if you want them to form well. Favorite loose-leaf types for us are Salad Bowl, Ruby, and Prizehead. Prizehead has red fringes and Ruby is red all over. Both are very heat resistant and are good midsummer lettuces. Our favorite head lettuces are the Butterheads—Bibb, Boston, Buttercrunch, Butter-King. We often use transplants of head lettuces to aid in efficient successional planting. Lettuce tolerates shade—it even grows well under our grape arbor. Although it likes cool soil and lots of moisture in trials here it has never shown an increase in yield from being mulched.[7] It's known to be salt sensitive, which would explain why seaweed isn't beneficial, but it doesn't seem to like straw or leaf mold either.

Melons Other people have succeeded with melons here on the Cape, although we can't seem to grow good ones. One summer we had very nice canteloupes from a plot with black plastic mulch, which no doubt heated up the soil. We also get good melons by planting them near a south-facing white concrete wall. Start seedlings in April in peat pots—they won't tolerate transplanting. Well-rotted manure is good for melons. Pick off small fruits and pinch off the growing tips of the vines as the season draws to a close; this concentrates the productive energy in the fruits that might mature.

Mustard Mustard greens are good to have for salads as well as for cooking. We always have lots of volunteers in the garden, so once your crop goes to seed, you may never have to seed again. Dark, smoother varieties tend to be less hot than curly yellow-green ones.

Okra Okra may be the best of the Southern specialties. If you think you don't like okra, try slicing it thin, dredging it, and frying it. Okra needs a lot of heat and sun. You can start it early in peat pots (it hates transplanting), but it's very susceptible to damping-off. Our most successful method for growing okra is to direct seed in late May and cover it with a cloche until the weather is nice and hot in June. Pick frequently, or the pods get woody. Dwarf varieties are best for the North, and Cape Cod may be just about the northern limit of good production even for the dwarves.

Onions You can start onions from seed in flats, but the seedlings are delicate and slow growing. Sets are less work and give much bigger onions. If the sets have already sprouted when you plant them, they may put up a hard seed stalk instead of making a firm onion. Sets can go out in April here, before frost danger is past. It's tempting to use onions as border plants because they're so tidy and compact, but they hate being disturbed or having their roots exposed. They do best in the center of beds or rows and can tolerate partial shade. Snip the tops back to use in salads and to encourage larger bulb formation. When the tops start to yellow, bend or break them over. Harvest when the tops are brown and dry. Of course, you can snitch a few green onions throughout the season.

Bunching Onions *Perennial.* Start from seed in flats and set out young plants six inches apart in spring. They'll form clumps of green onions; harvest as you need them by taking an onion from a bunch and leaving others to multiply. Mulch well in the fall so they'll pull easily and for protection against freezing.

Parsley We use parsley in large enough quantities for it to qualify as a vegetable rather than an herb. Start seeds in flats as early as late February. The single Italian parsley is prolific but not as tender or sharp as the curled. Parsley can be treated like a perennial by allowing it to reseed itself. Shade-tolerant.

Peas Peas can go in the ground in late March here if you have a thaw, but we usually don't get them in until April. Inoculate with nitrogen-fixing bacteria for best results. Peas, like corn, are relished by quail and by sparrows as well, so protect them with brush or nets until they're several inches high. Then the rabbits will eat them, with some help from the woodchucks. Seed thickly to compensate for loss. Use rows to save space. Peas need some help to climb. Edible pod peas are at least as good as shelling peas and give you a lot more food for the space they take; you're relieved of the shelling drudgery, as well. The new sugar snaps are a cross between the two types of peas, and some people here like them best of all.

(Others think they have a peculiar soapy flavor.) Wando is the standard shelling pea to grow latest in the season because it withstands heat well.

Peppers Another heat-lover. Start in flats in March, set in late May. Cutworms prefer cutting down pepper plants to any other activity. We wrap paper collars around the stems as we plant. Green bell peppers are the most common, but try some others like the sweet or hot bananas, Hungarian wax, hot or sweet cherries for pickling, or some of the special Mexican peppers for stuffing. Aconcagua is big, thick, and yellow, perfect for chili rellenos. Horticultural Enterprises, Box 340082, Dallas, Texas, has an exciting collection of Mexican pepper seeds. Too much nitrogen will give you lots of leaves and not much fruit, as will even partial shade. Don't mulch until they've blossomed. Pick off small peppers near the end of the season so the plant's strength can go to the bigger ones that have a chance to mature.

Potatoes They take up a lot of space, so they aren't for the very small garden. Potatoes have a hard time in heavy soil. Buy seed potatoes locally, and cut them into pieces no smaller than 1½ inches square with at least two eyes per piece. Let the pieces dry for 24 to 48 hours before planting. We plant in early April. You can plant sprouted potatoes from the year before, but there's more chance of disease than with certified disease-free seed. We've always gotten really healthy early plants from potatoes left in the ground from the year before, ones that we missed during the harvest. This year these volunteers had scab, though. Potatoes like an acid soil, so don't lime. One method of planting potatoes is to dig deep (16-inch) trenches, put the seed potatoes in the bottom, and fill in with leaves, using no soil. We tried this method year before last and they did splendidly, giving us big potatoes—lots of them—and no blight. Blight is encouraged by heat and dryness, and the deep planting and thick mulch keep the plants cool. This past summer we had a long drought. The potatoes planted in soil did fine, while the ones in trenches covered with leaves did miserably. They were slow to come up and then the leaf mulch dried out completely. From now on, we'll dig shallow six-inch trenches, and fill back in one-half the soil, adding the rest as the plants emerge. Then we'll mulch thickly. Potatoes are very fond of seaweed, as the Irish have known for a long time.

Sweet Potatoes We've found that the trick with sweet potatoes is not over-feeding them. We finally had great ones this year, grown in terrible sandy, unimproved soil. You can buy plants, or "slips," from Southern companies. Rose Centennial has done best for us. It yields well and is delicious, creamy, and deep rose-colored. Don't let your mail-ordered slips dry out; keep them in moist paper until you're ready to put them in the ground.

Fig. 9 Sweet potato
mounds

You can make your own slips by putting a potato part way into a jar of
water in a warm place, or by cutting the potato in half lengthwise and laying the pieces in a pan of water. They'll sprout, and the sprouts will form
rootlets. Sweet potatoes really must have warm soil, so don't put them out
until late May. Loosen the soil and then shovel it up into foot-wide ridges.
Dig the dirt from a foot-wide strip, piling it up onto the foot-wide loosened
strip next to it, to make a ridge. Skip over two feet to do the next one. Figure 9 shows some sweet-potato mounds. Set the slips into the ridges about
a foot apart, watering well as you transplant. The ridges heat up more than
a flat garden surface. To encourage better heating, either use black plastic
or don't mulch at all. Harvest before frost or they may be ruined.

Pumpkin and Squash   We like to start pumpkins and squash in peat pots
about the third week in April and set them out in late May, when they have
several true leaves. They're better able to withstand the attacks of the
striped cucumber beetle when they have some size—plus the beetles are
most prevalent here in early May, so our timing is a preventative control.
We've noticed that volunteer plants outgrow spring-seeded or transplanted ones and seem to be more resistant to insect attack, so we tried to
imitate that by winter seeding. Only a few plants germinated last spring
from a winter seeding, but they were early and strong. Pumpkins and winter squash take a lot of space. Put them at the edge of the garden if your
space is limited, and let them run out. We often interplant them with corn
and let the vines run around under the corn. Plant in little mounds with
depressions in the top to hold water better, two or three plants per site,

with about six inches between "hills." It's good to put rotted manure in the hills. Fresh manure will cause diseases. Smaller pumpkins are usually more flavorful than the big Halloween-style ones. The most reliable winter squash for us is Butternut. Blue Hubbard and Acorn do well for us, too. Spaghetti squash is a mellow-tasting, yellow-fleshed squash that cooks up in spaghetti-like strands. They do well here and we like them a lot. Mulch well, close to the plants.

Summer Squash Plant summer squash the same way you plant winter squash. However, because summer squash is a bush crop (rather than a vine), it needs far less space. Two feet between hills is fine. Summer squash can be planted until the end of July here. Straightneck yellow squash is tender at a larger size than crookneck is. Dark-green zucchini is more flavorful than the paler hybrids. Pick summer squash frequently; these vegetables can go from babies to giants overnight, or so it seems. The plants will stop producing if the fruits get big. Inevitably some zucchinis go undetected until they reach a size and condition suitable only for a war club. Reseed midsummer for a late harvest.

Radishes You'll probably over-plant radishes, as they can be seeded really early when you're most zealous, and they give such quick results. Plant just a few and reseed every week or so until late spring for a small continual supply of sweet tender ones. Thin them to stand an inch apart. For later radishes, seed in shade and give them plenty of water.

Rhubarb *A perennial.* Buy local root stock. Set the roots a foot apart in well-prepared, composted soil. Don't harvest until the second year. *Pull* the stalks free from one base—don't cut. Never take small spindly stalks or you'll weaken the plant. Mulch well every fall. Rhubarb likes rather acid soil.

Sorrel Another *perennial.* It's the little spade-shaped weed that plagues your strawberry patch, if your strawberry patch is like ours. It has a nice sour taste and French garden varieties grow big and succulent. Start in flats or seed directly. Sorrel will produce very early in the spring.

Spinach Seed as soon as the soil thaws in the spring. It's quick to bolt, so an early start is essential. Transplanting encourages bolting. We've had little success with late-summer seeding for a fall crop. We've found that the dark, heavily curled types do better than the smoother varieties.

Malabar spinach and New Zealand spinach are not true spinaches. Malabar is less common and much better. It makes big, broad, thick leaves on long semi-vines. There's a red-stalked type with pink flowers and a

Malabar spinach

green-stalked type with white flowers. Keep the flowers pinched back for continued production of large leaves. Can be started early in flats, but care must be taken in transplanting, or it will bolt. Cuttings are rooted easily in water. Malabar is a mainstay at our lowlands Costa Rican farm, and grows very well in the greenhouses here all summer.

New Zealand spinach will grow in poor soil and isn't affected by extreme heat either. It tends to reseed itself and provide volunteers. Very prolific. The seeds are hard and prickly and germinate more quickly if soaked or scarified (to scarify, nick seeds with a knife). Both Malabar and New Zealand spinach are rather mucilaginous and most people prefer them cooked.

Squash See Pumpkin.

Swiss Chard Seed directly in early April. A single seeding will continue to produce until December. Rhubarb chard has beautiful red stalks that look like stained glass in the sunlight, but it's a bit stronger flavored than green chard. A variety named Perpetual has tender light-green leaves. Chard loves seaweed mulch and tolerates partial shade.

Tomatoes Seed in flats in mid-March or eight to ten weeks before all danger of frost is past. The plants get too big and leggy if you seed earlier. Here there's some danger of frost until late May, so we wait until then to set them out. Cutworms are fond of tomatoes, too, so you may want to supply your plants with paper collars as you place them in the ground. Remove some of the lower branches and set the plants deeper then they were in the pots; this induces more root growth. If the stem is long, lay the plant over on its side and cover quite a bit of the stem. Tomatoes need full sun and shouldn't be mulched until they've blossomed. Plants can be staked or trellised if you want them to take up less space. We like to use the bamboo that we grow here for stakes and trellises. Mulch keeps the fruits of unstaked plants from rotting on the ground. Our favorite variety for flavor is Rutgers. Sweet 100's are delicious cherry tomatoes that grow in big bunches. Good early northern varieties are available from Johnny's Selected Seeds.

Turnips Seed directly in early spring and again in midsummer for fall turnips or rutabagas. Mulch the fall crop well, because turnips don't like heat. Oriental varieties are excellent for greens; they also produce crisp, small, white turnips. We always have a lot of trouble with root maggots in regular purple-topped white turnips. A thick mulch protects the turnips for part of the winter.

Crop areas delineated
with colorful marigold
blossoms

RECORD KEEPING

As the active gardening season begins, start recording information about your garden. Get a special notebook for this purpose—don't try to do it on the backs of seed packages or random scraps of paper. Note which rock minerals you've applied, how much, and when. Record seeding and transplanting dates, and the variety names for *everything* you plant. Make notes during the season on how various crops performed. Did you like the flavor of the tomatoes? Did one variety of potato yield a lot better than the other? Did certain types of squash make it through the summer with no vine borers? Were a dozen zucchini plants too many? Did your pole lima beans fail to mature, while the bush ones produced prolifically? When did you seed your fall carrots and did they reach full size? Note the arrival dates and forms of insect pests and record pertinent weather data. Each year your knowlege will increase along with your ability to observe. And you'll never have to spend hours trying to trace that elusive variety of sweet cherry tomato or arguing about which year the broccoli was most productive!

DIRECT SEEDING

The earliest crops that do well when seeded directly into the garden soil are dill, lettuce, peas, radishes, and spinach. The next-earliest are beets, Chinese greens, carrots, kohlrabi, chard, and turnips. After frost danger is past, you can seed beans, corn, cukes, squash, and pumpkin. Wait until the ground warms up more to seed melons, okra, and lima beans. Flowers that prefer direct seeding are nasturtiums, morning glories, portulaca, sunflowers, tithonia, balsam, and larkspur, although any of them can be started in individual plantable containers for earlier blossoming.

Carefully prepare the area to be seeded. The soil surface should be raked smooth so that all clods are broken up. This is very easy in a sandy soil like ours, not so easy in clay soils. Again, don't work a clay soil at all when it's wet or you'll make more clods rather than fewer. On intensive beds, we rake the entire bed surface smooth, first with the tines of the rake, then with the back, pushing and pulling the soil to round the bed edges. Don't heap the soil up in the middle of the bed or you'll get runoff and erosion. It's better to leave the middle a little lower, banking the dirt up slightly at the edges.

Small-seeded crops can be seeded in blocks rather than in rows. We often plant carrots, dill, and greens of all sorts in blocks. Just loosen the soil well, sprinkle on the seeds, pat them in, and water. Be prepared to thin if you over-plant.

When planting in rows, use a string and sticks to mark a straight line. Label the rows clearly. We've actually had rows intersect and cross each other when we've tried to be free-form, and have seeded twice in the same spot when we didn't mark the rows right away. A sharp-pointed hoe is useful for making shallow trenches for seeding. If the soil isn't damp and you're not expecting rain, water the rows before seeding. That's usually necessary only in midsummer here. The general rule of seed-planting depth is three- to four-times the thickness of the seed. Pushing the dirt back in with your feet and firming it as you walk is a fine method of covering seeds (don't walk on intensive beds), but most people probably use a hoe. Firming the soil over the seeds keeps them from drying out in air pockets, makes it harder for birds to get at the seeds, and keeps rain from exposing them.

This is a good time for another reminder not to seed too much at one time, but to space out the seeding of any particular crop so that you have a long season of fresh yield.

TRANSPLANTING

As we described in Chapter 2, you can start your own seedlings indoors for your outdoor garden. As the time for outdoor planting approaches, you should till your garden or put it into raised beds. If you're planting in a permanent mulch, you should move it back to expose the planting rows to the spring sun, according to our earlier suggestion about mulches.

Moving Into a Cold Frame or Cloche

It's wise to harden off seedlings before exposing them to outside conditions, especially in the early part of the season. This means moving them first into a cold frame or cloche, then later to the unprotected outside. For further information on hardening off, refer back to Chapter 3.

Moving Into the Garden

Comfortable assurance about when it's safe to plant which crops will come only after several seasons of observation. The location of your garden is significant. Our valley garden is more frost-prone than one on higher ground would be.

The first transplants to go out will be the brassicas, lettuce, parsley, onions, chard, and the perennials in late April. Occasionally a hard frost may do them in, but it's rare. May 15 is our frost-free date, but we generally wait until the third week of May before we put out the sensitive crops. This includes tomatoes, peppers, celery, okra, squash, and annual herbs. If you get a cold day and temperatures start to drop in late afternoon, be prepared to cover your sensitive seedlings. Plastic gallon milk jugs with the bottoms cut out are handy to put over individual plants. Push a stick through the neck of the bottle down into the ground to keep it from blow-

ing off. You can put these bottles on your tomatoes, peppers, eggplant, and other cold-sensitive plants when you set them out and just leave them on for a couple of weeks; this makes it safe to set them out earlier.

It's better to transplant in the afternoon, when the plants' activities are slowing down and the sun is milder. Avoid windy days or the increased transpiration will shock the transplants. An overcast day leading to an evening spring rain is perfect. Transplanting is the same throughout the season, but as the days get hotter you have be more careful about watering, and late afternoon planting becomes more essential.

Dig a hole big enough to easily accommodate the roots, and set the plant in a little deeper than it was in the carton. Handle the roots carefully, as you did in the earlier transplanting. Make sure the containers are watered adequately ahead of time to help the roots separate. Water the hole, too, and allow it to soak in before you introduce the plant. Fill in with dirt—or better, compost—and firm it around the plant. Water again. Newly transplanted seedlings should be watered frequently—probably daily—until they're established.

Tending the Garden

Once the garden is planted, you can't just forget about it and wait for the bounty to come. It won't. You'll find that it pays to spend a little time in the garden every day, noticing what needs to be done. At first you'll pull a few weeds and water the new transplants if they look a bit dry. Later you'll smash the first bean beetle munching on your plants, pull back the mulch from the baby carrots, and reseed a row of beets that germinated poorly or thin the lettuce that germinated better than you could have imagined.

The most successful gardeners are those who provide their crops with consistent care. Many individuals develop a regular routine in the morning or evening of walking through the garden and attending to its changing needs. In addition to being productive, this is a wonderful way to begin or end the day. If this schedule is impractical for you, you can become a "weekend gardener" and concentrate your activities into fewer—but more intensive—blocks of time.

The amount of work a garden requires is really arbitrary; basically, the more effort you expend in gardening, the more food yield you can expect. An untended plot can produce a lot of weeds (many of which are edible) and some vegetables. On the other hand, an immaculate garden prized for its beauty and high yield can be a full-time occupation. Between those extremes, the well-managed family garden of approximately 400 to 600 square feet will require about 30 to 45 minutes of labor per day from April through October. Keep in mind that this is an *average* figure and that the exact time required will vary throughout the season. May is a very busy month with lots of soil preparation and planting. By August and September it will be mostly a matter of weeding and harvesting.

Exactly how long a garden can go untended depends upon the weather, the types of crops, and your methods of production. Often a well-mulched plot can be left alone for a week or more without serious consequences. However, if you plan on vacationing away from home for more than a week, it's advisable to enlist someone to check on the garden. They may find it necessary to weed, water, harvest, or even deal with an outbreak of pests.

MULCHING

A mulch is any material you put on to cover the soil surface. Earlier in this chapter we discussed mulch as a method of soil-building, as a way of preparing a new garden plot, and as an alternative to the winter cover crop. You'll discover that mulch has a number of other useful functions, too.

Mulches retain soil moisture so that when you irrigate, or when there's rain, the moisture remains in the soil longer. Instead of evaporating, it can be used by the plants. Mulching prevents water run-off from soils that would otherwise crust or form an impermeable dust layer. Mulches control weeds if you mulch thickly enough—at least six inches after the material settles down. It's better to mulch a small area thickly and be relieved of weeding than to cover a large area thinly and end up having to weed through the mulch.

Soil temperature is moderated by a mulch cover. On a hot August day it may be 20 degrees cooler in a well-mulched area than in an area with no mulch. And the same mulch holds in the heat longer, come fall. Not long ago we were digging new ditches into two adjacent intensive beds, one well-mulched and the other rather sparsely mulched. The time was early December. We found the soil soft and easy to dig in the well-mulched bed but frozen hard in the other one. Soil doesn't heat up as fast under a mulch, so heat-loving plants shouldn't be mulched until they've blossomed. This group includes tomatoes, peppers, eggplant, okra, and melons. The only exception to that rule would be the use of a black plastic mulch which would warm the soil faster. The black absorbs heat and plastic is so thin that it doesn't insulate the soil like a thick organic mulch does.

Our primary mulch materials are seaweed and leaf mold. In trials here, seaweed has increased yields of tomatoes, peppers, beets, and chard, but it has decreased lettuce yields.[8] Neither straw nor leaf mold has increased yields as much as seaweed, but any organic mulch will add some nutrients and perform the other mulch functions of weed control, moisture retention, and temperature modification. Many people who visit here are surprised to see that we use oak leaves on our garden because they're very acidic. We don't have any problem with increased acidity, because the soil is well-limed and has a well-developed stable humus. If you're just starting a new garden in poor acidic soil, it's probably not advisable to use lots of oak leaves. Pile them up and allow them to rot first, and they'll be much better.

Another thing people are curious about is whether or not the salt in seaweed is damaging to plants and whether or not it builds up in the soil. Two plants that have responded badly to seaweed mulch are lettuce and strawberries. Salt levels in the soil do go up after we put on a seaweed mulch, but we've found that after a single winter's leaching, there are no measurable differences in salt levels in areas that have or haven't been mulched with seaweed.

You may get a lot of weed seeds in straw or hay, but if you put the mulch on thickly, the weeds won't be able to establish.

Newspaper is a good mulch, too. Although it doesn't provide as high a quality organic material as the other mulches we've talked about, it does an excellent job of preserving moisture. Put the newspaper on several sheets thick and cover it well with manure or sawdust or straw. That prevents it from blowing away, which it surely will do otherwise; besides, it's terribly ugly left uncovered.

In very closely planted areas, it may be difficult to get mulch around plants. The plants themselves will shade the soil and perform some of the same functions the mulch would. Grass clippings are the easiest mulch to put around small, dense crops.

Generally, the sooner you mulch a crop the better, so weeds don't get started. Mulch as soon as the plant is big enough not to get smothered by the mulch shifting over on it. Rows can be mulched early and the mulch snuggled up around plants as they get bigger. The fruiting plants we mentioned earlier are the only exceptions to the early-mulching rule.

WEEDING

Weed seeds are very patient. Some friends had a stand of 25-year-old white pines that had grown so tall they were shading light from the house. They cut them down and broke up the soil a bit to plant some flower bulbs. Almost immediately, up popped an exuberant growth of common annual weeds! The seeds had been waiting for 25 years, ever since that spot had been a meadow.

Wherever your garden is, you'll have weeds. If you always destroy them before they go to seed, and if you use compost that's clean of weed seeds, your problem will be reduced each year.

Annual weeds are easiest to kill when they're young and shallow rooted. Beheading them with a hoe will cause death. Bigger weeds will re-sprout around the base. Here, lamb's-quarters, purslane, and pigweed, our most common weeds, can usually be controlled by early hoeing followed by a good mulch. Some weeds very easily re-root after they're pulled up. (Purslane is our weed most talented at resurrection.) Therefore be sure to remove all weeds from the field as you pull them.

Deep-rooted perennial weeds like dock and mullein must be *dug* out. Many grasses can propagate from every little piece of root left in the soil, so try to clean them out as completely as possible.

Don't cultivate too deeply too close to your plants or you'll damage the roots. Frequent light hoeing is easier and more effective than waiting until you have jungle to subdue. And if you mulch well, cultivation will be necessary only at the beginning of the season.

Don't let big weeds grow up at the edge of your garden long enough to produce seeds. Flowering is beneficial to local wild insects, but chop them down and recycle them before seed time. You can choose particular gardenside native perennials as a biological island for beneficial insects, if you want to try the method described in Chapter 3.

IRRIGATION

The amount of watering you'll need to do will depend on weather and soil conditions. Organic material in the soil is the best manager of soil moisture. If your soil is naturally sandy and porous, the organic material will act like a sponge, absorbing and holding rain or irrigation water. If the soil is dense and heavy, the organic material will loosen and lighten it, provide air spaces, and prevent it from becoming waterlogged.

Plants must have water when they're young, delicate, and not well established. After seeding or transplanting, water lightly every day. Once the plants' roots go down deeper where the ground is more moist, they'll not need watering so often.

When you do water, water well. We like to saturate the soil six to twelve inches down. Constant shallow irrigation will keep the plants' roots up near the surface, where they're subject to temperature fluctuations and dryness. Be sure you've watered enough so that it really sinks in. Often the soil will *look* dark and wet but if you stir it up a little, you'll see that the water hasn't penetrated past the surface. A single large tomato plant will need several gallons of water to penetrate to the roots. During a typical Cape Cod summer, this kind of thorough weekly watering should be adequate even during the hottest and driest weeks.

We prefer to irrigate in the late afternoon, at least in summer. In the heat of the day you'll lose a lot of the water to evaporation immediately, and those water drops on the leaves can burn them. However, in a lovely book, *Better Vegetable Gardens the Chinese Way*, Peter Chan says over and over that the Chinese always water their gardens early in the morning.

If you're going to use a hose to water your garden, drive in a stake at the corner of each bed or row or place a heavy rock there, so you can pull the hose against the stake and not drag it over the plants. When watering with a hose, we like to "rain" the water down on the plants to wash their leaves; then we water deeply and directly around the bases of the plants.

The most efficient type of irrigation is drip irrigation. Pipes or tubes are laid on the soil surface and the water is emitted in drops through small holes onto the soil surface. The advantage of drip irrigation is that the water goes directly into the soil with no loss to evaporation or wind. With conventional overhead sprinkler irrigation, up to 60 percent of the water is lost before it hits the ground. Run-off will be less with drip irrigation, too, because the soil can absorb the small drops emitted over a longer period of time.

There are inexpensive, easy-to-install drip systems made from flexible plastic tubing that can be laid out however you want it in your garden. Emitters can be punched into the tubing at the desired spacing. Inexpensive timers are available that automatically stop the water flow after the selected amount has been applied. Your labor is reduced by this method.

If you grow fish for home consumption (see Chapter 5), an extra benefit is the fertile water from your fish pond. Many fish growing together in a small space produce a lot of waste, and from time to time, you'll need to drain off some of the enriched water and replace it with fresh water. We've found that this fish-pond water is beneficial to many crops.

Careful use of water has become crucial as our clean water supply diminishes. An efficient method of irrigation, a rich spongy humus to hold the water, and a thick mulch to prevent run-off and evaporation combine to conserve moisture effectively. With good organic soil management, water usage is thus reduced to a minimum.

A very informative book that thoroughly covers all aspects of the interactions between plants and the environment, including water, temperature and soil, is *Environment and Plant Life*, by S.A. Searle.

PEST CONTROL

When we started to garden organically, all those testimonies in organic-gardening literature seemed almost too good to be true. Again and again they held that healthy plants coming from healthy soil wouldn't be destroyed by insects and diseases. Why is conventional agriculture so dependent on poisons? The answer *is* largely in the soil. As our garden soil has improved each season, insect damage truly has diminished.

There have been some very striking visible examples. A garden plot where we planted corn and squash is bordered by woods at the back. A wide strip of coarse perennials grows between the garden and woods, but no doubt the trees are still sending some roots over into the garden to compete for nutrients. The corn decreased in height as it approached the back of the field, the squash plants were smaller, and both corn and squash plants yellower and less healthy looking than the plants at the front of the garden. We had both corn earworms and squash vine borers. Healthy plants at the front of the plot may have had a few borers or earworms, but they pulled through just fine with little crop damage. The unhealthy plants in the poorer soil succumbed to insect attack—the corn ears were virtually destroyed and the squash plants died.

Supposedly, in addition to the fact that weakened plants have less stamina, insects actually prefer the high carbohydrates present in unhealthy plants and thus concentrate on them. An old, experienced biodynamic gardener tells us that insect attack is always an indication of imbalance in the plants.

This summer a man who grows and sells squash and pumpkins came by to ask us what we do about squash vine borers. He had been growing squash for years with no problem, but in the last two seasons his crop was badly damaged by borers. We told him about the poor-soil/good-soil theory and also that our squash seemed to do better with a thick mulch to keep the soil moist and cool. He said he'd always dug trenches, filled them with rotten manure, covered the manure with soil, and set in his squash plants—*until* the last two years, that is. He left immediately to go get a load of good rotten manure from a friend with a dairy.

Another real-life example of growing conditions helping plants to withstand insect attack occurred with our cabbages this summer. The flea beetles were the worst ever this year (see Fig. 10). Normally they come in the early spring, nibble little holes in our early brassicas and radishes, and hop on their way. But this year they stayed on and reproduced prolifically,

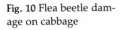
Fig. 10 Flea beetle damage on cabbage

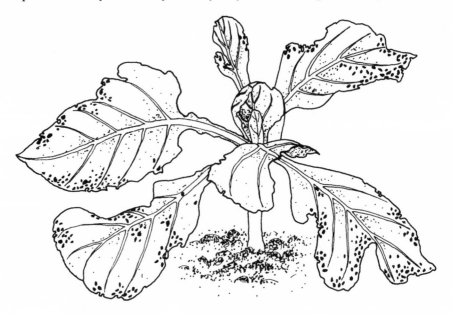

covering the young cabbage seedlings. We immediately mulched some of the cabbages thickly with fresh seaweed; others, we didn't get to right away. The mulched ones lived; many without mulch wilted and died. There was too much moisture loss through the many tiny holes in the leaves of the unmulched plants, but the mulched plants had enough extra moisture to survive.

Our general approach to pest control is to be sure that the plants have all their needs met and then not to panic. Many gardeners and farmers resort to poisonous sprays when a little patience would have proved them unnecessary. In growing trials here, we found that cabbages badly damaged by cabbageworms early in the season often recover and produce perfectly fine cabbage heads with no control of any kind.

Many gardeners are concerned about pest damage because they want their plants and produce to look perfect. Wouldn't it be preferable to have a few spots on your apples, or even an occasional worm hole, than to consume a little poisonous residue?

Prevention

Our pest management strategy begins with prevention, which is, after all, worth pounds of cure.

Good soil management is a preventative approach to pest control. Such management is effective against diseases as well as insects. Pathogens in the soil can be inhibited by a high humus content, and the multiplication of pathogenic spores is inhibited by the beneficial microorganisms present in soil that is rich in organic material.[9]

Removing diseased or pest-infested plants is another good preventative pest-control strategy. Destroy the plants to prevent further spread of the disease or pest. If you've had squash vine borers, for example, remove the plants from the field and compost them instead of plowing them in or using them as mulch.

Another important preventative control is selection of *resistant varieties*. So far, there are more crops effectively bred for disease resistance than for insect resistance. Check catalog descriptions for varieties resistant to pests and diseases in your area. For instance, we use varieties of cucumbers and peas that are resistant to various wilts. Butternut squash seems to be less affected by squash vine borers than other types of squash. Certain corn varieties have tighter husks that inhibit the entrance of corn earworms. Appendix E and Appendix F at the end of this chapter list varieties resistant to various pests and diseases.

Proper timing can often reduce insect damage. If you observe when an insect population is at its peak, you may be able to avoid exposing your plants at that time in future years. As we described earlier, we've learned to hold our squash plants until late May when the cucumber beetle population is way down. Early-seeded beans have less Mexican-bean-beetle damage because they are past the preferred flowering stage by the time the beetles amass.

Perhaps the best precaution of all is *attention* to insect behavior. Keep your eyes open; look for egg clusters on the backs of leaves and remove them before they hatch. Record appearance dates for various insects so you can anticipate their arrival next year. Experiment with ways to make your plants less appealing to the pests.

Cultural Controls

We employ various cultural controls, also. These are methods used to minimize damage by altering the pest's habitat to make it less favorable for reproduction and survival.

Rotating crops is an old-time cultural control. The crop is grown away from the place where the pests were the year before. Rotations are probably more effective for pest control on a farm scale than they are in the family garden.

Interplanting and companion planting also deter insects. Such planting makes it harder for insects to hone in on their preferred food plants. Flowers and herbs attract predaceous insects too. And there are plants that act as repellents to various insects. See Appendix D for a table of plants that often help discourage common pests.

Physical Controls

Physical controls are methods used to physically keep out pests or to trap them once they've found your crop. Netting to prevent quail from getting at your peas, sunflower stalks to protect your corn from blackbirds, and paper collars to stop cutworms are all physical controls. Another physical control is to hand pick pests as you find them.

For a few insects, *traps* are effective. Many gardeners use the beer-in-a-dish method of attracting and drowning slugs. Squash bugs like shade. They'll gather under an old board or shingle, making mass murder easier. Traps with bait are available for Japanese beetles.

Using *trap plants* is another physical control. A trap plant is used to attract a pest and is then removed and destroyed. If you know the time of year when certain insect pests are likely to attack, you can plant a small quantity of the target crop so that it will be at the desired stage of development for that pest's preferences. Delay slightly the seeding of the main crop. Then when the pest has infested the trap plants, pull the plants and destroy them.

Biological Controls

If the preventative, cultural, and physical controls cannot contain a pest population, we look next to biological controls. Biological control

FOR THE EAST	
Autum olive (25)	Sumac (17)
Gray-stemmed dogwood (16)	Holly (22)
Cherry (40)	Highbush cranberry (34)
Silky dogwood (10)	Moutain ash (15)
Bittersweet (10)	Amur honeysuckle (8)
Crabapple (18)	Firethorn (17)
Flowering dogwood (36)	Highbush blueberry (36)
Hawthorn (25)	Red cedar (68)
Redosier dogwood (19)	Tatarian honeysuckle (17)
Virginia creeper (37)	

Table 4 *Plants that attract Birds to the Yard and Garden**

*The figures in parentheses indicate the approximate number of bird species that utilize the plants in the East.
Reprinted from *Organic Plant Protection*, © 1976 by Rodale Press, Inc. Permission granted by Rodale Press, Inc., Emmaus, PA 18049; p. 158.

refers to the use of predaceous and parasitic organisms and insect diseases that destroy enough pests to hold down their population levels. These organisms include birds, lizards, and other insects.

The use of biological control requires attention and care, but most, methods are well within the capacity of the average gardener. You must learn about insect life cycles and habitats as well as how they're affected by weather, length of day, and other insects.

Many *native predators* probably already live in your garden. *Birds* prey on many destructive insects. You can attract birds by providing food, housing and a desirable habitat. Swallows specialize in flying insects, as do purple martins, and both are quite happy in our garden. Table 4 tells you which plants will attract birds to your garden. Wild areas around the garden encourage birds, too. If you have honeysuckle, sumac, and greenbrier growing near your garden, leave it there! *Note:* Not all birds will help you out. English sparrows, starlings, and quail, among others, can be fairly obnoxious. Eviction is probably the best course. Shooting them is a possibility, although some folks around here get a bit queasy at the idea.

Lizards, snakes, chameleons, frogs, toads, and spiders are all welcome in our garden; they can eat as many insects as they like.

In addition to encouraging native predators, it is sometimes helpful to *introduce natural enemies.* For example, you can introduce common beneficial insects such as the ladybug and praying mantis. The adult ladybug can eat as many as 40 aphids an hour! Among the beneficial insects found in our garden are syrphid flies, ladybird beetles, ground beetles, praying manti, parasitic wasps, grasshoppers, and lacewings.[10]

There are a number of effective tiny *parasitic wasps*. Normally they lay their eggs in the body of the host insect, which dies as the eggs develop. Braconid wasps parasitize aphids, coddling moths, gypsy moths, tomato hornworms, and many others. *Trichogramma* parasitizes the cabbage worm and other caterpillars. *Pediobius foveolatus* is a very effective parasite of Mexican-bean-beetle larvae.

Bacillus thuringiensis is a disease-causing bacteria that infects coddling moths, corn borers, cabbageworms, and many other soft-bodied larvae. It's marketed under such names as Dipel and Thuricide. *Milky spore* is a disease that controls Japanese beetles.

Many biological control agents are not commercially available. Urge your county agent and agricultural supply store to stock biological control agents. There's no reason why you shouldn't be able to buy a carton of wasps instead of a bottle of pesticide. There's a lot more money to be made in chemical controls, and the concept is simpler (or more simplistic), but biological controls will pay off in the long run. For a list of biological control sources, see Chapter 3.

Applications

Next (in general order of ascending nastiness) are several applications that will help reduce pest damage. *Diatomaceous earth* falls into this category. It's the remains of little sea creatures (diatoms) that have shells made of silica—very sharp when ground up. These sharp edges pierce the bodies of insects from the outside, or from the inside when they're ingested. We use it against thrip, cabbageworms, and cutworms, and it's supposedly effective against many others including flies, corn earworms, mites, slugs, and nematodes. The cheapest source of diatomaceous earth we've found is swimming-pool service companies. They use it in pool filters.

Homemade sprays can be made from garlic, red pepper, onions, soap, and various herbs such as yarrow and tansy. Soak or steep the plant materials. Go easy on the hot peppers! We use about a teaspoon of soap (not detergent) per gallon of water. These substances can be harmful to beneficial insects and to soil organisms, so treat them carefully. A high-pressure water spray is often effective on aphids; the addition of a little soap makes the spray more effective.

As a last resort, we sometimes use a *plant-derived insecticide*. The three common ones are rotenone, pyrethrum, and ryania. These substances don't have the persistence of the chemical pesticides; they'll break down into harmless substances very quickly. They are supposedly never harmful to warm-blooded animals, but they will kill cold-blooded ones. This means *never use them in greenhouses with fish ponds!* Our plant-derived pesticide use is confined to using rotenone on an occasional heavy pest outbreak that looks like one clean sweep might take care of the problem. We've used rotenone on Mexican bean beetles and on Colorado potato beetles. We are reluctant to use these poisons, and often we don't use them at all.

The direct-attack method most common in conventional agriculture is the use of *chemical pesticides*—insecticides, herbicides, fungicides. And yet, poisons are *poisons*. Not only do they damage the target organism but they disturb the life process of beneficial insects, soil organisms, wildlife— and eventually human beings. Pesticides are typically very stable chemicals, which means that they persist in the environment. You eat vegetables with pesticides on them and the toxins accumulate in your body fat. Or you eat meat from animals whose feed contained pesticide residue, and you consume the poisons that accumulated in their flesh. Pesticides find their way into bodies of water, where they damage fish populations; they can contaminate our drinking water. Bird populations are being decimated by pesticides, as are honeybees. Long-range effects on the environment and human health promise to be even worse. It is suspected that 80 to 90 percent of cancer in humans is caused by chemical contamination of food and the environment,[11] and that because cancer takes a long time to develop, it has not yet hit its peak. Appendix G compares chemical pesticides and organic controls.

Throughout the next few pages you'll find drawings that illustrate the most common garden pests in the northeastern United States. As we discuss them individually, we'll suggest special control methods beyond soil building, diversified planting, crop rotation, and bird predation.

A good identification book will be a wise investment if you are troubled by other insect problems. *A Golden Guide to Insect Pests*, by George S. Fichter, is cheap and good. *Rodale's Color Handbook of Garden Insects*, by Anna Carr, is expensive and good. Try your county extension agent for a free garden pest identification book.

Cabbageworm   The green caterpillar of the cabbage butterfly. Spray with *bacillus thuringiensis* in solution. Dust leaves with diatomaceous earth. The butterflies are seen early in May; caterpillar damage is worst in early summer. Hand-picking is effective for very small gardens.

Colorado Potato Beetle   (See Fig. 11.) The larvae are coral colored smushy folk with black dots; they do most of the damage. The adults are yellow with black markings. Plants in cool, moist fertile soil are less attractive. Plant in trenches or mulch thickly. Sprinkle diatomaceous earth on the leaves. A single application of rotenone will set back a heavy infestation. Populations highest in midsummer.

Corn Earworm   (See Fig. 12.) Another one that seems to be attracted to dry, underfed, stressed plants. Select tight-husked varieties if possible. Sup-

Fig. 11 Colorado potato beetle

Fig. 12 Corn earworm

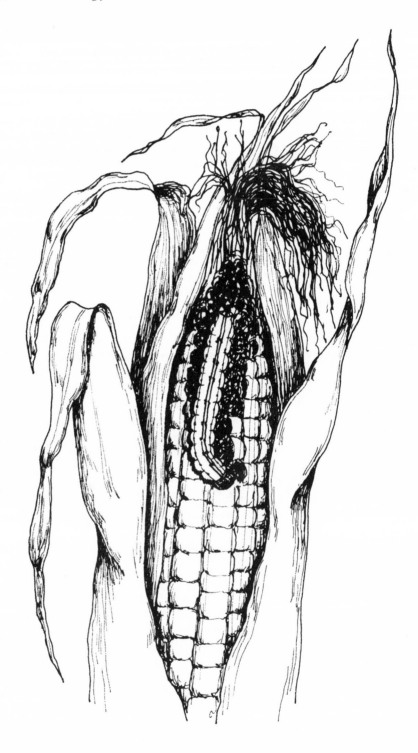

posedly, the application of mineral oil to the silk will deter the worms, as will trimming the silks, but we haven't tried either method. Diatomaceous earth on the silk might be worth trying. Normally, the damage to healthy corn is bearable, if you don't mind just breaking off the top inch of the ear.

Cutworm   (See Fig. 13.) Gray or green worms that do most of their damage at night, curling up in the soil near the base of plants during the day. They cut plants off at ground level. Individual paper collars wrapped around stems of peppers and brassicas, the cutworm's favorites, are sure protection (see Fig. 14). Rings of wood ash or diatomaceous earth are helpful. Digging around the base of plants in the group attacked often turns up the sleeping enemy. Braconid wasps will parasitize them. Present only in early spring.

Fig. 13 Cutworm

Flea Beetle   Tiny beetles that make lots of tiny holes in the leaves of cabbage-family plants, radishes, potatoes, and eggplant. Usually limited to spring. Damage worse on plants without adequate moisture. Mulch and irrigate target plants. Dusting leaves with wood ash or diatomaceous earth gives some control. Garlic sprays supposedly repress them.[12]

Japanese Beetle   (See Fig. 15.) Shiny metallic greenish-brown beetles. The grub is very common in sod and in garden soil. Green beans, grapevines, and roses seem to be the adults' favorites around here. Milky spore disease is the best control, although it's most effective when used on a town or county-wide scale. Traps containing attractive baits are commercially available. Population is highest here midsummer.

Fig. 14 Cutworm collar around young pepper plant

Mexican Bean Beetles   (See Fig. 16.) The yellow larvae cause the most damage. Found on the undersides of leaves. Watch for the adults, who emerge the beginning of July around here. They look like ladybugs, but are larger. Bean beetles are yellow when young and turn coppery brown after a few days. Damage is worst here during August. *Pediobius foveolatus* is a parasitic wasp that is an excellent control but is not commonly commercially available. Early plantings mature before the population peaks. Rotenone can be used if all else fails. Interplanting of marigolds and potatoes is supposed to be effective but hasn't worked for us. We used to pay the kids to hand-pick them, but their rates went up.

Fig. 15 Japanese beetle

Squash Vine Borer   (See Fig. 17.) These ugly white larvae are found inside the stem at the base of squash vines. You may not notice them until the plant wilts and then it is often too late. The worst damage occurs from late July into August when the weather is at its hottest and driest. Grow squash in fertile soil and keep plants well-mulched and watered. We've tried slit-

Fig. 16 Mexican bean
beetle

ting the vines and dragging the worms out, but the surgery often kills the plants as well as the pests. Heaping dirt up around the base stem may help, and putting dirt over sections of vines at the joints will encourage the formation of extra roots. Put all dead squash plants in the compost pile.

For more detailed information on the dangers of pesticides, read Rachel Carson's *Silent Spring,* or *The Pesticide Conspiracy* by Robert van den Bosch. Yepsen's *Organic Plant Protection* touches on just about everything to do with pests and their control.

Fig. 17 Squash vine
borer

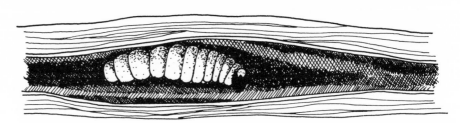

Harvest Fresh to Eat or Preserve

Harvesting may be the most enjoyable part of gardening for you. It should be done faithfully and well. This will keep your plants healthy and your garden productive. Many plants will stop producing if fruits are allowed to mature. Harvest thoroughly and frequently. Don't pick beans or work around them when they're wet, or you'll encourage diseases. Some varieties of certain crops will keep their quality longer after maturity—a few types of cabbages will stand in the field longer without splitting, and some beets will stay sweet and non-woody for a long time. Many crops don't wait for you once they're ready—broccoli will flower, okra turns woody, spinach will bolt, green beans get big seeds, corn loses its sugar, peas turn to starch and fiber, melons get mushy, zucchini swell into tasteless giants. Learn to harvest when things are at their peak rather than just going to look for an eggplant the day you decide you want an eggplant. Be responsive—it's not a grocery store, it's a living garden.

Freshly harvested vegetables can be eaten immediately or preserved for later. See Chapter 9 for storage tips. Eating fresh food really is the simplest strategy. In addition to being economically prudent, it's also challenging and quite pleasurable to plan your diet around what's available in the garden at a particular time. People say, "Hey, I just went to the garden and couldn't find a zucchini." Meanwhile, there's gorgeous broccoli right at the peak of perfection. The next week they *want* broccoli and all they can find is zucchini—and scraggly yellow flowers on the broccoli stems. You may announce enthusiastically that there are "tons of beans ready to pick." Two weeks later someone will lament that the beans are big and tough. If they had been picked when ready, they'd already be putting out a new crop of tender beans. If the corn and squash are ready, don't buy potatoes from the store! And who wants a melon from Florida when the raspberries are ripe? If there's a midsummer lettuce slump, eat cucumber-and-tomato salad. You can derive a lot more pleasure from the seasonal variation of fresh foods than from having constant access to everything year 'round. In the spring, eat your fill of spinach and peas and asparagus, since you won't taste fresh ones again for a year. Midsummer, relish your sweet corn, stuff your peppers, and eat juicy tomatoes right off the vine. In the fall, fat white leeks and kale sweetened by frost make the end of the garden season as good as the beginning. And when you take some beans out of the freezer next winter, liven them up with a sprig of thyme from the pot on your windowsill.

REFERENCES

1. For more information, contact GARDENS FOR ALL, The National Association for Gardening, 180 Flynn Avenue, Burlington, VT 05401.
2. Hills, Lawrence. *Fertility Without Fertilizers.* New York: Universe Books, 1977, p. 11.
3. Mollison, Bill. *Permaculture Two, Practical Design for Town and County in Permanent Agriculture.* Tasmania, Australia: Tagari Community Books, 1979, pp. 40-41.
4. Hills, L. *Fertility Without Fertilizers,* p. 24.
5. Ervin, Susan. "Further Experiments on the Effects of Mulches on Crop Yields and Soil Conditions," *The Journal of the New Alchemists,* 6.
6. *Ibid.*
7. *Ibid.*
8. Ervin, S. "Garden Notes," *The Journal of the New Alchemists,* 7. Brattleboro, VT: Stephen Greene Press, 1981, p. 53.
9. Oelhaf, Robert C. *Organic Agriculture.* New York: Halstead Press, 1978, p. 48.
10. Yepsen, Roger B. (ed.). *Organic Plant Protection.* Emmaus, PA: Rodale Press, 1976. p. 80.
11. Oelhaf, p. 60.
12. Yepsen, R., p. 508.

Brattleboro, VT: Stephen Greene Press, 1980. p. 55.

BIBLIOGRAPHY

Belanger, Jerome D. *Soil Fertility.* Waterloo, WI: Countryside Publications, 1977.

Brady, Nyle C. *The Nature and Properties of Soil.* New York: Macmillan, 1974.

Berry, Wendell. *The Unsettling of America.* New York: Avon Books, 1977.

Bubel, Nancy. *The Seed-Starter's Handbook.* Emmaus, PA: Rodale Press, 1978.

Carr, Anna. *Rodale's Color Handbook of Garden Insects.* Emmaus, PA: Rodale Press, 1979.

Carson, Rachel. *Silent Spring.* Boston: Houghton-Mifflin, 1962.

Carter, Vernon Gill, and Tom Dale. *Topsoil and Civilization.* Oklahoma City: University of Oklahoma Press, 1976.

Chan, Peter. *Better Vegetable Gardens the Chinese Way.* Portland, OR: Graphic Arts Center, 1977.

Doscher, Paul, Timothy Fisher, and Kathleen Kolb. *Intensive Gardening Round the Year.* Brattleboro, VT: The Stephen Greene Press, 1981.

Ervin, Susan. "Further Experiments on the Effects of Mulches on Crop Yields and Soil Conditions," *The Journal of the New Alchemists,* 6. Brattleboro, VT: The Stephen Greene Press, 1980.

Ervin, Susan. "Garden Notes," *The Journal of the New Alchemists,* 7. Brattleboro: VT: The Stephen Greene Press, 1981.

Fell, Derek. *How to Plant a Vegetable Garden.* Barrington, IL: Countryside Books, 1975.

Fichter, George S. *A Golden Guide to Insect Pests.* Racine WI: Western Publishing Co., 1966.

Fukuoka, Masanobu. *The One-Straw Revolution.* Emmaus, PA: Rodale Press, 1978.

GANSER, STEPHEN. *Vegetable Production in a Living Sod.* Emmaus, PA: Rodale Press, 1979.

GILBERTIE, SAL. *Herb Gardening At Its Best.* New York: Atheneum, 1978.

GRIEVE, M. *A Modern Herbal.* New York: Dover Publications, 1971.

HILLS, LAWRENCE D. *Comfrey: Past, Present, and Future.* London: Faber and Faber Ltd., 1976.

HILLS, LAWRENCE D. *Fertility Without Fertilizers.* New York: Universe Books, 1977.

HILLS, LAWRENCE D. *Grow Your Own Fruits and Vegetables.* London: Faber and Faber Ltd., 1971.

HILLS, LAWRENCE D. *Organic Gardening.* London: Penguin Books, 1977.

HYLTON, WILLIAM W. (ED.). *The Rodale Herb Book.* Emmaus, PA: Rodale Press, 1974.

JACKSON, WES. *New Roots for Agriculture.* San Francisco: Friends of the Earth, 1979. (Distributed by Brick House Pub. Co., Andover, MA.)

JEAVONS, JOHN. *How to Grow More Vegetables.* Palo Alto: Ecology Action of the Mid-Peninsula, 1979.

JEAVONS, JOHN, J. MOGADEN GRIFFIN, *et al. Beginning to Mini-Farm.* Palo Alto: Ecology Action of the Mid-Peninsula, 1980.

JORDAN, WILLIAM H. *Windowsill Ecology.* Emmaus, PA: Rodale Press, 1977.

KING, F.H. *Farmers of Forty Centuries.* Emmaus, PA: Rodale Press, 1973 (reprint of 1911 edition).

KRAMER, JACK. *The Natural Way to Pest Free Gardening.* New York: Charles Scribner's Sons, 1972.

LANGER, RICHARD W. *Grow It!* New York: Avon Books, 1972.

LOGSDON, GENE. *The Gardener's Guide to Better Soil.* Emmaus, PA: Rodale Press, 1978.

MARTIN, ALEXANDER, HERBERT S. ZIM, AND ARNOLD NELSON. *American Wildlife and Plants: A Guide to Wildlife Food Habits.* New York: Dover Publications, 1961.

MERRILL, RICHARD (ED.). *Radical Agriculture.* New York: Harper Colophon Books, 1976.

MOLLISON, BILL. *Permaculture Two.* Tasmania, Australia: Tagari Books, 1979.

NEWCOMB, DUANE. *The Postage Stamp Garden Book.* Los Angeles: J.P. Tarcher, 1975.

OELHAF, ROBERT C. *Organic Agriculture.* New York: Halsted Press, 1978.

OLKOWSKI, HELGA, AND WILLIAM OLKOWSKI. *The City People's Book of Raising Food.* Emmaus, PA: Rodale Press, 1975.

PHILBRICK, HELEN, AND JOHN PHILBRICK. *The Bug Book.* Charlotte, VT: Garden Way Publishing Co., 1974.

PHILBRICK, HELEN, AND RICHARD GREG. *Companion Plants and How to Use Them.* New York: Devin-Adair, 1966.

RATEAVER, BARGHYLA, AND GYLVER RATEAVER. *The Organic Method Primer.* Pauma Valley, CA, 1973.

RAYMOND, DICK. *Down to Earth Vegetable Gardening.* Charlotte, VT: Garden Way Publishing Co., 1976.

RIOTTE, LOUISE. *Success with Small Food Gardens.* Charlotte, VT: Garden Way Publishing Co., 1977.

RIOTTE, LOUISE. *Companion Planting.* Charlotte, VT: Garden Way Publishing Co., 1975.

RODALE, J.I. (ED.). *The Encyclopedia of Organic Gardening.* Emmaus, PA: Rodale Press, 1970.

RODALE, J.I. (ED.). *How to Grow Vegetables and Fruits by the Organic Method.* Emmaus, PA: Rodale Press, 1970.

VAN DEN BOSCH, ROBERT, AND P.S. MESSENGER. *Biological Control*. New York: Intext Educational Publishers, 1973.

WOLF, RAY (ED.). *Solar Growing Frame*. Emmaus, PA: Rodale Press, 1980.

YEPSEN, ROGER B. (ED.). *Organic Plant Protection*. Emmaus, PA: Rodale Press, 1976.

SEARLE, S.A. *Environment and Plant Life*. London: Faber and Faber, 1973.

STOUT, RUTH. *How to Have a Green Thumb Without An Aching Back*. New York: Cornerstone Library Publications, 1973.

VAN DEN BOSCH, ROBERT. *The Pesticide Conspiracy*. New York: Doubleday, 1978.

APPENDIX A
NPK Percentages in Common Organic Materials

	N	P	K
Manures*			
Cow	.4	.3	.44
Horse	.65–.76	.3–.6	.5–.65
Pig	.3	.3–.4	.45
Sheep and goats	.65	.46	.23
Chicken	1.1–1.8	1.0	.5
Turkey	1.3	.7	.5
Rabbit	2.0	1.0	.5
Commercially available materials			
Blood meal	9.0–15.00	1.0–1.3	.7–1.0
Bone meal (steamed)	1.0–4.0	20.0–30.0	0–.2
Bone meal (raw)	3.0–4.0	20.0–24.0	0
Cottonseed meal	6.5–8.0	2.0–3.0	1.0–2.0
Fish emulsion	5.0	2.4	1.2
Fish meal	8.0–10.5	4.0–9.0	2.0–3.0
Hoof and horn meal	7.0–15.0	0–2.0	0
Kelp meal	1.0	0	12.0
Greensand	0	1.5	5.0–6.7
Granite dust	0	0	3.0–5.0
Hard rock phosphate	0	0	25.0–33.0
Soft rock phosphate	0	0	15.0–20.0
Collectible and grow-your-own materials			
Alfalfa green manure	3.0–4.0	NA	NA
Alfalfa hay	1.5–2.5	.3–.5	1.5–2.1
Winter rye green manure	1.7–2.3	.18	1.05
Seaweed	.5–3.3	.1–2.0	1.0–5.0
Kentucky bluegrass	.66–1.2	.19–.4	.71–1.6
Oak leaves	.8	.35	.2–.3
Red clover hay	2.0–3.2	.25–.5	1.28–2.0
Sawdust and wood chips	.2	.1	.2

*NPK Levels in rotted manures can be slightly higher if kept under cover from rain. If manures are leached, nitrogen and potassium levels will be lower than the values shown.

	N	P	K
Coffee grounds	2.1	.3	.3
Wood ashes (unleached)	0	1.0–2.0	4.0–10.0
Wood ashes (leached)	0	1.0–1.5	1.0–3.0
White clover green			
Manure	.5	.15	.60
Sewage sludge	.74–6.0	.33–4.0	0–.24
Timothy hay	1.25	.55	1.0
Cow peas (green forage)	.45–3.0	.12–.25	.45–1.45
Oats, green manure	1.3–1.4	.17	1.09

SOURCES:

John Jeavons, *How to Grow More Vegetables*, Berkley, CA: Ten Speed Press, 1979.

J.I. Rodale, *The Encyclopedia of Organic Gardening*, Emmaus, PA: Rodale Press, 1970.

J.I. Rodale, *How to Grow Vegetables and Fruits by the Organic Method*, Emmaus, PA: Rodale Press, 1970.

APPENDIX B
Northeast Planting Table

CROP	SEED OR PLANT PER 100' OF ROW	DEPTH TO SOW SEED (INCHES)	DATE OF OUT-DOOR PLANTING (AVERAGE)
Plants That Stand Sharp Frost **Plant As Soon As Soil Can Be Worked**			
Root crops			
Beets	1 oz	¾	April 1–July 15
Carrots	1 oz	½	April 1–July 15
Onion (sets)	2 lbs	1	April 1
Parsnips	½ oz	½	June 1
Peas	1 lb	1	April 1
Radishes	½ oz	½	April 1
Rutabaga	2 pkts	½	July 1
Turnip	2 pkts	½	April 1–July 15
Greens & salad crops			
Broccoli	50 plants	½	April 1–July 6
Cabbage, early	50 plants		April 1
Cabbage, late	50 plants		July 5–10
Endive	⅛ oz	½	April 1 & August 15
Kale	1 pkt	½	April 1 & August 15
Lettuce (leaf)	1 pkt	½	April 1–August 1
Spinach	½ oz	½	April 1 & August 15
Swiss chard	1 oz	½	April 1
Crops That Stand Light Frost **Plant When Danger Of Soil Freezing Is Past**			
Green snap bean	1 lb	1	May 1–July 15
Yellow snap bean	1 lb	1	May 1–July 15
Pole snap bean	½ lb	1	May 1–July 15
Sweet corn	¼ lb	1	May 1–June 25
Squash, summer	1 oz	1	May 1
Squash, butternut	1 oz	1	June 1
Squash, winter	1 oz	1	June 1

CROP	SEED OR PLANT PER 100' OF ROW	DEPTH TO SOW SEED (INCHES)	DATE OF OUT-DOOR PLANTING (AVERAGE)
Crops That Cannot Stand Frost Plant When Frost No Longer Expected			
Bush lima bean	1 lb	1	May 10–June 10
Pole lima bean	1 lb		
Peppers	50 plants		May 15
Tomatoes	50 plants		May 15

Reprinted from material prepared by New Jersey Cooperative Extension Service, with permission.

APPENDIX C
Companion Planting Guidelines

HERB	COMPANION AND EFFECTS
Basil	Companion to tomatoes; dislikes rue intensely. Improves growth and flavor. Repels flies and mosquitoes.
Bee balm	Companion to tomatoes; improves growth and flavor.
Borage	Companion to tomatoes, squash, and strawberries; deters tomato worm; improves growth and flavor.
Caraway	Plant here and there; loosens soil.
Catnip	Plant in borders; deters flea beetle.
Chamomile	Companion to cabbages and onions; improves growth and flavor.
Chervil	Companion to radishes; improves growth and flavor.
Chives	Companion to carrots; improves growth and flavor.
Dead nettle	Companion to potatoes; deters potato bug; improves growth and flavor.
Dill	Companion to cabbage; dislikes carrots; improves growth and health of cabbage.
Fennel	Plant away from gardens. Most plants dislike it.
Garlic	Plant near roses and raspberries; deters Japanese beetle; improves growth and health.
Horseradish	Plant at corners of potato patch to deter potato bug.
Hyssop	Deters cabbage moth; companion to cabbage and grapes. Keep away from radishes.
Lamb's-quarter	This edible weed should be allowed to grow in moderate amounts in the garden, especially in corn.
Lovage	Improves flavor and health of plants if planted here and there.
Marigold	The workhorse of the pest deterrents. Plant throughout garden; it discourages Mexican bean beetles, nematodes, and other insects.
Marjoram	Plant here and there in garden; improves flavor.
Mint	Companion to cabbage and tomatoes; improves health and flavor; deters white cabbage moth.
Nasturtium	Companion to radishes, cabbage and cucurbits; plant under fruit trees. Deters aphids, squash bugs, striped pumpkin beetles. Improves growth and flavor.
Peppermint	Planted among cabbages, it repels the white cabbage butterfly.

HERB	COMPANION AND EFFECTS
Pigweed	One of the best weeds for pumping nutrients from the subsoil, it is especially beneficial to potatoes, onions, and corn. Keep weeds thinned.
Pot marigold	Companion to tomatoes, but plant elsewhere in the garden, too. Deters asparagus beetle, tomato worm, and general garden pests.
Purslane	This edible weed makes good ground cover in the corn.
Rosemary	Companion to cabbage, beans, carrots, and sage; deters cabbage moth, bean beetles, and carrot fly.
Rue	Keep it far away from sweet basil; plant near roses and raspberries; deters Japanese beetle.
Sage	Plant with rosemary, cabbage, and carrots; keep away from cucumbers. Deters cabbage moth and carrot fly.
Southernwood	Plant here and there in garden; companion to cabbage; improves growth and flavor; deters cabbage moth.
Sowthistle	This weed in moderate amounts can help tomatoes, onions, and corn.
Summer savory	Plant with beans and onions; improves growth and flavor. Deters bean beetles.
Tansy	Plant under fruit trees; companion to roses and raspberries. Deters flying insects, Japanese beetles, striped cucumber beetles, squash bugs and ants.
Tarragon	Good throughout garden.
Thyme	Plant here and there in garden. It deters cabbage worm.
Wormwood	As a border, it keeps animals from the garden.
Yarrow	Plant along borders, paths, near aromatic herbs; enhances essential oil production.

This information was collected from many sources, most notably the Bio-Dynamic Association and the Herb Society of America.

Reprinted from *The Seed-Starter's Handbook,* © 1978 by Nancy Bubel. Permission granted by Rodale Press Inc., Emmaus, PA 18049: pp. 102–103.

APPENDIX D
Insect Repelling Plants

PEST	REPELLENT PLANT
Leafhopper	Petunia, geranium
Mexican bean beetle	Marigold, potato, rosemary, summer savory, petunia
Mice	Mint
Mites	Onion, garlic, chives
Mole	Spurge, castor beans, mole plant, squill
Nematode	Marigold (African and french varieties), salvis (scarlet sage), dahlia, calendula (pot marigold), asparagus
Plum curculio	Garlic
Rabbit	Allium Family
Rose chafer	Geranium, petunia, onion
Slug (snail)	Prostrate rosemary, wormwood
Squash bug	Tansy, nasturtium
Striped pumpkin beetle	Nasturtium
Tomato hornworm	Borage, marigold, opal basil
Whitefly	Nasturtium, marigold, nicandra (Peruvian ground cherry)
Wireworm	White mustard, buckwheat, woad

Reprinted from *Organic Plant Protection* © 1976 by Rodale Press, Inc. Permission granted by Rodale Press, Inc., Emmaus, PA 18049; pp. 42-43.

APPENDIX E
Insect-Resistant Plant Varieties

PLANT	PEST
ALFALFA	ALFALFA APHID *Resistant:* Cody, Lahontan, and Zia *Susceptible:* Buffalo
BARLEY	GREENBUG *Resistant:* Omugi, Dictoo, and Will *Susceptible:* Rogers and Reno
BEANS	MEXICAN BEAN BEETLE *Resistant:* Wade, Logan, and Black Valentine *Susceptible:* State, Bountiful, and Dwarf Horticultural
BROCCOLI	DIAMONDBACK MOTH *Moderately resistant:* Coastal, Italian Green Sprouting, and Atlantic *Susceptible:* De Cicco HARLEQUIN BUG *Resistant:* Grande, Atlantic, and Coastal *Moderately resistant:* Gem STRIPED FLEA BEETLE *Resistant:* De Cicco, Coastal, Italian Green Sprouting, and Atlantic *Moderatley resistant:* Gem
CABBAGE	CABBAGE LOOPER AND IMPORTED CABBAGEWORM *Resistant:* Mammoth Red Rock, Savoy Chieftan, and Savoy Perfection Drumhead *Moderately resistant:* Special Red Rock, Penn State Ball Head, Early Flat Dutch, Badger Ball Head, Wisconsin Hollander, Red Acre, Danish Ball Head, Charleston Wakefield, Premium Late Flat Dutch, Glory of Enkhuizen, Globe, All Seasons, Midseason Market, Bugner, Succession, Early Round Dutch, Stein's Early Flat Dutch, Badger Market, Large Late Flat Dutch, Jersey Wakefield, Marion Market, Wisconsin Ball Head, Large Charleston Wakefield, Early Glory, Green Acre, Round Dutch, Resistant Detroit, and Wisconsin All Season *Susceptible:* Golden Acre, Elite, Coppenhagen Market 86, and Stein's Flat Dutch DIAMONDBACK MOTH *Resistant:* Michihli Chinese and Mammoth Red Rock *Moderately resistant:* Stein's Early Flat Dutch, Savoy Perfection Drumhead, Early Jersey Wakefield, and Jerry's Round Dutch. *Susceptible:* Copenhagen Market 86

PLANT	PEST
	HARLEQUIN BUG *Resistant:* Copenhagen Market 86, Headstart, Savoy Perfection Drumhead, Stein's Flat Dutch, Early Jersey Wakefield *Susceptible:* Michihli Chinese MEXICAN BEAN BEETLE *Resistant:* Copenhagen Market 86, Early Jersey Wakefield *Susceptible:* Michihli Chinese STRIPED FLEA BEETLE *Resistant:* Stein's Early Flat Dutch, Mammoth Red Rock, Savoy Perfection Drumhead, Early Jersey Wakefield, Copenhagen Market 86, and Ferry's Round Dutch *Moderately resistant to susceptible:* Michihli Chinese *Susceptible (Canada):* North Star and Northern Belle
CANTALOUPE	MEXICAN BEAN BEETLE *Cantaloupe is generally resistant to this pest, but serious damage was done to Rocky Ford Earliest during an infestation.* SPOTTED CUCUMBER BEETLE *Resistant (foliage):* Edisto 47, Edisto, and Harper Hybrid *Susceptible (seedlings):* Edisto, Edisto 47, Harper Hybrid, and Honey Dew *Susceptible (foliage):* Honey Dew
CAULIFLOWER	DIAMONDBACK MOTH *Moderately resistant:* Snowball A HARLEQUIN BUG *Resistant:* Early Snowball X and Snowball Y STRIPED FLEA BEETLE *Resistant:* Snowball A and Early Snowball X
COLLARD	DIAMONDBACK MOTH *Resistant:* Green Glaze *Moderately resistant:* Morris Headings, Vates, and Georgia Southern HARLEQUIN BUG *Resistant:* Vates, Morris Improved Heading, and Green Glaze *Moderately resistant:* Georgia LS and Georgia MEXICAN BEAN BEETLE *Resistant:* Georgia LS, Green Glaze, and Vates STRIPED FLEA BEETLE *Resistant:* Vates, Georgia, and Georgia LS *Moderately resistant:* Morris Heading *Susceptible:* Green Glaze
SWEET CORN	CORN EARWORM—Any corn with long, tight husks physically helps to prevent ear penetration. *Resistant:* Dixie 18 (field crop), Calumet, Country Gentleman, Staygold, Victory Golden, Golden Security, Silver Cross Bantam, and Silvergent

PLANT	PEST

Susceptible: Ioana, Aristogold, Bantam Evergreen, Seneca Chief, Spancross, North Star, and Evertender

FALL ARMYWORM—Late sweet corn crops and second crops are especially vulnerable. Resistance depends upon the planting time and tolerance of a variety. The varieties are arranged by survival rates, from best to worst.

Resistant: Golden Market, Long Chief, Golden Security, Evertender, Marcross, Golden Regent, Silver Cross Bantam, Calumet, Victory Golden, Golden Sensation, Spancross, Golden Cross Bantam, Aristogold Bantam Evergreen, Golden Beauty, Triple Gold, Deep Gold, and Ioana

SAP BEETLES—Any corn with long, tight husks physically helps to discourage the sap beetle.

Resistant: Country Gentleman, Deligold, Gold Pack, Golden Security, Harris Gold Cup, Tender Joy, Trucker's Favorite, Stowell's Evergreen, and Victory Garden.

Moderately resistant: Atlas, Duet, Eastern Market, Gold Strike, Golden Grain, Golden Security, Marcross, Merit, Midway, Royal Crest, Silver Queen, Spring Gold, Stowell's Evergreen, Tendercrisp, Wintergreen, and Victory Golden

Susceptible: (in many cases, sap beetles gain access to these varieties by way of entrances previously made by corn earworms): Aristogold, Bantam Evergreen, Calumet, Carmelcross, Corona, Deep Gold, Floriglade, Gold Mine, Golden Beauty, Golden Fancy, Ioana, Merit, Northern Belle, Seneca Chief, Seneca Explorer, Silvergent, Sixty Pak, Spancross, Spring Bounty, Titian, Vanguard, and White Silk Tendermost.

CUCUMBERS

MEXICAN BEAN BEETLE—While not normally a serious pest of cucumbers, this beetle severely damaged these varieties in an outbreak: Arkansas Hybrid No. 4, Colorado, Crispy, Hokus, Marketer, NK804, Nappa 63, Piccadilly, Pico, Pixie, and Triumph.

PICKLEWORM

Resistant: Arkansas Hybrid No. 4, Cubit, Gemini, Nappa 61, Nappa 63, Pixie, Princess, Spartan Dawn, Stono, Ashley Colorado, Hokus, Long Ashley, Model, Piccadilly, Packer, and Table Green

SPOTTED CUCUMBER BEETLE

Resistant (seedlings): Ashley, Chipper, Crispy, Explorer, Frontier, Gemini, Jet, Princess, Spartan Dawn, and White Wonder.

Resistant (foliage): Ashley, Cherokee, Chipper, Gemini, High Mark II, Ohio MR 17, Poinsett, Stono. (Stono is reported resistant to both striped and spotted cucumber beetles, and

PLANT	PEST
	Fletcher and Niagra are moderately resistant to the two pests.) Also Southern Cross *Moderately resistant (seedlings):* Cubit, High Mark II, Hokus, Nappa 63, Poinsett, and SMR 58 *Moderately resistant (foliage):* Colorado, Crispy, Explorer, Frontier, Long Ashley, Nappa 61, Pixie, and Table Green *Susceptible (seedlings):* Cherokee, Coolgreen, Model, Nappa 61, Packer, Pioneer, Southern Cross, and Table Green *Susceptible (foliage):* Coolgreen, Cubit, Hokus, Jet, Model, Nappa 63, Packer, Pioneer, Spartan Dawn, and SMR 58
KALE	DIAMONDBACK MOTH *Resistant:* Vates (protected by antibiosis, as a result of compact cell structure within the leaf) *Susceptible:* Early Siberian and Dwarf Siberian (has loosely arranged cells that are apparently easy for the larvae to mine) HARLEQUIN BUG *Resistant:* Vale *Susceptible:* Dwarf Siberian MEXICAN BEAN BEETLE *Resistant:* Dwarf Siberian STRIPED FLEA BEETLE *Resistant:* Vates, Dwarf Siberian, Dwarf Green Curled Scotch, and Early Siberian
MUSKMELON	STRIPED AND SPOTTED CUCUMBER BEETLE *Resistant:* Hearts of Gold *Susceptible:* Smith Perfect and Crenshaw
MUSTARD	DIAMONDBACK MOTH *Resistant:* Southern Giant Curled *Moderately resistant:* Florida Broadleaf HARLEQUIN BUG *Moderately resistant:* Old Fashion *Susceptible:* Southern Giant Curled, Green Wave, and Florida Broadleaf MEXICAN BEAN BEETLE *Resistant:* Green Wave *Susceptible:* Southern Giant Curled STRIPED FLEA BEETLE *Resistant:* Florida Broadleaf *Moderately resistant:* Southern Giant Curled and Green Wave
POTATO	APHIDS *Resistant:* British Queen, DeSota, Early Pinkeye, Houma, Irish Daisy, and LaSalle *Tolerant:* Red Warba, Triumph, President, Peach Blow, and Early Rose

PLANT	PEST
	Susceptible: Katahdin, Irish Cobbler, Idaho Russet, Segabo, and Sequoia
	COLORADO POTATO BEETLE
	Resistant: Sequoia and Katahdin
	Susceptible: Fundy, Plymouth, and Catoosa
	POTATO LEAFHOPPER
	Resistant: Delus
	Moderately resistant: Sebago, Pungo, and Plymouth
	Susceptible: Cobbler
PUMPKIN	SERPENTINE LEAF MINER (only 4 varieties were tested)
	Resistant: Mammoth Chili and Small Sugar
	Susceptible: King of the Mammoth and Green Striped Cushaw.
	SPOTTED CUCUMBER BEETLE
	Resistant (foliage): King of the Mammoth, Mammoth Chili, and Dickinson Field
	Susceptible (seedlings): Green Striped Cushaw, King of the Mammoth, Mammoth Chili, and Small Sugar
	Susceptible (foliage): Connecticut Field, Green Striped Cushaw, and Small Sugar
RADISH	CABBAGE WEBWORM
	Resistant: Cherry Belle
	Moderately resistant: Globemaster
	Susceptible: White Icicle, Red Devil, and Champion
	DIAMONDBACK MOTH
	Resistant: Cherry Belle, White Icicle, Globemaster, and Champion
	HARLEQUIN BUG
	Resistant: Red Devil, White Icicle, Globemaster, Cherry Belle, Champion, and Red Prince
	Moderately Resistant: Crimson Sweet
	MEXICAN BEAN BEETLE
	Susceptible: Sparkler, Champion, and White Icicle
	STRIPED FLEA BEETLE
	Moderately resistant: Champion and Sparkler
	Susceptible: Globemaster, Cherry Belle, and White Icicle
RUTABAGA	DIAMONDBACK MOTH
	Moderately resistant: American Purple Top
	HARLEQUIN BUG
	Susceptible: American Purple Top
	STRIPED FLEA BEETLE
	Resistant: American Purple Top
SORGHUM	CHINCH BUG
	Resistant: Atlas

PLANT	PEST

CORN LEAF APHID
Resistant: Sudan
Susceptible: White Martin

SQUASH

MEXICAN BEAN BEETLE—Although this beetle is not normally a serious pest of the squash, White Bush Scallop was damaged severely in an outbreak.

PICKLEWORM
Resistant: Summer Crookneck, Butternut 23, Buttercup, Boston Marrow, Blue Hubbard, and Green Hubbard (Butternut 23 is also resistant to the squash vine borer.)
Moderately resistant: Early Prolific Straightneck, Early Yellow Summer Crookneck, and White Bush Scallop
Susceptible: Black Beauty, U Conn, Marine Black Zucchini, Seneca Zucchini, Cozella Hybrid, Long Cocozelle, Benning's Green Tint Scallop, Short Cocozelle, Zucchini, Caserta, Black Zucchini, and Cozini Serpentine

LEAF MINER
Resistant: Butternut 23 and Cozella
Moderately resistant: Blue Hubbard, Zucchini, Benning's Green Tint Scallop, Summer Straightneck, Boston Marrow, Buttercup, and Pink Banana
Susceptible: Seneca Prolific, Green Hubbard, Seneca Zucchini, Summer Crookneck, Black Zucchini, Cozini, and Long Cozella

SPOTTED CUCUMBER BEETLE—These beetles are attracted to the odor of the germinating seeds of some varieties, and often dig through the soil to eat seedlings even before they've grown to the surface. Mature varieties with flowers having a strong, sweet smell attract these beetles in greater numbers than do other varieties.
Resistant (seedlings): Blue Hubbard, Green Hubbard, Long Cozella, Seneca Prolific, Summer Crookneck, and Summer Straightneck
Resistant (foliage): Black Zucchini, Benning's Green Tint Scallop, and Blue Hubbard (Royal Acorn and Early Golden Bush Scallop were found to be resistant to both the striped and spotted cucumber beetles.)
Moderately resistant (seedlings): Boston Marrow, Buttercup, and Pink Banana
Moderately resistant (foliage): Green Hubbard, Pink Banana, Seneca Zucchini, Summer Crookneck, and Summer Straightneck
Susceptible (seedlings): Benning's Green Tint Scallop, Black Zucchini, Cozella, Cozini, Seneca Zucchini, and Zucchini
Susceptible (foliage): Boston Marrow, Buttercup, Cozella, Cozini, Long Cocozelle, Seneca Prolific, and Zucchini

PLANT	PEST

SQUASH BUG
Resistant: Butternut, Table Queen, Royal Acorn, Sweet Cheese, Early Golden Bush Scallop, Early Summer Crookneck, Early Prolific Straightneck, and Improved Green Hubbard
Susceptible: Striped Green Cushaw, Pink Banana, and Black Zucchini

STRIPED CUCUMBER BEETLE
Reistant: Early Prolific Straightneck, U Conn, Long Cocozelle, White Bush Scallop, Benning's Green Tint Scallop, Early Yellow Summer Crookneck, Cozella Hybrid, Marine Black Zucchini, Butternut 23, Short Cocozelle, Summer Crookneck, and Zucchini (Royal Acorn and Golden Bush Scallop were found to be resistant to both the striped and spotted cucumber beetles.)
Susceptible: Black Zucchini, Cozini, Caserta, and Black Beauty.

SWEET POTATO SOUTHERN POTATO WIREWORM
Resistant: Nugget and All Gold
Moderately Resistant: Porto Rico, Centennial, Georgia Red, and Gold Rush
Susceptible: Nugget, Red Jewel, Georgia 41, Nemagold, and Julian

TOMATO TWO-SPOTTED MITE
Resistant: Campbell 135
Moderately resistant: Campbell 146
Susceptible: Homestead 24

TURNIP DIAMONDBACK MOTH
Resistant: Seven Top and Purple Top White Globe
HARLEQUIN BUG
Susceptible: Amber Globe, Purple Top White Globe, and White Egg
MEXICAN BEAN BEETLE
Susceptible: Amber Globe and Purple Top White Globe
STRIPED FLEA BEETLE
Moderately resistant: Seven Top
Susceptible: Purple Top White Globe and Amber Globe

WATERMELON SPOTTED CUCUMBER BEETLE
Resistant (foliage): Crimson Sweet and Sweet Princess
Susceptible (seedlings): Blue Ribbon, Charleston Gray, Crimson Sweet, Sugar Baby, and Sweet Princess
Susceptible (foliage): Charleston Gray, Blue Ribbon, and Sugar Baby

Reprinted from *Organic Plant Protection* © 1976 by Rodale Press, Inc. Permission granted by Rodale Press, Inc., Emmaus, PA 18049; pp. 531-538.

APPENDIX F
Disease Resistant Plant Varieties

CROP	DISEASE	VARIETY
APPLE	*Alternaria cork rot*	Delicious, Rome Beauty, Winesap, and Stayman Winesap
	Apple blotch	Grimes Golden, Jonathan, Stayman Winesap, and Winesap
	Bitter rot	Delicious, Rome Beauty, Stayman Winesap, Winesap, York Imperial, and Yellow Transparent
	Black pox	Transparent, York Imperial, and Gano
	Cedar apple rust	Baldwin, Delicious, Rhode Island, Northwestern Greening, Franklin, Melrose, Red Astrachan, Stayman, Transparent, Golden Delicious, Winesap, Grimes Golden, and Duchess
	Collar rot	Delicious, Winesap, and Wealthy. Moderately resistant varieties include Jonathan, Golden Delicious, McIntosh, and Rome Beauty. A susceptible variety can be grafted onto a resistant one, with good results; Grimes Golden on a Delicious trunk is a standard practice. Also, Malling XI and VII rootstocks are resistant.
	Fire blight	Baldwin, Ben Davis, Delicious, Duchess, McIntosh, Nothern Spy, Prima, Stayman, and Winter Banana
	Mildew	Prima
	Quince rust	Jonathan, Rome, Ben Davis, and Wealthy
	Scab	Prima
	Scar skin	Golden Delicious (tolerant)
ASPARAGUS	*Asparagus rust*	Supplanting the older Mary and Martha Washington are Waltham Washington, Seneca Washington, and California 500
BEAN	*Bacterial blight and wilt*	Tendergreen (some types)
	Common mosaic	Robust, Great Northern, U.. No. 5, Refugee, Idaho Refugee, and Wisconsin Refugee
	Powdery mildew	Contender
	Rust	Tendergreen (some types), Harvester, and Cherokee Wax (yellow)
DRY BEAN	*Bean halo blight*	Many, including Pinto, Great Northern, Red Mexican, and Michelite

CROP	DISEASE	VARIETY
LIMA BEAN	*Downy mildew*	Thaxter
SOYBEAN	*Bacterial blight*	Flambeau and Hawkeye
BEET	*Boron deficiency*	Detroit Dark Red
BLACKBERRY	*Orange rust*	Eldorado, Orange Evergreen, Russell, Snyder, and Ebony King
	Yellow rust, Cane rust	Nanticoke, Austin, Thornless, Boysen, Brainerd, Burbank Thornless, and Jersey Black, as well as most European varieties
BLUEBERRY	*Blueberry canker*	Weymouth, June, and Rancocas
	Mildew	Stanley, Rancocas, Harding, and Katherine
CABBAGE	*Yellows and Fusarium wilt*	Many, including Jersey Queen, Marion Market, Wisconsin Golden Arce, Resistant Detroit, Charleston Wakefield, Globe, Wisconsin All Season, Wisconsin Hollander, some strains of Jersey Wakefield, Market Topper, Market Prize, Greenback, King Cole, Resistant Danish, Vanguard II, Savoy King, Red Danish, Red Ball, and Red Head
CANTALOUPE	*Downy mildew*	Texas Resistant No. 1 and Georgia 47 (also resistant to aphids)
CAULIFLOWER	*Yellows*	Early Snowball
CELERY	*Fusarium wilt, Yellows*	Grow green petiole varieties or somewhat resistant Michigan Golden, Cornell 19, Tall Golden Plume, Golden Pascal, and Emerson Pascal.
SWEET CORN	*Bacterial wilt*	Many, including Golden Cross, Bantam, Golden, Beauty, F-M Cross, Carmelcross, Ioana, Marcross, Seneca Chief, N.K. 199, Iochief, and two white varieties, Silver Queen and Country Gent
	Helminthosporium smut	Gold Cup and Silver Queen (white); Golden Cross Bantam and Country Gent (white)
CUCUMBER	*Downy mildew*	Burpee Hybrid, M&M Hybrid, Saticoy, Salty, and Poinsett (also resistant to anthracnose and leaf spot)
	Mosaic	Spartan Dawn, SMR, and Salty
	Scab	Maine No. 2, Wisconsin SR 10 and SR 6, Highmoor, and Salty
RED CURRANT	*White pine blister beetle*	Viking and Red Dutch
DEWBERRY	*Orange rust*	Leucretia
EGGPLANT	*Phomopsis*	Florida Market and Florida Beauty
GRAPE	*Anthracnose*	Concord, Delaware, Moore Early, and Niagra

CROP	DISEASE	VARIETY
Dutch Iris	Iris rust	Early Blue, Gold and Silver, Golden West, Imperator, Lemon Queen, and Texas Gold
Lettuce	Downy mildew	There are many strains of this disease, so consult your county extension service.
	''Multiple Resistance''	Grand Rapids and Salad Bowl
	Tipburn	Slobolt, Summer Bibb, and Ruby
Mimosa	Mimosa wilt	Charlotte and Tryon
Muskmelon	Alternaria blight	Harper Hybrid
	Fusarium wilt	Gold Star, Harvest Queen, Samson, Chaca, and Supermarket
	Mosaic	Harper Hybrid
	Powdery mildew	Samson, Supermarket, and Chaca
Mustard	Turnip anthracnose	Southern Giant Curled
Onion	Fusarium rot	Early Yellow Globe and Southport Red Globe
	Pink root	Nebuka (Welsh onion), Beltsville Bunching and Brown Beauty (in Arizona, Granex bears best)
	Smudge	Early Yellow Globe, Downings Yellow Globe and Southport Red Globe
	Smut	Evergreen (bunching)
Parsley	Septoria blight	Paramount
Parsnip	Root canker	Model
Pea	Fusarium wilt	Wisconsin Early Sweet, Little Marvel, Thomas Laxton (all early varieties), and Frosty, Pride, Early Perfection, Sparkle, Wando, and Green Arrow (all medium to late varieties)
Pear	Fire blight	Old Home, Orient, and Kieffer
	Leaf blight and fruit spot	Kieffer shows some resistance
	Leaf spot	Kieffer, Flemish Beauty, Duchess, and Winter Nellis are moderately resistant.
	Pear scab	Bartlett
Pecan	Zinc deficiency	Money-maker
Pepper	Bacterial leaf spot	Sunnybrook (sweet salad variety) and two hot varieties, Long Red Cheyenne and Red Chili
	Mosaic	Sweet stuffing varieties; Bellringer, Keystone Resistant Giant, and Yolo Wonder
Plum	Armillaria root rot	Myrobolan 29 and Mariana 2624
Potato	Common scab	Menonimee, Ontario, Cayuga, Seneca, Superior, Haig, Pungo, and Norchip

CROP	DISEASE	VARIETY
	Late blight	Kennebec, Essex, Pungo, and Cherokee are resistant or tolerant to some strains
	Leaf roll	Katahdin
	Potato crinkle, mild mosaic	Katahdin, Chippewa, Houma, and Sebago
	Southern bacterial wilt (also known as brown rot, bacterial ring disease, and slime disease)	Northern seed varieties; Sebago and Katahdin
RADISH	*Fusarium wilt*	Red Prince
ROSE (GRAFTED)	*Black mold*	Ragged Robin
SHALLOT	*Pink root*	Evergreen
SPINACH	*Downy mildew*	Califlay and Texas Early Hybrid 7
SQUASH	*Bacterial wilt*	Table Queen (acorn), Butternut, and Buttercup
STRAWBERRY	*Hop mildew*	Sparkle, Puget Beauty, Siletz, and India
	Leaf scorch	Catskill, Midland, Fairfax, Howard 17, Blakemore, and Wouthland
	Red stele disease	Aberdeen, Steelmaster, Redchief, Darrow, and Guardian
SWEET POTATO	*Black rot*	Allgold
	Internal cork	Allgold, Centennial, and Nemagold
	Root-knot	Nemagold
	Soil rot	Allgold
	White rust	Goldrush
	Wilt	Allgold, Centennial, Goldrush, and Nemagold
TOMATO	*Blossom drop*	Summerset, Hotset, Summer Prolific, and Porter
	Curly top	Owyhee and Payette
	Early blight	Varieties that do not bear heavily are somewhat more resistant: Manalucie, Southland, Floradel, and Manahill
	Fusarium wilt	Heinz 1350, Heinz 1370, Campbell 1327, Jet Star, Better Boy, Supersonic, Burpee VF, Small Fry, Springset, Fantastic Manapal, Manalucie, Roma VF, Rutgers, Kokoma, Marion, Porter, and Homestead
	Gray spot	Manahill, Manalucie, and a number of Hawaiian varieties
	Graywall	Manalucie, Tropi-red, Tropi-grow, Indian River, Ohio WR Seven, and Strain A Globe
	Late blight	New Hampshire, Surecrop, New Yorker, Nova (a paste tomato), West Virginia, and Rockingham

CROP	DISEASE	VARIETY
	Leaf mold	Tuckcross 520, Ohio Hybrid O, Manalucie, Manapal, Vantage, Veegan, Vinequeen, Waltham, This fungus has mutated into new forms, and the older resistant varieties may no longer work well. Keep an eye out for new varieties.
	Mosaic virus	Moto-red, Ohio M-R9, Ohio M-R12, and Vendor
	Nailhead spot	Marglobe, Pritchard, Glovel, and Break O'Day
	Root-knot	Better Boy
	Spotted wilt	Pearl Harbor
	Verticillium wilt	Galaxy, Supersonic, New Yorker, Jet Star, Tom Tom, Roma VF, Heinz 1350, Campbell 1327, Better Boy, Burpee VF, Springset, Small Fry, and Loran Blood
WATERMELON	*Fusarium wilt*	Chareston Gray, Crimson Sweet, Sweet Princess, Improved Kleckly Sweet, and Klondike
	Melon anthracnose	Charleston Gray, Congo, Fairfax, Black Keckly, Crimson Sweet, Sweet Princess, and two seedless varieties, Tri-X313 and Triple Sweet

Reprinted from *Organic Plant Protection*, Roger Yepsen (ed.). Emmaus, PA: Rodale Press, 1976, pp. 539–545. With permission.

APPENDIX G
Comparison of Chemical Pesticides and Biological Controls

CHARACTERISTIC	CHEMICAL PESTICIDES	BIOLOGICAL CONTROLS	METHOD FAVORED*
R&D and Marketing; R&D support	Large, private and public	Some, mostly public	C
Private profit	Patentable	Generally not patentable	C
Market potential	Large, broad-spectrum	Small, specific	C
Advertising	Heavy	Minimal	C
On-the-Farm application costs	Comparitively large annual	Small or zero	B
Visibility	High	Low	C
Timing of effects	Fast positive action; Slow negative effects later		C
Percent control	Complete at first	Generally only partial	C
Long-range planning and careful timing?	Not needed	Needed	C
Inter-farm coordinator needed?	No	Often	C
Effectiveness depends on weather? Climate?	Usually not much	Yes, often	C
Compatible with other modern technology?	Highly	Varies	C
Compatible with other stages of the food system?	Highly	May conflict	C
Safety in use	Varies	Absolutely safe	B
Pest resistance?	Yes	Most, none	B
Appeal to ego?	Yes	None	C
Externalities			
Damage to wildlife	May be great	None	C?
Danger to consumers	May be great	None	C?
Public good?	Generally not	Often	C

"C" indicates chemical control favored; "B" indicates biolgical. (R&D indicates Research and Development expenditure.)

Reprinted from *Organic Agriculture*, Robert C. Oelhaf. New York: Halsted Press, Roman & Allanheld Publishers, 1978. With permission.

Chapter 5

Aquaculture

Michael Greene and Merryl Alber

Why raise food in water? If you are fond of eating fish and have bought any lately, you'll realize that one incentive to raise your own fish is its prohibitive market cost. Those of you who are energy conscious know that fish are perhaps the most efficient converters of feed into animal protein. In terms of nutrition and health, no other meat animal can compete with the low-fat, low-cholesterol fish. Yet today's polluted oceans, lakes, and streams have turned many of our fish into virtual storehouses of heavy metals and PCBs. And if these weren't reasons enough for raising your own fish, the difference in flavor would be! Even the taste of really fresh, home-grown fish is superior, just as vegetables fresh from the garden are superior to supermarket produce.

At New Alchemy, we have been exploring various fish culture techniques for more than 12 years. Our focus has been on three types of culture systems: floating cages, backyard ponds, and greenhouse solar-algae ponds. Each offers numerous advantages— and disadvantages—depending on your site and species preference. This chapter gives you a general description of each system. Keep in mind that the experimental results presented here will have been updated by the time you read this. When you're ready to begin at your own home, check back with us for further details about our most recent methods.

Michael Greene, the principal author of this chapter, was fortunate to have apprenticed in all three New Alchemy aquaculture programs during his years of work here. It would be impossible to list every one of the creative fish farmers who have contributed to our understanding of these efficient food-production systems, but we are particularly grateful to Carl Baum, Peter Burgoon, David Engstrom, Linda Gusman, Bill McLarney, Meredith Olsen, Jeff Parkin, John Todd, John Wolfe, and Ron Zweig for their advice on this subject.

THE EDITORS

EACH YEAR approximately 75 million tons of fish are caught in the world's oceans, seas, rivers, and lakes. It is estimated that sustainable annual yields may reach levels of about 110 million tons. This increase will not be nearly enough to keep pace with a rapidly expanding human population and its need for protein. Here in the United States, consumer prices can only rise.

One solution to this problem is aquaculture, the growing of foods in water. Aquaculture is a rather broad term for the raising of aquatic organisms: fish, lobsters, mussels, seaweed, and so on. The aquatic animals chosen for culture are usually high in protein. In well-managed aquatic systems, the yield of protein produced per unit area and per unit of feed is often higher than in land-based systems. In this chapter, we focus mainly on fish farming. Chapter 10 offers some suggestions for additional aquatic crops and ways in which aquaculture can be integrated with agriculture and the raising of other livestock.

In certain European and Asian countries, fish farming traditionally has supplied an important part of the people's diet. Recently, some aquaculture projects have been started in the United States. In fact, the fish filet served at McDonald's probably was grown on an aquaculture farm in the South or Midwest.

Since most American fish farming is done for commercial purposes, it is usually practiced on a relatively large scale. During the past few years, however, a number of researchers have experimented with smaller facilities that would allow an individual or family to raise fish as a means of supplying some of their own food (see Fig. 1).

A number of fish species are well suited for small-scale aquaculture. In cold, pristine water (always below 70°F), trout may be raised. In warm water (above 60°F), catfish, tilapia, bluegills, or certain species of carp are suitable. Although some of these fish may be unfamiliar as food, they are all quite tasty.

Each species has different nutritional requirements, oxygen demands, tolerance to poor water quality, temperature sensitivity, and ability to

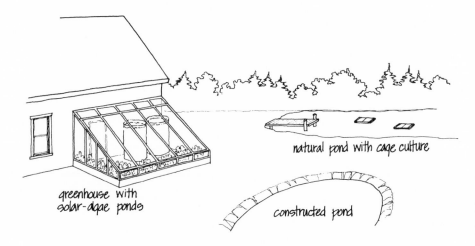

greenhouse with
solar-algae ponds

natural pond with cage culture

constructed pond

Fig. 1 Backyard aquaculture systems. This diagram illustrates several methods of small scale aquaculture. 1. Fish can be stocked in cages that are set out in a natural body of water such as a lake or pond. 2. A small backyard pond can be built and stocked with several species of fish. 3. Fish ponds can even be placed in a greenhouse.

breed in captivity. Publications that address the specific requirements of each fish are listed in the Bibliography at the end of this chapter.

Backyard fish farming does not require excessive amounts of time. Most of the work involves inspecting the operation and feeding the fish. Usually this interesting activity takes only a few minutes each day. Some dirty, time-consuming work can be expected at the beginning and end of the season. Early activities include filling a small pond, obtaining equipment, and handling live fish. Harvesting at the end of the season includes cleaning and gutting the fish and will take the better part of a day.

The physical activities involved in maintaining a backyard fish farm are less difficult—and require considerably less time—than gardening. However, since fish are not visible under the water, it is easier to spot trouble in the garden than it is in the pond. In addition, plants can usually get by adequately for a few days without maintenance, even under difficult conditions such as drought and insect attack. But when there is a problem with fish, they often need immediate attention if they are to survive. Fortunately, problems such as overfeeding, poor water quality, and low oxygen levels can be corrected easily if they are spotted in time.

Often an initial stock of young fish can be trapped at a local pond. Knowledge of the species' breeding habits will be of great assistance in this undertaking. For instance, fingerlings (young fish) of the local catfish species on Cape Cod can be netted easily in May, when they congregate in the waist-deep water of swampy ponds. If suitable fish cannot be obtained locally, various species can be purchased from commercial hatcheries. Each year, *Aquaculture* Magazine puts out a Buyers Guide that lists sources of all types of aquaculture supplies—from fish to feed to cages. After the first year, you may be able to overwinter certain fish so that they can breed and supply the next year's stock. (*Note:* See the section labeled Legal Guidelines toward the conclusion of this chapter for information regarding legal restrictions on importing or trapping fish.)

Fish must be fed on a daily basis in order to grow rapidly. A number of commercial feeds have been developed to meet the nutritional requirements of different species. (Yes, there's even a Purina Trout Chow®.) Floating feeds are usually preferred to those that sink, because they allow you to observe whether or not your fish are consuming all of their daily ration. Feeding levels should be reduced if some food remains uneaten 20 minutes after it has been placed in the pond.

Daily feeding portions are determined by calculating the total weight of fish in a pond and then feeding them between 1 and 5 percent of this figure. As the fish grow they need more feed. To adjust feeding portions accurately, you'll need to know the food conversion rate, the total weight of fish, and the feeding rate of your system.

The *food conversion rate* is the ratio of total dry feed to total wet fish growth, and ranges between 0.9 and 4.0 pounds of dry food to produce a pound of fish. You can periodically weigh all the fish, or, more practically, you can weigh a percentage of your fish and estimate the *total weight* of all the fish in your pond. The *feed rate*, as stated above, ranges from 1 to 5 percent.

You can determine the new feeding portion by using the following formula: Take the total weight of the food added, divide by the food conversion rate, and add this number to the initial fish weight. Then multiply this new weight by the feeding rate to get the new feeding portion.

For example, let's say you stock 5 pounds of fish in a backyard pond. The feeding rate is 3 percent. The fish receive 3 percent of their total weight (5 pounds), which is 0.15 pounds of food per day. The food conversion rate of your system is 1.5 (this is an average figure). If you feed the fish six out of seven days per week, after two weeks you'll want to adjust the feeding rate as follows: Take the total weight of food added (0.15 pounds per day × 12 days), which is 1.8 pounds, and divide by the food conversion rate (1.5). This equals 1.2 pounds. You now know that the fish have grown 1.2 pounds. Add this number to the initial fish weight (5 pounds) to get a total of 6.2 pounds; now multiply this new weight by the feeding rate of 3 percent to get the new feeding portion of 1.9 pounds per day.

Feeding levels should be adjusted regularly throughout the season. You might consider supplementing your fish's diet with "home-grown" feeds such as worms, insects, or kitchen and garden scraps. These feeds are 75 to 90 percent water, whereas commercial products are dry. Therefore, unless large quantities are used, they should not affect the amount of commercial feed given to the fish. Even in small doses, some of these natural feeds can have a positive effect. Research at New Alchemy suggests that the growth rate of young fish (particularly tilapia and bullheads) is greatly enhanced when small amounts of insects are included in their feeding regimen.

Unless the fish are consistently neglected, underfeeding will rarely be a serious problem; it will just result in decreased yields. Overfeeding, on the other hand, can be quite harmful, particularly in semiclosed systems (small ponds or tanks with high fish densities and little or no water flow-through). Uneaten food will decay and pollute the water. In addition, the more food the fish eat, the more they excrete. Their wastes contain ammonia and other toxic nitrogenous compounds. High concentrations of these toxins will inhibit fish growth and can even cause their death. The task of the fish farmer is to remove the polluted water or to convert its harmful compounds into a more benign form. One of the most distinguishable features of the different fish systems discussed in this chapter is the manner in which they deal with this problem.

The most successful backyard fish farmers are the ones who remain observant and interested in their project. Reading the literature, questioning others, and experimenting with new ideas will develop your abilities and give you a deeper understanding of the inner workings of the pond.

Begin the undertaking with realistic expectations. Small-scale aquaculture is a young field, just beginning to be explored. At this time it does not offer all the economic advantages of gardening. However, it does seem to offer a special sense of adventure; and you can't beat the satisfaction of sitting down with friends and family to a meal of fresh, home-grown fish.

Cage Culture

Cage culture is the method of raising fish in floating cages made of wire, plastic, or other mesh materials. The cages are placed in natural bodies of water—lakes, streams, or ponds—and are stocked densely with young fish. While the fish are confined to this small area, surrounding water passes easily through the mesh material. Water that has been polluted by the fish excrement is removed from the growing area and replaced with fresh water. This effective cleansing process, combined with intensive feeding, promotes fish growth at a rate 5 to 100 times greater than the unassisted productivity of a small pond of the same size.

Do you have access to a pond or lake suitable for cage culture?

Fresh waterways can serve a number of concomitant useful purposes, such as providing the opportunity to fish, swim, and go boating. In addition they may be water sources for people or livestock, or they may be conservation areas. Cage culture integrates easily with these other uses. Cages will rarely interfere with the pond's recreational uses. However, people engaged in these activities may disturb your cages.

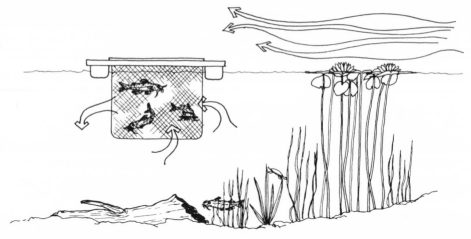

Fig. 2 Cage culture pond. All natural bodies of water have some wind or convective currents. These currents, combined with the movement of the contained fish, force constant interchange between water inside the cage and the water in the pond.

Is the water clean enough for swimming?

Consider the quality of the pond's water. Some of the pollution can hinder fish growth or make the fish unsuitable to eat. If the pond water is clean enough for swimming, usually it is safe for fish culture. If you want more information about pollution levels and legal constraints for a particular pond, call your town's conservation officer or the district fisheries-and-game service.

Cage culture has many advantages:

- Cages are relatively small and unobtrusive. They don't interfere with the recreational or aesthetic value of a pond or stream.
- Cages can be used in bodies of water which otherwise would be difficult to harvest due to dense plant growth, excessive depth, or rocky/muddy bottoms.
- Cages are easy to inspect, clean, and harvest.
- There is a minimum of wasted feed. In open ponds without cages, food can be eaten either by the species being cultured or by other fish in the water. Cages restrict the feed from drifting away and ensure that it is used mainly by the selected species.

Prospective fish farmers should also consider some of the disadvantages of the cage-culture method:

- When many fish are confined to a small area, there is risk that if some contract an infectious disease, it will spread quickly.
- Fish can't swim to more favorable zones to avoid problems such as low levels of oxygen or high water temperatures.

- Although the cages can prevent loss of stock to such natural predators as larger fish and birds, they are quite vulnerable to human theft and vandalism.
- State or local laws may block the use of a potential site or the culture of a given fish species.

Cages can vary in size, although approximate dimensions of two feet wide, four feet long, and four feet deep will be satisfactory for most small-scale applications. They can either be purchased from a manufacturer or constructed at home. While building the cages is time-consuming, you can save quite a bit of money this way.

Cages can be made from a rigid half-inch plastic mesh or plastic-coated wire. If the mesh is not stiff enough, polyvinyl chloride (PVC) tubing or wood can be used as a frame. You may want to treat the wood so it won't rot in the water, but make sure your treatment is not toxic to fish. You'll want a hinged lid that you can open and close to add food. Styrofoam can be used to keep the cage afloat, and you'll need a concrete block or something else that's heavy to anchor it. You may want to put a lock on the cage to secure the fish against human predation.

Properly constructed cages will require very little maintenance. During the growing season, an occasional scrubbing of the inside and outside of the mesh should be all that is required. Inspect the cages frequently. If a crack or hole develops in the material, fix it at once or you may soon lose all your finned friends.

To ensure adequate circulation of water, always place your cages where there's at least one or two feet of water between them and the pond bottom. If you line up several cages (along a raft, for example), be sure to leave at least a foot between them. Maintenance will take less time if the cages are accessible from the shore, although going out in a boat can be a real pleasure. Since water in the cages will not contain much natural feed, the grower must provide the fish with their nutritional needs. Feeding is a simple process that takes just a few minutes a day; but to ensure maximum growth, you must feed your fish regularly.

Experiments to determine optimum stocking densities for cages have yielded interesting results. The behavior of aggressive fish (like catfish, for example) seems to be greatly influenced by their level of population. At low densities they stake out territories that they are usually able to defend without much conflict. At intermediate densities, territories are too small for comfort. Actual fighting develops, and fish mortality may occur. At really high densities, however, the fish do *not* exhibit these territorial and aggressive traits. Therefore stocking 200 to 300 catfish per cubic yard is preferred to stocking levels of 20 to 30 catfish per cubic yard.

During one season of growth, we've raised catfish from fingerlings to a size ranging from one-third to two-thirds of a pound. They are edible at this size and make fine pan-fried meals.

One of the more successful cage-culture experiments conducted at New Alchemy was with yellow bullheads, a type of catfish. They were chosen for this experiment because they accept feed, are disease resistant, are reasonably available in many regions, and taste good. Young fish trapped in a pond in central Massachusetts provided the initial stock.

In a $2 \times 4 \times 3$-foot cage, we raised 100 fish from an initial weight of 12.1 pounds to a final weight of 35.6 pounds (that is, from an average weight of 0.12 pounds to 0.36 pounds each) in a little over three months. This means approximately one pound of fish growth per cubic foot. The experiment was initiated in late June, about a month after good growing conditions actually began on Cape Cod. Yields probably would have been higher if the experiment had started earlier.[1]

Our overview of cage culture has been presented solely as an introduction to this aquaculture method. If you're intrigued and want more complete instructions, you'll find them in *The New Alchemy Back Yard Fish Farm Book* by William O. McLarney and Jeffrey Parkin (Brick House Publishing, 1983). This useful volume is available at bookstores and by mail from the New Alchemy Institute for about $8.95 plus postage. Other relevant publications are listed in the chapter Bibliography.

Backyard Ponds

Perhaps you're one of the many people who can establish a fish pond on their own property. Backyard ponds can be almost any size: quite large or no bigger than a small swimming pool. Their shapes can vary to fit the surrounding landscape. Our discussion will focus on the relatively small type of pond that takes up about 200 square feet of land and has a three- to five-foot depth. The volume of water would range between 4500 and 7500 gallons.

Do you have access to a piece of land where you can construct a small pond? Also, is there a source of tap or well water (or a stream) nearby?

A backyard pond will be your most accessible form of aquaculture if you own some land that can be used for this purpose. Before deciding on a specific location, take a walk around your property and review the potential of each site. Will a small pond pose any physical danger to people or livestock? Will creating a small pond interfere with—or contribute to—the land's current function?

You can hand-dig a pond, but we must warn you that it takes a lot of time and hard work. (Don't even think about it, though, if you have a

rocky soil.) Perhaps you could persuade a few friends to help with this unusual project by offering them food and drink in return for a day of cooperative labor. Most people, however, will find it worthwhile to rent a backhoe. Although this equipment is comparatively expensive, it will get the job done quicker.

How well does the soil hold water?

If the soil has a high clay content, it may not need a special seal to hold water. Otherwise it's necessary to seal the bottom.

One way to seal the bottom and sides is with a large plastic sheet. Make sure you remove rocks and other objects that could puncture the plastic. As a further precaution, you can line the pit with soft organic material such as grass clippings or manure *before* you lay the plastic sheet.

Or you can use a process known as *gleying* to seal the bottom. Damp organic material decomposing anaerobically (without the presence of air) can produce a sticky impermeable layer known as gley. This material can prevent ponds from leaking. If you want to make this natural seal, construct the pond sides with a gentle slope. Line the sides and bottom to a depth of one foot with thin layers of very succulent green vegetable matter and fresh wet manure. Cover the materials with several inches of dirt, pack it down well, and *then* fill the pond.

Figure 3 shows a pond that is to remain plastic-lined. So long as the soil under the plastic lining does not settle, the sides of the pond may have a sharp slope. Edges of the plastic lining may be held down with a heavy layer of soil.

Fig. 3 Plastic-lined
pond, steep slope

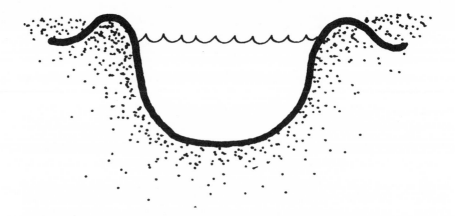

Figure 4 shows a pond that has a temporary plastic liner but will eventually be sealed only with the gley. If large amounts of organic matter are placed in the trench, the sides of the pond should have a gentler slope. Edges of the plastic lining need not be permanently secured.

The amount of fish produced in a small pond will depend largely on the activities of the grower. If you just place a few fish in the water and let them find food for themselves, total growth will be quite limited. Natural ponds of average fertility will support between one-third and three pounds of fish growth per year per 200 square feet of surface area. Regular feeding of the fish can increase your pond's productivity tenfold.

As we noted earlier, commercial products can be supplemented with home-grown feeds. One interesting possibility is that of placing a "bug light" over the pond. During the night, this mechanism will attract and electrocute flying insects. The deceased bugs then fall into the water, where the fish hungrily snatch them up. Bug lights catch enormous numbers of insects in windless inland areas; in coastal wind-blown areas like Cape Cod the catch is slimmer. Even so, on a still, dry June night we've collected one-quarter pound of bugs.[2]

As fish eat greater quantities of food, they produce greater quantities of wastes. If large amounts of food are added to the pond, provisions should be made to remove the resulting pollutants. This can be accomplished by regularly draining the pond and adding fresh water.

If your garden is at a lower elevation than your pond, install a drainage pipe and use the nutrient-rich water for irrigation. If your garden is higher than your pond, you'll need a submersible pump to help the water move uphill.

One alternative to regularly draining the pond is cleaning and recycling the water through a biological filter. These filters contain gravel or shells that provide a large surface area on which billions of bacteria can grow. The bacteria convert the harmful chemical compounds excreted by

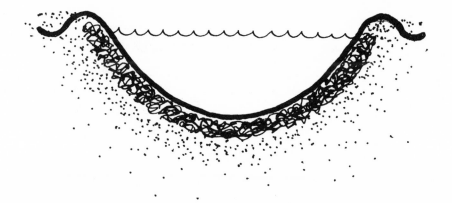

Fig. 4 Plastic and gley-lined pond, gentle slope

the fish into less toxic forms. This process will not occur, however, unless adequate levels of oxygen are sustained within the filter. Oxygen levels are substantially reduced when the shells or gravel become clogged with particulate matter. Therefore we advise you to establish a settling tank upstream of the bacterial filter. That way, water from the pond must flow through the settling tank before entering the filter. This allows some of the tiny suspended particles to settle out before the water passes through the shells or gravel. Sediments from the settling tanks should be regularly drained and used in the garden.

Even the best settling tanks can't remove *all* the particulate matter from the water. Therefore at some point the filter will tend to become clogged with wastes. To maximize its effectiveness, you should clean your filter at least once or twice during the growing season. This chore will be much less offensive if the filter is designed carefully. One approach is to make sure your tank can be tipped over for easy removal and washing of filter materials. Another method is to place the shells or gravel in a number of flow-through bags (made of wire or strong plastic mesh) that can be cleaned individually when they are removed from the tank.

You can design filters in ways that will increase oxygen levels in the pond. Instead of returning the water through a hose, allow it to fall through the air and splash into the pond. Splashing water can add a significant amount of oxygen to the pond. Oxygen levels may be increased through the use of an electrical or wind-driven aerator, also.

At New Alchemy, we are experimenting with several types of filtering systems. One that shows great potential is the combination bacterial and hydroponic filter. (*Hydroponics* refers to growing plants directly in water without soil.) Wastes that would be detrimental to fish growth serve as the nutrient supply for food plants.

We have had excellent results in growing copious amounts of watercress and Chinese spinach through this method. Current hydroponic

Fig. 5 Settling tank and shell filter with watercress

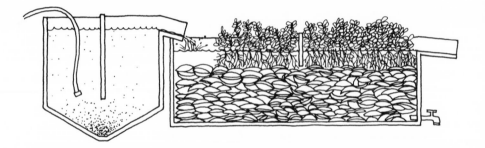

experiments include the use of celery, cucumbers, tomatoes, and lettuce. The roots of these crops require higher levels of oxygen than watercress (which is an aquatic plant). Therefore, instead of placing these plants directly *in* the bacterial filter, you should build a separate hydroponic tray (see Fig. 5).

If you decide to use this system, design it so that the water contains high levels of dissolved oxygen and flows quickly through the hydroponic trench. Current experiments suggest that this type of system is effective even without the use of an additional bacterial filter.

The total size of the filtration system can vary according to the needs of the grower. The larger and/or more efficient the filter, the faster pollutants can be removed from the water. This increases the pond's productivity, as fish can be stocked at higher densities and fed larger quantities of food. As it increases productivity, however, filtration also increases costs; you must purchase additional equipment, supply electrical or mechanical energy to pump water, and spend more time on the project.

To date, only a few species of fish have been used in experiments measuring the potential of small backyard ponds, and even this research is scant. Since the backyard pond is a miniature replica of a natural body of water, it is likely that many types of fish can adapt successfully to its environment. Ponds may be stocked with one or several species. *Polyculture* (growing several species together) can increase total fish production when each variety requires different kinds of food. In China, the world leader in the production of freshwater fish, large and small ponds usually contain four types of carp: One feeds on higher aquatic plants; one eats algae; a third type feeds on microscopic animals; and a bottom-dweller eats the feces of the other fish as well as small aquatic animals.

At New Alchemy, our most successful experiments have involved small ponds stocked solely with tilapia. These tropical fish are native to Africa and the Middle East, but they are available from fish hatcheries in this country. Although their use in outdoor ponds is somewhat restricted by their need for warm water (they die at temperatures below 52°F), they have a number of impressive attributes for the home aquaculturist. Tila-

Solar-algae pond in
New Alchemy
Bioshelter

pia are able to use a wide variety of feeds efficiently: commercial pellets, worms, insects, algae, and garden scraps. They can tolerate such unfavorable water conditions as low oxygen levels and high amounts of organic pollution. In addition, they seem to be quite forgiving of our mistakes; many a tilapia has survived an accidental fall from our hands.

Solar-Algae Ponds

As we observed in Chapter 3, the attached greenhouse has gained lots of recent popularity among homeowners. When built on the southern side of a residence, a greenhouse acts as a solar collector, heating the interior as well as providing the family with a year-round food-growing area. If you have an attached greenhouse, you can use the space to raise fish as well as vegetables.

One way to do this is by building a concrete pond inside the greenhouse. If you provide adequate filtration, such a pond can be highly productive. The dynamics of this system actually are quite similar to those of a backyard pond, and the indoor environment extends the growing season. An excellent booklet describing this type of system is *Fish Farming in Your Solar Greenhouse*, by William Head and Jon Splane. It's available through the Amity Foundation of Eugene, Oregon. (See the chapter Bibliography for further details.)

Another method is to grow your greenhouse fish in large fiberglass cylinders, known as *solar-algae ponds*. To fit your space requirements, you may purchase the tanks ready-made, or buy fiberglass sheets and epoxy them together at home. (Plans for building a tank at home can be purchased from the New Alchemy Institute.) One advantage of a solar-algae pond (as opposed to an in-ground, cement pond) is that if you place your tanks in sunny areas, they will absorb great amounts of solar energy. Since the winter sun is always low in the sky, side walls absorb much more light than the horizontal water surface of an in-ground pond. Thus the water in a solar-algae pond will be warmer than water in a concrete pond and more advantageous for fish culture. It will also maintain the heat of the greenhouse, buffering the effects of falling temperatures during cold winter nights (see Fig. 6).

Does your greenhouse contain sufficient space for solar ponds to produce fish and store heat?

The standard solar-algae ponds that we use are cylinders five feet high by five feet in diameter. Not all greenhouses are designed to accommodate ponds of this size. If there is insufficient space for a standard-size pond, a smaller solar pond, three feet high and two foot in diameter can be used. If ponds smaller than five by five feet are used, total fish production and heat

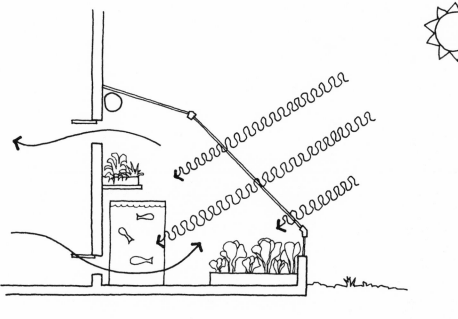

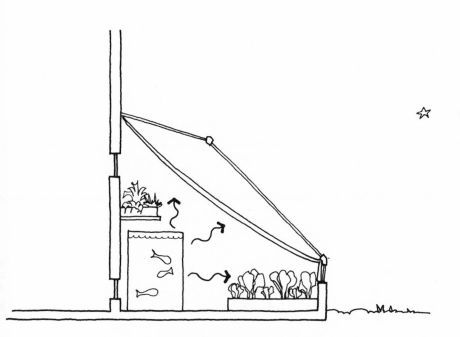

Fig. 6 Solar-algae ponds as heat storage. In addition to providing an environment in which to raise fish, solar-algae ponds also act as heat storage units for a greenhouse. They absorb sunlight during the day and release it back into the greenhouse at night.

storage per tank will decrease, although not necessarily proportionately. Smaller ponds are likely to fit more easily into existing greenhouses, but because of the larger surface-to-volume ratio, daily temperature fluctuations will be greater. This can be hard on the fish that inhabit the pond.

Can your greenhouse or garden use periodic irrigation with warm, fertile water?

Solar-algae ponds are essentially small aquatic ecosystems, which can be beneficial in many ways if used properly. First you must understand the dynamics and limits of these living systems. We've already mentioned that solar-algae ponds can be an efficient medium for growing fish protein. Algae and bacteria are also important components of the system. The "wastes" from this ecosystem can also be used as a convenient source of high-quality nutrients required for plant growth.

Simply stated, the dynamics of a solar-algae pond are as follows: The fish eat both algae and the commercial feed provided. They excrete wastes. They also respire through their gills and give off nitrogen in the form of ammonia. Part of this "waste" is taken up by algae. Some is converted by nitrifying bacteria into less toxic forms. However some remains and builds up to a point where it is harmful to the fish and must be removed. What better place for these nutrients than your nearby plants? They will love you for it!

The word *algae* in the name solar-algae pond, is emphasized with good reason. Algae benefit the aquaculture system in several ways:

- Algae increases the pond's ability to capture solar energy. High levels of light and dissolved nutrients encourage a dense population of algae, as indicated by the deep green color in the water.   The darker the water color, the more sunlight is absorbed.
- Algae reduce the need for aeration. When these microscopic plants are exposed to light, they photosynthesize and release oxygen into the water. Therefore, even on partially overcast days, it's not necessary to aerate the pond. However, the algae's rate of photosynthesis is sharply reduced during prolonged periods of cloudy weather and completely ceases at night. A small electric aerator should be used to supply oxygen to the pond at these times.
- Algae act as a feed source for the fish. Tilapia, for instance, can filter some algae from the water and use it as a minor source of food, although additional feed must be added to attain rapid rates of growth.
- Algae absorb fish wastes. Ammonia and other nitrogenous compounds that are poisonous to the fish act as fertilizer for the algae. By absorbing these wastes, algae allow relatively large amounts of food to be added to the pond without causing water pollution.

Many kinds of fish can be raised in solar-algae ponds. Most of the work at New Alchemy has been with tilapia, a fish native to the Middle East and Africa. We favor tilapia because they are semi-tropical and grow well in a warm greenhouse environment. They eat algae and green plants. They are easy to handle and, most important, they taste good.

The pond management schemes described in the following pages are specific for tilapia. If you raise other types of fish, appropriate modification will be necessary.

POND MANAGEMENT GUIDELINES

Like any natural system, the solar-algae pond ecosystem changes throughout the year. During the winter months, ponds function primarily as heat storage inside the greenhouse. During the spring and summer, ponds are moved outside for fish production. In managing a pond, you need to consider several variables including the *total fish weight, fish density, feeding rate,* and *water quality* of the pond.*

Summer Management

Moving ponds outside during the warmer months (from May through November) means the loss of heat storage in the greenhouse; consequently greenhouse temperatures are not as well moderated. However, ponds will receive more solar energy and thus fish and algal growth will increase. You'll need to determine your own compromise. If you have many ponds (as we do), you can move some of them outside and leave some inside the greenhouse for the summer months.

We've found that our outdoor ponds do best when they're managed in six-week cycles. A pond can support 2 to 22 pounds of tilapia, although they do best when the *total weight* of the fish is about 11 to 15 pounds.

Fish density is another matter to consider. If fish are small (e.g., .15 ounces each), you can stock between 75 and 100 fish. If they're larger (e.g., 8 ounces each), we've found that density can be reduced to as few as 35 fish—as long as total weight is still around 11 pounds. If there are fewer than 35 fish (or more than 100), the ecosystem is not balanced and the fish do not grow as quickly.

During the first two weeks, we add 2.12 ounces (60 grams) of feed per day to the ponds, six days per week. Please note: this is independent of both fish density and total weight, as long as the density and weight are in the ranges stated above. You're actually feeding the algae that take up the fish waste, and the food requirements are based on the algal population.

---

* The standard solar-algae pond is five feet high and five feet in diameter, holds approximately 630 gallons of water and is made of either one or two layers of fiberglass glazing. All of the work presented here is based on this pond size.

We feed 3.18 ounces (90 grams) daily for the third and fourth weeks and 4.24 ounces (120 grams) per day during the last two weeks of the cycle. Again remember to feed only six days per week.

To maintain *water quality*, ponds are partially drained and refilled with clean water periodically. This is not to dilute the fish waste per se, but rather to remove dead algae and other particulate matter which would otherwise begin to build up and shade the living algae. Draining maintains a healthy algal population, which in turn continually metabolizes fish waste.

Starting the second week, we drain our solar-algae ponds by 20 percent once a week. Thus a 630-gallon tank is drained approximately 130 gallons every week for four weeks, so that most of the original water has been replaced by the end of the cycle. At the end of six weeks, the pond is completely drained, any accumulated algal matter is scrubbed off the sides of the tank, and the pond is refilled with fresh water.

This cycle can be extended to nine weeks if you attach settling tanks to the ponds. Settling tanks are cylinders 5 feet high with 18-inch diameters, connected in series with one or more solar-algae ponds. They are used to allow dead algae and other particulate matter to settle out of the water, thus they are not stocked with fish. Settling tanks should be drained two or three times a week, but full drain-downs of the solar-algae pond can be delayed for up to three weeks.

It is worthwhile to coordinate drain-downs with garden activities. Twenty percent of the water in a 630-gallon tank provides enough water to irrigate 200 square feet of land with an amount of moisture equivalent to one inch of rain. It also contains as much nitrogen as about five pounds of horse manure. As we've mentioned, frequent use of pond water can provide valuable supplemental fertilizer to growing vegetables.

Over the six-week period, you will have added a total of 7 pounds, 2.5 ounces (3240 grams) of food, and fish will have grown approximately the same amount. At this point, you should harvest some of the fish to return the total fish weight to the initial 11 pounds, and, if necessary, add some smaller fish to keep the population above 35 individuals. Now you can repeat the cycle.

In this climate, we usually get in four 6-week cycles between May and November. In 24 weeks, with 28.6 pounds of feed added, we can get 20 to 25 pounds of fish growth. However, new growers should realistically expect something in the range of 15 to 20 pounds. As home aquaculturists gain experience, and as researchers continue to improve managment strategies, yields should increase.

Winter Management

As the weather gets cooler, solar-algae ponds are moved inside the greenhouse to help heat the building. Since the water is necessary for heat

Outdoor solar algae ponds at the New Alchemy Institute.

storage, it is important to conserve warmed pond water and drain as little as possible. In addition, both fish and algal metabolisms slow down with the cooler weather. Algae will not produce as quickly without high light and temperature levels; the ponds switch to a bacterial-based system, where the nitrifying bacteria begin to predominate over the algae.

If you begin with fresh water, it takes at least two weeks for the bacterial population to build to the point where it can handle the fish waste. The process can be speeded up by "seeding" the pond with old, bacterial laden water.

Initial stocking density and total fish weight can be slightly greater than in the summer system.

During the winter, we feed each pond approximately 60 grams of food per day. We add more on sunny, warm days, when the algae are more active, and less on cloudy, cool days.

To help maintain water quality, you have several options. The least appealing of these is to drain some of the water, as we do during the sum-

Fig. 7 Nutrient recycling and irrigation options

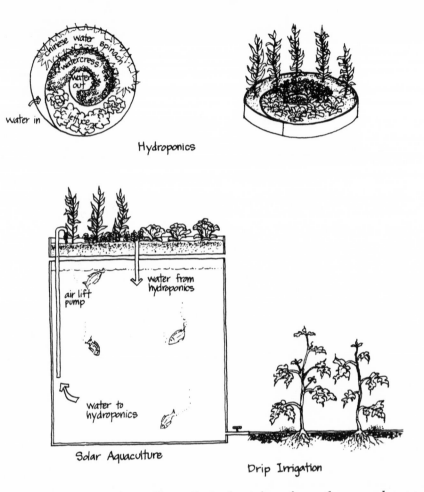

Hydroponics

Solar Aquaculture

Drip Irrigation

mer. In the winter, this will result in heat loss from the greenhouse, although the loss can be minimized by using the water for growing beds inside the greenhouse instead of pumping it outside. An alternative to drain-downs is to add a low concentration of salt to the pond and rely on good bacterial cultures. The salt reduces the toxic effects of the nitrogenous compounds and allows the fish to better tolerate higher levels of wastes.

Perhaps the most appealing solution is to set up a hydroponic system and use the nutrient-rich water to grow plants. As the plants grow, they clean the water by removing the wastes. Figure 7 shows a solar-algae pond using both hydroponics and a drip irrigation line to recycle and remove excess nutrients.

Because this is such a new technology, the costs of solar aquaculture are difficult to assess. The cost of the pond itself is paid back over five or six years by the amount saved on heating oil (approximately 30 gallons per season). At current oil prices we estimate the annual heating oil savings at about $35 per year. Thus the fish grown in the pond can be looked at as an added benefit that an oil furnace would never provide. Other costs to consider are initial stocking costs, electricity (for aerators and heaters, when necessary), fish food, and labor. Nothing beats the taste of freshly cooked fish from your own greenhouse!

Our description of solar-algae ponds has been designed to help you determine whether or not you're interested in learning more about this method of home food production. If you feel tempted to give it a try, New Alchemy publications on solar aquaculture, especially the *New Alchemy Solar Aquaculture Book,* (to be published in 1984) will provide you with comprehensive information. These and other useful publications are listed in the chapter Bibliography.

LEGAL GUIDELINES

Most states have rules and regulations that affect home aquaculture. Some states require that you secure a license or permit for one or more of the following activities

- Importing new types of fish to the state.
- Collecting young fish from natural waters.
- Propagating any type of fish (particularly in a pond or lake).

Check out the legalities in your home state *before* you begin!

REFERENCES

1. McClarney, William O., and Jeffrey Parkin. "Cage Culture," *Journal of the New Alchemists,* 6. Brattleboro, VT: The Stephen Greene Press, 1980, pp. 83-87.

2. McClarney, William O. and Jeffrey Parkin. "Alternatives to Commercial Feeds in the Diets of Cultured Fish," *Journal of the New Alchemists,* 7. Brattleboro, VT: The Stephen Greene Press, 1981, pp. 74-82.

BIBLIOGRAPHY

NEW ALCHEMY PUBLICATIONS

The New Alchemy Institute publishes a number of reports and articles related to small-scale aquaculture. A number of these articles are in the Aquaculture section of the Institute's annual Journals and Quarterlies. These publications may be obtained by writing to: The New Alchemy Institute, 237 Hatchville Road, East Falmouth, MA 02536.

BAUM, CARL. "Gardening in Fertile Waters," *New Alchemy Institute Quarterly, No. 7.* East Falmouth, MA: New Alchemy Institute, 1981. ($2.00)

ENGSTROM, DAVID, ET AL. *The New Alchemy Solar Aquaculture Book.* Andover, MA: Brick House Publishing Co., 1984 (in process).

GUSMAN, LINDA. "Breeding in Bioshelters," *New Alchemy Institute Quarterly, No. 9.* East Falmouth, MA: New Alchemy Institute, 1982. ($2.00)

NEW ALCHEMY INSTITUTE. "Solar Aquaculture: Perspectives in Renewable Resource-Based Fish Production." Results from a workshop at Falmouth, MA, September 28, 1981, supported by the National Science Foundation under grant number ISP-80-16577. The New Alchemy Institute, 237 Hatchville Rd., East Falmouth, MA 02536.

McLARNEY, WILLIAM O., and JEFFREY PARKIN. *The New Alchemy Back Yard Fish Farm Book.* Andover, MA: Brick House Publishing Co., 1982. ($8.95)

McCLARNEY, WILLIAM O. and JEFFREY PARKIN. "Cage Culture," *Journal of the New Alchemists,* 6. Brattleboro, VT: The Stephen Greene Press, 1980, pp. 83-87.

McCLARNEY, WILLIAM O. and JEFFREY PARKIN. "Alternatives to Commercial Feeds in the Diets of Cultured Fish," *Journal of the New Alchemists,* 7. Brattleboro, VT: The Stephen Greene Press, 1981, pp. 74-82.

NEW ALCHEMY INSTITUTE. Progress Reports Numbers 3,4,5, and 6 to the National Science Foundation: "Assessment of a Semi-Closed Renewable Resource-Based Aquaculture System," 1979-1982. Available from New Alchemy Institute. ($5.00)

Other Useful Publications

Aquaculture magazine, P.O. Box 2329, Asheville, NC 28802. Published bi-monthly, subscription $15.00 a year.

BARDACH, JOHN, JOHN RYTHER, and WILLIAM O. McLARNEY. *Aquaculture: The Farming and Husbandry of Freshwater and Marine Organisms.* New York: Wiley-Interscience, 1972.

CHAKROFF, MARILYN, *Freshwater Fish Pond Culture and Management.* Mt. Rainer, MD: Vita Publications, 1976. (3706 Rhode Island Avenue, Mt. Rainer, MD 20822)

HEAD, WILLIAM, and JON SPLANE. *Fish Farming in Your Solar Greenhouse.*

Eugene, OR: Amity Foundation, 1979. (P.O. Box 11048, Eugene, OR 97440)

LING, SHAO-WEN. *Aquaculture in Southeast Asia: A Historical Overview.* Seattle: University of Washington Press, 1977.

LOGSDON, GENE. *Getting Food From Water.* Emmaus, PA: Rodale Press, 1978.

LUTZ, F. E., P. S. WELCH, P. S. GALTSOFF, and J.G. NEEDHAM. *Culture Methods for Invertebrate Animals.* New York: Dover Publications, 1937.

MASTERS, CHARLES O. *Encyclopedia of Live Foods.* Neptune City, NJ: TFH Publications, 1975. (P.O. Box 27, Neptune City, NJ 07753)

MCLARNEY, WILLIAM O. *Aquaculture.* Seattle: Coldburst Press, 1981. (85 S. Washington St., Seattle, WA 98104)

SPOTTE, S.H. *Fish and Invertebrate Culture: Water Management in Closed Systems.* New York: Wiley-Interscience, 1970.

WHEATON, FREDRICK W. *Agricultural Engineering.* New York: Wiley-Interscience, 1977.

Chapter 6

Chickens
and a Word or Two about Honeybees

Gary Hirshberg and Denise Backus

In this chapter, we introduce you to chickens and honeybees, two of the most productive and conveniently managed food-producing animals. We New Alchemists are particularly fond of these critters and with good reason. Chickens are the most popular domestic food animals in the world. Their major attraction, of course, is their ability to provide a constant daily supply of high-quality protein—eggs. Honeybees, while providing volumes of scrumptious honey, also ensure the pollination of the plants in your garden.

A few years ago New Alchemy phased out its chickens in favor of weeding geese, but many staff members still maintain home flocks. Earle and Hilde consider chickens an integral part of their backyard "foodscape," and Colleen has built an elegant "Coop-de-Ville" in her yard. Denise and Dick and friends have an annual "Chicken-Pickin and Dickerin" party where they talk about chickens and select exotic breeds from the catalogs. Gary, an admitted neophyte as a poulter, has managed several flocks over the years.

Chicken raising can be fun, profitable, and rewarding. Once you've gotten the hang of it, your home flock will become an indispensable component of your home food system. You'll wonder how you ever did without them. They'll consume your kitchen and garden wastes and return a rich fertilizer, or perhaps food for a worm bed. Their hen-house bedding makes a great garden or nursery mulch as well.

Chicken raising can also be a complete headache if you haven't prepared yourself for the routines that are part of the job. A home flock doesn't have to alter your lifestyle dramatically, but you must make sure that the birds' basic needs of nutrition, sanitation, and protection are met.

This chapter provides a basic introduction to most of the major considerations in chicken-rearing. Gary and Denise will supply you with enough information to help you get started. But, they warn, as in all aspects of food production, you've got to get your hands dirty to develop a feel for the fine art of poulting.

THE EDITORS

Chickens

POULTRY IS AN IMPORTANT ASSET to the home food producer in several diverse ways. Besides offering the obvious advantages of fresh eggs and meat, a small flock of fowl will convert your kitchen wastes into high-quality fertilizer. A few geese or chickens are all it takes to keep the lawn clipped and well fertilized. In fact, at New Alchemy we use geese to keep field grasses and weeds from outcompeting young fruit and nut trees for nutrients. The geese will not eat woody plant matter (i.e., the young trees), but will (1) eliminate unwanted plant matter, (2) consume "drops" and excess fruits, and (3) fertilize our orchard. They do all this while simultaneously providing us with eggs and meat.

Maintaining a healthy poultry flock can be a simple, enjoyable task. So long as you give proper attention to regular feeding, watering, and protection from varmints, the rewards and satisfactions will abound.

Here we will focus on managing a backyard layer flock of hens. One can start small in this enterprise, and the up-front financial investment is modest. We'll try to provide you with enough information to get underway, and we'll supply a few guidelines to help you avoid some of the common errors. For the enthusiastic chicken farmer, a number of excellent detailed guides are listed in the Bibliography at the end of the chapter.

GETTING STARTED

One question to answer before you begin raising chickens is whether zoning and health regulations permit chickens in your area. Our town meeting held a lengthy debate on poultry several years ago; after an hour's exchange, the pro-chicken constituency won out. Check at your Town Hall or with a game warden to determine just what your own local restrictions may be. If you consider them unfair or questionable, speak out! You may find yourself among a large number of equally frustrated fellow residents.

Building A Proper Home for Your Flock

First you need an enclosed hen house and yard. The fenced yard provides daytime protection and the house provides sanctuary at night, providing you close the connecting entryway. Both house and yard should have convenient entryways for you, and should be fitted with hasps or other sure-fire closure mechanisms.

Home poultry flocks inevitably attract predators, especially raccoons. You must build as secure a house and yard as possible, though even then you'll need to assume a constant attitude of caution and alertness. Every yard faces different predatory dilemmas, but soon your own common sense will help you devise protective solutions appropriate to your site. You may choose to start with just a few birds so as to minimize potential losses during your initial season of chicken farming.

The number of birds or types of breeds you need will depend on whether you want meat or eggs. For an average breed, you can usually count on three hens to produce a dozen eggs per week. A flock of 25 birds is quite manageable, but 50 hens will begin to push reasonable limits, especially for a beginner. You may choose to start with a dozen hens, planning your space to accommodate future expansion.

The Hen House

Is there an existing structure that can be modified to make a chicken house? Does the site receive direct sunlight? Will the chicken house be near the garden?

One rule of thumb calls for four to five square feet of hen house per bird. A 10 × 12 house is ample for a flock of 25 birds.

You may choose to modify a section of your existing barn, or you may prefer to construct a freestanding shelter. In either case, there are five essential characteristics to consider:

- It must exclude rain, snow, and wind.
- It must be strong enough to support itself plus a considerable snow load.
- It should be easy and inexpensive to construct.
- It should not interfere with good ventilation.
- It should provide ample headroom.

A shed roof meets these criteria best, and is the most common. It requires very little lumber, is simple to construct, sheds snow or water effectively, and requires only one roof gutter. If the house faces south or east, it will be warmer.

You want lots of windows for ventilation and light. Most experts recommend one square foot of glass per 12 to 15 square feet of floor space. The most sensible strategy is to put plenty of glass on your south face and add smaller windows elsewhere. Probably you'll want screens and storm windows for the changing seasons.

The floor of your house should be dry, rat-proof, and easy to clean. For a new, permanent structure, cement is best. If you must build a wooden floor, you may want to put it on a gravel pad to avoid wicking up ground moisture. A double floor on 2×6 joists is safe, and plywood is best for avoiding leaks and cracks, as well as for ease of cleaning. Purists carefully paint their wooden floors with a sealant to protect them from the moisture produced by their hens.

Your hen-house walls should be tight with as few air leaks as possible. You may want to insulate, since warm hens always produce more eggs than cold birds do. Your insulation costs will be offset by a savings on feed. For more light and a cleaner surface, whitewash your inside walls. Make them weather-tight on the outside through any means that is convenient.

To produce well, chickens are supposed to need 14 to 16 hours of light per day. The usual recommendation for artificial light is one watt per four square feet of floor space. A 60-watt bulb is ample for a small house. Morning light is generally preferred; this means the birds will go to their roosts by dusk. When evening lighting is needed for chores, serious poulters use a timer with a dimmer to simulate twilight, which sends the birds to their roosts.

When planning your interior layout, you will want to consider space for nesting, roosting, feeding and watering, and enough headroom for you. A sample layout is shown in Fig. 1. Don't forget that you'll want approximately six to eight inches of floor bedding.

The *nest* provides a location for depositing eggs; it should not be a bird's sleeping place. Slept-in nests become fouled with the hens' wastes and are not at all attractive for laying. Provide individual nests for every three or four hens. These nests should be approximately 14 inches high and 12 inches deep. They can be stacked or adjacent to one another and should be off the floor. A community nest can work: 48 inches by 24 inches will accommodate up to 35 layers. In either case, the top of the nest should be sloped so that hens cannot stand, sleep, or walk on it. This action would disturb the layers below.

The *roost* is a horizontal pole or perch used as a sleeping place. Roost construction requires only 2×2s or saplings, preferably rounded on top. Position your roosts about 2½ feet off the floor; space perches 10 to 12 inches apart, providing about 6 to 8 inches for each adult bird. A solid dropping board can be placed a foot below the roosts for convenient weekly cleaning.

Feeding and watering is a simple matter that we'll discuss a little later. For now, keep in mind that the food and water containers must be off the

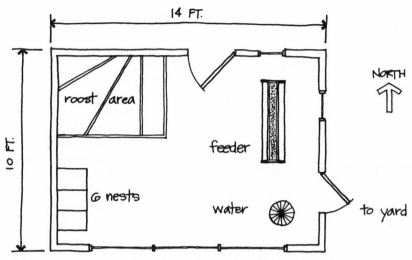

Fig. 1 A typical hen house layout

floor, so the birds can't foul them. However, they must also be *lower* than the roosts, so the hens won't roost in them at night.

Something to remember is that chickens tend to protect themselves at night by seeking the highest roost you can provide, so always place your roosts above the easy reach of local predators. This explains why many chicken farmers in Third World countries allow their birds to roost in trees at night.

The Chicken Yard

The small opening between the hen house and the yard should be no larger than your biggest bird, and it requires a sure-fire closure mechanism. We had a simple vertical sliding door on one of our hen houses, but we didn't bother to install a latch or clasp. One night, a raccoon slid the door open, grabbed a hen, then reopened the door, and made its exit. A hungry predator is a crafty predator—think as they do, and you'll be safe.

Unfortunately, most of us do not live in places where we can allow our chickens free range. Domestic dogs, automobiles, and neighbors usually preclude this possiblity. An enclosed chicken yard is the typical solution, designed to serve the two principal functions of permitting exercise and providing access to green food.

Your hens will get exercise in any size and shape of yard. But to maintain sod cover on our sandy Cape Cod soil, we must provide 100 to 150 square feet per bird. Your soil quality may permit you to provide less space.

The shape of the yard is important in subtle ways. You can't "corner" a hen in a circular yard. Avoid triangular yards altogether, as their acute corners become catch-alls for leaves and rubbish. A rectangular yard—or still better, a square one—is the most convenient shape for replanting and foraging.

Fencing height will depend on the breeds to be contained. A five-foot fence is adequate for most brown egg strains. For the lighter, more active breeds you may need a seven-foot fence or a net covering the yard. Some light breeds can fly even when all their wing feathers are gone.

If you have a problem keeping your flock inside a hen yard or outside a garden with a short fence, wing clipping is the likely solution. The wings are most easily clipped at night, when the birds are passive. Enter the hen house with a flashlight, grasp the bird by the feet and let it hang upside down. Then, using sheers, clip the feathers on only one wing; this leaves the bird free to scoot around but helpless to take off on long excursions. Keep in mind, however, that a clipped bird has a harder time escaping from predators.

You may want to seed your yard on a rotational basis to provide a continual cover crop. Peas, oats, barley, buckwheat, rye, vetch, clover, mustard, and amaranth are good crops. Ending the growing season with a rye, vetch, and clover planting ensures an early source of green feed when spring arrives.

A double-yarding system makes green-feed rotations easier. Divide your yard into equal-sized pens, allowing about 25 square feet per bird. When one pen is eaten down, move the hens into the other. Let the new growth in each replanted yard reach a height of four to six inches between rotations.

Comfrey is a plant that's particularly useful as chicken food. You can plant it along the outside of the chicken fence, where it will receive some nutrients from the chicken yard and will be nibbled through the fence by the chickens. Or it can be planted *in* the chicken yard, so long as you protect it from total destruction by the chickens (see Fig. 2). Chickens have a habit of constantly scratching around any plant and will normally make the ground in their exercise area bare and dusty. Allow them to create at least one dusty area in which to roll and take "dust-baths," a practice that is thought to help control lice and mites.

Selecting Your Hens

When it's time to purchase chickens, make absolutely sure that the selling place is clean and that your birds are healthy. Always ask whether or not they've been vaccinated for Marek's disease, bronchitis, and Newcastle disease.

There are three approaches to purchasing stock:

1. Raise them from chicks at a cost of about 40¢ each. You can place orders for day-old birds at any number of local suppliers. (Even Sears,

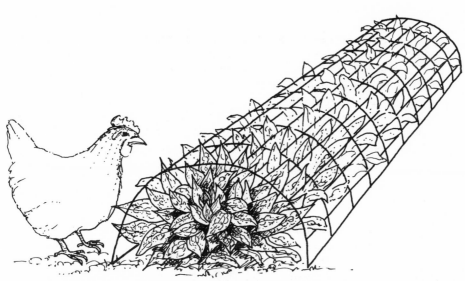

Fig. 2 Growing feed in the chicken yard

Roebuck handles mail-order chicks.) Call your agricultural extension service for a list of those nearest you. On their arrival date you'll receive a call from the post office telling you about a noisy package of peepers that just came in. These little cuties must be raised indoors and kept warm at first (95°F for the first week, decreased by 5°F for each week until you reach 70°F). Keep them at 70°F for about two months, or until it is relatively warm outside. You can expect them to begin producing at about six months of age.

2. Purchase six-month-old started pullets, which will begin laying immediately. (They'll cost approximately $2 to $4.) Allow for about a one-percent mortality per month during the laying period. Birds of this type should weigh between 2.7 and 3 pounds apiece, and should be well-feathered with a good, pink comb. Each survivor will lay approximately 250 eggs in the first year. Be wary of bargain deals on young cockerels. Usually these are the rejects from a commercial flock.

3. Purchase second-year layers from a poultry farmer who is selling birds after one year of lay. They will not produce nearly so many eggs as young birds, and will have a high (20-percent) annual mortality rate. Probably they will go through a molt or rest period during the year. However, second-year layers may offer the easiest way to get started, and surely they'll help you become accustomed to home poultry management.

We've found that backyard poulters are usually pleasant, enjoyable folks. Buying and trading can be something of a hobby and lots of fun.

Roosters

The most often-asked question is, "Do I need a rooster?" The only biological reason to have one is for fertilized eggs. Some people believe that fertilized eggs are more nutritious; others disagree.

The main reason to have one of these lively fellows is sociological—that is, for the entertainment factor. Our common word "cocky" accurately describes these wild characters, and we think they are well worth the fun. Roosters add an important dimension to the flock's social antics.

Two roosters will inevitably add up to a cockfight until the hierarchy or pecking order is established. Don't worry—this is absolutely normal, instinctual behavior. If it goes on too long and two cocks are perpetually mauling each other, it may be time to separate them; eat one, or just give one away.

One other important factor is a legal one. Roosters are illegal in many places precisely because of the noise. You may want to investigate this before you purchase your own noisemaker. At least you should check with your neighbors to determine their feelings.

Choosing Breeds

The commerical crossbreeds are the most popular chickens nowadays. These are the birds that will most economically produce meat or eggs. When it comes to breeding, however, their offspring are rarely the producers that their parents were.

Brown layers are the preferred hens in New England. Russ Bodwell of Litchfield, Maine, provides the following standards for brown egg layers:

- Livability—day-old to production: 95%.
- Total eggs per hen housed per 52 weeks: 240 or more.
- Average egg weight per laying year: 27 oz./dozen.
- Average feed per dozen eggs: 4 to 4.75 lb.
- Percent grade-A eggs: 90% or above.
- For eating spent layers, look for a body weight of five pounds or more at maturity.

In the case of meat birds, your selection criteria is simpler. You will want to select for rapid weight gain; something approaching four pounds live weight in eight weeks for a straight-run flock is good. The Cornish strains are common birds of this type.

For the all-purpose egg, meat, and breeding bird, you will want to choose from among the American Class dual-purpose fowl. They are slow growers and don't lay as early or as well, but they'll serve you adequately. The common dual-purpose breeds are New Hampshire, Rhode Island Red, Barred Plymouth Rock, and White Plymouth Rock.

"Well, we don't need a rooster!"

The American Poultry Association recognizes over 100 varieties of large fowl. For more information on breeds, we recommend their publication, *Standard of Perfection* (see the chapter Bibliography for further details).

Breeding

It is beyond the scope of this discussion to detail in depth the many considerations of poultry breeding. However, we'll go so far as to tell you that developing a self-sustaining flock can be a rewarding and even an addicting pastime. Breeding and hatching requires an incubator, so it's not economical for the home grower who raises birds at one hatch per year. For those of you who may wish to experiment with breeding on a home scale, information is provided by Robert O. Haws (Department of Animal and Veterinary Science, University of Maine, Orono) in the special "Poultry" supplement of the April 1981 *Maine Organic Farmer and Gardener*.

Fig. 3 A waterer for
older birds

DAY-TO-DAY-CARE

Now we'll look at the areas on which you'll focus the daily care of your birds: equipment, feeding, and the prevention, detection, and control of disease.

Equipment

Layers require a lot of water. One hundred layers will drink from four to five gallons per day when the temperature is below 40°F, six to seven gallons per day when the temperature is 60° to 80°F, and seven to eleven gallons as the temperature rises beyond that. Good waterers are the only devices that are difficult to make at home, but they are also among the most essential tools you'll need. The easiest answer is to buy a plastic one-gallon waterer. These cost $2, are easy to handle, and should last from three to five years.

Day-old chicks must be shown how to take their first sips. A simple tray or shallow pan will do. Be sure always to have water available for these youngsters.

When the birds are four to five weeks or older, they can graduate to a larger watering device. The easiest and cheapest solution is to get an open circular pan with a wire-grill covering (Fig. 3). You will want to (1) elevate the waterer off the ground to prevent it from filling with dirt and bedding; (2) insert the container in a frame so that larger birds cannot tip it over; and (3) provide a platform on which the birds can stand. Figure 4 shows a typical device.

Fig. 4 A waterer with
platform

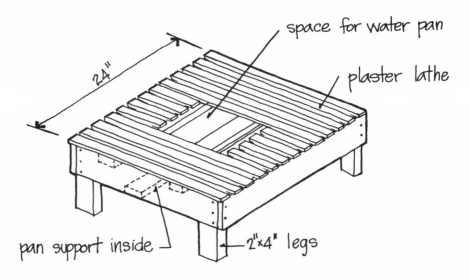

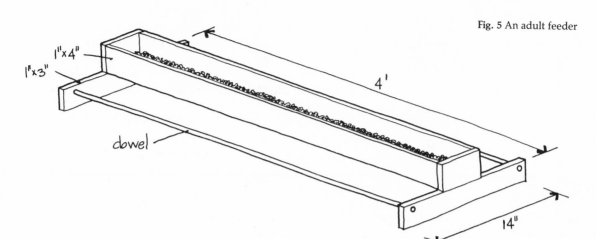

Fig. 5 An adult feeder

Making your home feeder is easy; in fact, we've never bought a commercial device. You'll need two types of feeders during your flock's lifetime. The first is a shallow trough for your young (up to 10-week-old) chicks. Older birds require a more stable elevated or hanging feeder. A 16-inch by 3-foot trough will feed about 25 hens adequately (see Fig. 5).

Feeding Your Flock

You can meet your hens' nutritional requirements in one of two ways: either mix your own feed or purchase commercial feed and scratch. For the part-time backyard poulter, buying a commercial preparation is simpler and more convenient. Prepared feeds come in mash, pellet, or crumb form. We've found that birds tend to spill and waste more of the mash than they do of the pellets or crumbs.

If you decide to mix your own feed, we recommend this well-balanced formula:

65% grains—use *at least two* of the following: barley, corn, milo, oats, wheat
7% alfalfa meal or ground hay
5% meat scraps, fish meal, or soybean meal
13% dried peas or additional soybean meal
6% crushed oyster shells or limestone
3% bone meal
1% trace mineral salt
    Add one cup cod-liver oil to each 100 pounds of feed.

Use a commercial chick starter for the first eight weeks. Sprinkle the feed all over their floor for the first three days; then use a low, flat feeder. Never let the chicks run out of feed.

Commercial mash provides all the essential vitamins, minerals, fats, carbohydrates, and proteins for older birds. However, you may want to supplement the mash with some corn scratch so that your birds will work in the litter and stay sharp and alert. A good average daily feeding routine for 25 adult (20- to 72-week-old) birds is 5 to 6 pounds all mash or 3 to 4 pounds mash plus 2 pounds scratch.

Layers of the heavier strains will consume 10 to 15 percent more feed. Keep a watchful eye on your birds and make sure that they don't get too fat. If your birds do start looking fatty, reduce the mash and increase the scratch.

For best results, offer about 75 percent of the feed in the morning; give them the remainder along with the scratch in the afternoon. From time to time, add grit or crushed shells to the feed. This will help the birds crush up and digest the ingested food. It's especially helpful to the young ones.

We feed our birds when they are let out in the morning and just before they come in at dusk. Our hen house is not rat-proof, so we *never* put food inside; it inevitably attracts rats. Rats pass on lice and other problems that are more difficult to eliminate than to prevent. Thus all our feeding is done outdoors, even in the winter. If you feed at regular intervals, and don't *over*feed your birds will consume all the food before any rodents can get their turn. If you have a rodent-proof hen house, you can feed indoors.

A common tendency among eager chicken farmers is to overfeed. Just as eating anything and everything available has not contributed to human well-being, you can assume it's not too good for livestock, either. A chicken that must do a bit of scrounging for food will be superior in health, vigor, and egg production. A hungry hen will consume table scraps, grass clippings, and other greens. She will also chase down grasshoppers, flies, and other insects, and will scratch for worms and grubs. Her continued search for food will keep her active and alert, more aware of predators, and in better shape to escape danger.

Don't underestimate the value of letting your birds roam outside the yard for feed; even a few minutes of this activity each day will improve their health and egg production. The hens will find some of their own food and thus reduce your need for commerical feed. Experiment with different amounts of feed. We found from experience that one can obtain better egg production from a healthy, active flock.

A handful of corn thrown on the ground will attract a hungry chicken. Using this trick, you can let your hens outside for a while during the day and then entice them back into the yard, although it's more than likely that the birds will return voluntarily to the hen house at dusk. Avoid chasing them, if possible; otherwise you'll find yourself dealing with a flock of skittish, nervous hens.

Poultry Diseases

If you take good care of your birds, keep them well fed and exercised, make sure they have no contact with rats and other rodents, and maintain a clean hen house, you will not have much worry about disease.

On the other hand, if your birds become cold, hungry, thirsty, or over-crowded for extended periods, you're likely to have problems. Some of these problems and recommended cures are listed here.

Lice and Mites   If any of these critters appear, get them under control immediately, as they spread quickly and cause great discomfort among your flock.

Head lice infest the birds' necks and bodies. Lice powders are effective, but you may want to take the extra precaution of painting a preventative compound on the walls of your coop and/or on the roosts.

The Northern Fowl Mite and Red Mite both live all over the hens' bodies; the Red Mite goes a step further and inhabits cracks in the floor or walls. Both types multiply rapidly in warm weather. Again, commercial powders are quite effective.

Marek's Disease   This illness takes many forms, including paralysis (droop-ing wing, loss of movement in a leg, a twisted neck) and internal tumors. It is a virus that infiltrates major nerves in the birds' bodies and cannot be cured. Birds that show signs of Marek's disease should be culled. Usually commercial poultry fanciers vaccinate day-old chicks against this disease.

Coccidiosis   This is the most common backyard-flock disease; usually it strikes when birds are five to eight weeks old. You'll first notice a cocci-diosis infection when the bird looks sick, with ruffled feathers and a gener-ally droopy, sluggish demeanor. If you see bloody droppings, try to iden-tify the unhealthy bird and immediately cull her out.

The key to controlling coccidiosis is good flock management. The birds must develop immunity, and this means exposing the flock to the ever-present organism in *small* doses. Don't clean your coop too perfectly, and don't disinfect. Mother Nature has taken care of these situations for milennia.

Once the birds are older, they will be safe from coccidiosis—it is the disease of the growing chick, not of the adult bird.

Newcastle Disease   The typical symptoms of this illness are the same as those of our own common cold: watery eyes, wheezing, and coughing. Again, good management seems to be the only preventative cure.

SLAUGHTERING CHICKENS

If you raise some of your chickens for meat, are you willing to slaughter and prepare them?

If you plan to eat some of your birds, the day of slaughter will inevitably come, and you should prepare for it. It is best to not feed birds for 12 hours before processing. Give them plenty of water, however, as this will help flush out the digestive system.

There are two common killing and bleeding techniques.

- *Modified Kosher.* This is the most common method. Cut the bird's throat from the outside, just below the lower jaw; the bird will lose consciousness immediately. Cut the veins (*not* the esophagus, which may cause contamination) and drain the blood.

- *Beheading.* Using an axe or wringing the bird's neck is easy, but because the heart action is stopped when the spinal cord is severed, it does not remove as much blood. Also, this method permits the bird to thrash around, causing quite a scene and inviting contamination.

At once you must bleed the bird thoroughly. Begin defeathering immediately; it's much easier when the carcass is still warm. Many people use one of two scalding methods to loosen feathers; we've never found any need for this so long as the bird is warm. Hard-scalding involves dipping the birds for 30 to 60 seconds in water 160°F to 180°F. Subscalding requires a 30- to 75-second dip in water of about 140°F. Be especially careful when pulling feathers from the breast and thigh—the skin there tears easily.

Next, you must "vent" your birds by pressing on the abdomen to force fecal matter out from the posterior end of the breast bone down to the vent.

Cut open the abdomen. Remove the internal organs and separate the heart, liver, and gizzard from the intestines. These and the neck make up the "giblets." Split the gizzard lengthwise, remove the yellow lining, and wash thoroughly. Cut the green gall bladder out of the liver carefully: sacrifice a piece of the liver rather than risk spilling the gall liquid (it tastes horrible). If the chicken is to be stored frozen for less than three months, place the giblets inside the bird.

For more information, you can obtain *Home Slaughter of Poultry* (Bulletin No. A1478) by sending 50¢ and your request to Agricultural Bulletin Building, 1535 Observatory Drive, Madison, WI 53706.

Honeybees

Honeybees are a joy to watch as they alight on flowers and fly to and fro near their hive. Even if you never harvest any honey, the

enjoyment of watching honeybees and learning about the intricacies of their life is reward enough. At New Alchemy we always keep a few hives, usually managed by someone on the staff. In recent years we have begun to landscape the farm with special nectar- and pollen-producing plants both to help the bees and to provide us with more honey each fall. Similarly, in your own yard, you can develop a plant community that sustains your bees as it provides your food.

THE EDITORS

GETTING STARTED

Where is the closest beehive to your home?

The easiest way to begin keeping bees is to locate a beekeeper in your neighborhood and learn from that person. Generally it is best to start small, with only one hive, and expand over time if you find the activity rewarding. It is safest to buy the original hive and population of bees from an established commercial source. Ask the local beekeeper to recommend one.

A beehive does not require much room, but the location is important. The hive site should receive morning sun, should *not* receive direct midday summer sun, and should have protection from the worst winter winds. Also important is that it be placed where people do not usually walk within 10 feet of its front entrance. In urban and suburban situations, beehives often fit quite well on a porch or accessible rooftop surface.

You do not need enough flowers on your own land to feed your bees; they will fly up to two miles to find their necessary nectar, pollen, or water. Under absolutely optimum conditions, one acre of blooming plants will support an active hive, although two or three acres is the usual requirement. Thus it is likely that your bees will forage over a wide area to find suitable plants.

DAY-TO-DAY CARE

Management of the hive requires relatively little effort, but careful timing is essential. Each spring and fall you must spend part of a day checking, rearranging, and preparing the hive for the coming season. During summer, it's wise to check on the hive several times a month, providing additional hive sections for honey storage if needed. Finally in the fall, if all goes well, you must commit at least a day to harvesting some of the honey from the comb. Leave enough in the hive for the bees to live on throughout the winter.

A less obvious but important element of care for your bees is your choice of nearby plantings. It's widely agreed that to select specific plants for the benefit of the bees *only* is uneconomical—there should be another purpose for each plant. However, when you choose a food plant, a ground cover, an ornamental tree or shrub, or flowers for the lawn or landscape, give preference to types that will provide bee forage *in addition to* the primary ornamental or food-producing function.

Certain points in the yearly foraging cycle of a bee colony are critical to its well-being. Early spring is most important; it's warm enough for the bees to be active, they have nearly depleted their winter honey storage, and they must begin building up their numbers in preparation for the forthcoming fruit bloom. A pollen and nectar source at this time is of great value to the colony, and it's to your advantage to provide such a plant in your landscape. Swamp maples, willows, and dogwoods are prime candidates for this season, as are daffodils, viburnum, and deadnettles.

Second priority should be given to late July through early August, which are dry times on Cape Cod, with little nectar flow. Smooth sumac, many of the common culinary herbs (thyme, sage, marjoram, borage), and several wild flowering plants are useful as bee forage at this time. (For help in selecting plants, see the publications listed in the chapter Bibliography.)

BIBLIOGRAPHY

CHICKENS

American Bantam Association. *Bantam Standard.* Box 464, Chicago, IL 60690. (Similar to APA's *Standard of Perfection,* below, but deals only with Bantam chickens.)

American Poultry Association. *Standard of Perfection.* 1026 East Oak St., Cushing, OK 74023. (The "end-all/be-all" for those who show poultry. Includes pictures of most breeds and indicates judging standards for each class.)

Bodwell, Russ, *et al.* "Poultry," supplement to *Maine Organic Farmer and Gardener,* April 1981. (An excellent, comprehensive guide.)

Luttman, Rick, and Gail Luttman. *Chickens in Your Backyard: A Beginners Guide.* Emmaus, PA: Rodale Press, 1976. (Excellent guide for beginners who want to learn more about the fine art of raising poultry.)

Mercia, Leonard S. *Raising Poultry the Modern Way.* Charlotte, VT: Garden Way Publishers, 1974. (Good guide to maintaining small farm flocks.)

Poultry Press, Box 947, York, PA 17405. (A monthly newspaper that keeps poulters informed about shows and offers tips on bird care.)

HONEYBEES

Hooper, Ted. *Guide to Bees and Honey.* Emmaus, PA: Rodale Press, 1976.

Morse, R.A. *Complete Guide to Beekeeping.* NY: Dutton and Co., 1972.

Pellett, Frank C. *American Honey Plants.* Atlantic, IO 50022. (Brochure)

Root, A.I. *ABC and XYZ of Bee Culture.* Medina, OH: A.I. Root Co., 1975.

Chapter 7

Food-Producing Trees

John Quinney

Again I stood on a crest beneath a spreading chestnut tree and scanned a hilly landscape. This time I was in Corsica. Across the valley I saw a mountainside clothed in chestnut trees . . . as far as the eye could see. The expanse of broadtopped fruitful trees was interspersed with a string of villages and stone houses. . . . These grafted chestnut orchards produced an annual crop of food for men, horses, cows, pigs, sheep and goats, and a by-crop of wood. Thus for centuries, trees upon this steep slope had supported the families that lived in the Corsican villages. The mountainside was uneroded, intact, and capable of continuing indefinitely in its support for the generations of man.

When J. Russell Smith wrote these words in his magnificent text, *Tree Crops, A Permanent Agriculture,* he was comparing these lands with those of West China, North Africa, and the central plains of North America. Why, he asked, are the fields of the world losing topsoil at catastrophic rates when tree crop systems have been proven so effective in reversing these trends? And later in his text, he speculated,

These wonders of automatic production are the chance wild trees of nature. They are to be likened to the first wild animal that man domesticated and to the first wild grass whose seed was planted. What might happen if every wild crop-bearing tree was improved to its maximum efficiency?''

John Quinney, Earle Barnhart, and others at New Alchemy have been driven by a search for answers to the same questions J. Russell Smith voiced over thirty years ago. In tree crop explorations here on our Cape Cod farm and in other places in the United States and abroad, they have studied the current and potential use of trees for food, fuel, energy-conserving windbreaks, soil control, and diverse other functions. Here on the Cape, they have planted and evaluated hundreds of varieties for their usefulness and viability.

This chapter summarizes the most valuable ideas from seven years of experience with tree crops at New Alchemy. Here are a variety of commonsense methods you can use to make your property a productive, permanent agricultural landscape.

John Quinney, a tree farmer, teacher, and one of our resident curmudgeons, is a sardonic New Zealander who'll give any wit a run for his or her money. He fits into our Yankee landscape with surprising ease, as we're sure his ideas will fit into yours.

THE EDITORS

Why Tree Crops?

CERTAIN TREES AND SHRUBS provide nourishing food in the form of fruits, nuts, and berries. A variety of tree crops can supply a full range of food nutrients, from carbohydrates (chestnuts), to protein (highly concentrated in most nuts), to vitamins (fruits and berries). Tree crops are perennials; they remain year after year. For the home food grower, this means that once the plants are established, they needn't be replanted each year. Some annual work is required, but much of it can be done at times of year other than the busy spring.

What makes trees and other perennial plants particularly important are the many environmental benefits that they provide in addition to food production. These benefits include noise control, climate modification, air-pollution control, erosion control, energy conservation, and increased wildlife populations. Both the food and the environmental benefits of tree crops are continuous and actually improve as the trees grow.

Noise Control Trees and shrubs screen out noise by either absorbing or deflecting sound waves. Evergreens are commonly planted along roadsides for this purpose and various windbreaks planted around homes also provide some protection from noise.

Use shade-giving vines
to cool a south wall.

Climate Modification   Trees moderate local and regional climates by reducing temperature and humidity fluctuations. During the daytime, some heat is stored in leafy tissue, while some is removed in evaporated water. Transpiration from leaf surfaces adds large amounts of water to the atmosphere and raises humidity. At night, the stored energy is released slowly and makes for milder evening temperatures.

Trees planted as windbreaks reduce wind speeds on the leeward side and create an improved environment for other plants.

Air Pollution Control   Dust and other particulate matter in air is trapped by leaves and trunks and is eventually washed to the ground by rain.

Erosion Control.   Extensive root systems and leafy branches reduce the erosive power of wind and rain. Twigs and leaves dropped by trees and shrubs build up levels of organic matter in soil. This provides nutrients, improves the soil's moisture-holding capacity, and reduces erosion.

Energy Conservation   A windbreak or hedge will shelter a dwelling from winds and reduce winter heat loss and therefore reduce energy consumption. Deciduous trees planted on the southern side of a structure provide shade from the high summer sun yet allow the low winter sunshine to warm the interior. The same effect can be achieved by using deciduous vines. If a trellis is constructed above south-facing glass, vines can be trained to shade the window. This shading device is self-adjusting. In years when spring is cold, the vine will leaf out later, so solar heating can continue. During mild autumns, the vine will retain its leaves longer, and the cooling benefits of shade will continue.

In regions that have been largely deforested, or in cities barren of trees, the problems of noise control, climate modification, and erosion control are usually solved mechanically. The buildings and machinery that provide these services signify a large investment in materials and energy. Trees and shrubs, on the other hand, use only renewable solar energy to do the same work.

Increased Wildlife   Many trees and shrubs also provide food and habitat for wildlife. Particularly useful is their tendency to attract insectivorous birds, which help to establish a natural system of pest control in the backyard garden and orchard.

Even if your available land is planted extensively with vegetables, you can almost always find some room for food-producing trees and shrubs. For designing these areas, a number of models are available as guides. One is the so-called "dump-heap" garden/orchards of Central America. These small plots adjacent to the family dwelling are planted with trees that produce fruit, nuts, fiber, and animal fodder. Vegetables and self-seeding plants are interspersed throughout on mounds of compost. Many of the trees provide support for fruiting vines. These garden/orchards are highly productive yet require minimal human labor. Fertility is maintained by recycling wastes back into the soil. Because the ground is covered year 'round, erosion is minimal and the soil remains shaded and moist. In part, these gardens are effective because they are semi-wild and develop some of the complexity and stability of natural ecosystems.

In California, Robert Kourik, formerly of the Farallones Institute, follows a similar philosophy. His gardens are designed in the image of the forest. Dwarf fruit trees, perennials, edible weeds, and self-seeding annuals are combined in carefully designed arrays. The gardens are largely self-fertilizing, since they include some plants that fix atmospheric nitrogen and others that accumulate plant nutrients from deep soil horizons. Diverse planting mixtures ensure that the whole soil profile is exploited for nutrients and moisture.

Further valuable resources for backyard design are the books *Permaculture One* and *Permaculture Two*. (You'll find them listed under General Texts in the chapter Bibliography.) Permaculture is a strategy that attempts gradually to create a food-producing ecosystem of primarily perennial plants. We urge you to consult these and other references for help in planning your agricultural landscape.

Planning
SITE ANALYSIS

To choose plants best adapted to your site, you need good information about site conditions. Begin with the soil. As you would for a garden plot, determine the range of pH at various locations, the soil texture (sand, silt, clay), the organic matter content, and the level of fertility—relative amounts of nitrogen, phosphorus, potassium, calcium, magnesium, and sulphur.

It is equally important to examine your site for *microclimate* (the specific climate of a given area). Microclimates result from the combined effects of topography, vegetation, water bodies, and nearby structures. For example, south-facing walls receive more solar radiation than north-facing walls. Thus the environment in front of south-facing walls is generally warmer and dryer than normal. These sites are ideal for certain types of fruit trees. On sloping land, cold air flows downhill and can create frost pockets. In these cold spots many fruit trees lose their blossoms to late spring frosts. On north-facing slopes, blossoming occurs later than on flat sites; thus fruit blossoms on these slopes may survive spring frosts. Other areas of your landscape may be exposed to chilling winter winds that make them unsuitable locations for many fruit and nut trees. A thorough familiarity with your site will enable you to select the best plants for each specific microclimate.

SPECIES SELECTION

Do you expect to remain on your present site for three years? Five years? Ten years?

The length of time until food production varies considerably among perennial plants, and your choice of food plant species will depend somewhat on your future plans. A few unselfish people plant trees with no thought of personal gain, but most of us want to reap some benefit from our planting and tending work. The options range all the way from raspberries and dwarf fruit trees, which yield food the second summer, to some of the nut trees that bear only after 20 years. Generally speaking, most food trees and shrubs will reach good production in 5 to 10 years.

In a vegetable garden, bad choices usually can be corrected the next season. Though it is relatively simple to remove your mistakes and replant other trees and shrubs, this trial-and-error process is time-consuming and costly. Decide now whether you most desire food, wind protection, or more wildlife (or a combination); then pick the best plant available for that purpose or purposes.

Plant growth and survival is dependent on many factors, some of which are subject to human control, and others of which are not. In many areas of the Northeast, a crucial factor affecting plant survival is the *average annual minimum temperature.* The hardiness map shown in Fig. 1 gives this information for the continental United States. Plants are often described by the hardiness zones listed on this map. Cape Cod, for example, is within the boundaries of Zone 6. Many plants will grow in areas that are warmer than their minimum zone designation, but few will survive in colder, lower-numbered zones.

Nurseries commonly indicate hardiness zones for many of the plants they sell. This information gives only a rough idea of plant survival, however, because a number of microclimatic variations can exist. In some cases, these conditions will allow less-hardy plants to be grown successfully. On Cape Cod, the moderating effect of the ocean ensures that our winter is comparatively mild; thus we are able to grow plants that would not otherwise survive at this latitude. Consider the hardiness map as a guide, but be alert to the variations of your own site.

Plants vary in their tolerance to soil pH, soil moisture, salt spray, amount of shade, and so on. For many species these preferences have been collated and presented in a plant species information matrix, which appears in *The Future Is Abundant* (see chapter Bibliography). This species matrix was formulated for the temperate Northwest, but it will aid you in considering appropriate species for your particular region. As a rough guide, most fruit and nut trees prefer fertile, well-drained soil that is only slightly acidic (pH 6.5).

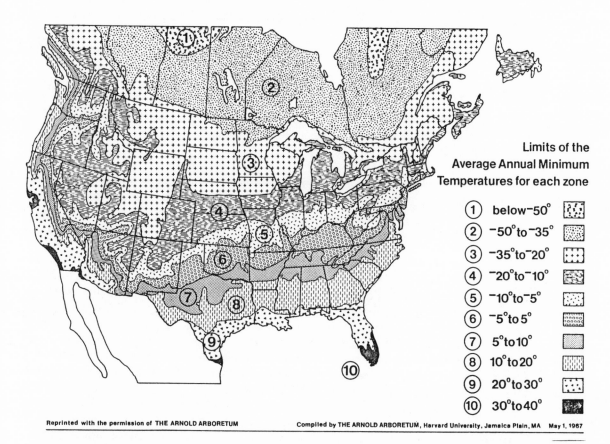

Limits of the
Average Annual Minimum
Temperatures for each zone

1) below⁻50°
2) ⁻50°to⁻35°
3) ⁻35°to⁻20°
4) ⁻20°to⁻10°
5) ⁻10°to⁻5°
6) ⁻5°to 5°
7) 5°to10°
8) 10°to20°
9) 20°to30°
10) 30°to40°

Fig. 1 Hardiness zones
of the United States
and Canada

USEFUL PLANTS
Popular Fruits and Berries

The common fruit trees (apples, pears, peaches, plums, nectarines, cherries) and berries (blueberries, raspberries, blackberries, currants) are described in many of the publications we've listed as Resources at the end of this chapter. In recent years, many new *cultivars* (cultivated varieties of a given plant) have been developed. Often they are particularly high yielding, will bear over an extended season, and may be resistant to disease. Often, however, these "special" trees are dependent on applications of soluble fertilizers and insecticides if they are to produce well. For your home orchard, you may want to consider the antique varieties that can produce good crops of tastier fruit with less intensive chemical management. Many antique varieties are commercially available through the nursery and seed sources that we list later.

Table 1 *Disease-Resistant Fruit Trees*

DISEASE (FRUIT)	RESISTANT VARIETY
Scab (Apple)	Liberty, Macfree, Nova Easygro, Prima, Priscilla, Sir Prize
Cedar apple rust (Apple)	Baldwin, Delicious, Jerseymac, McIntosh, Milton, Liberty, Nova, Easygro, Priscilla, Tydeman
Fireblight (Pear)	Kieffer, Maxine, Seckel, Magness, Moonglow
Bacterial spot (Peach)	Cullinan, Harbinger, Havis, Sentinel, Jayhaven

Selecting a disease-resistant variety is one way to minimize or avoid the use of toxic chemicals. Table 1 provides a reference to some resistant varieties of apple, pear, and peach. However, nurseries sometimes make exaggerated claims for their plants. Disease resistance is proven only by observation at your own site or in the immediate neighborhood.

For the home landscape, dwarf fruit trees offer the combined features of high yield and low space requirement. Dwarfs range in height from six to twenty feet according to the rootstock used or the particular selection made by the breeder. Many dwarfs begin bearing in the second year, whereas standard trees may take three years or longer to fruit. Dwarf apples are the most common, but dwarf pears, cherries, peaches, and plums are also available. Some antique varieties have been dwarfed.

Many fruit trees can be trained as *espaliers*—that is, grown and trimmed into flat forms against walls or fences (see Fig. 2). This technique requires skill, but it allows utilization of small areas. In Richmond, California, Emil Linquist is growing more than 200 espaliered fruit trees in an average-sized yard! By using dwarf trees and training them as espaliers, home orchardists can produce high yields of fruit from young trees.

Lesser-known Food Trees and Shrubs

It's easy to overlook what may be an excellent answer to your specific needs. Perhaps a particular food producer is not familiar to you. Maybe no one in your neighborhood grows it and you've assumed for this reason that it's an "exotic" species. The chances are good that it isn't.

The following lesser-known fruit- and nut-producing perennials all will grow in some areas of the Northeast. We can't promise that they'll do well for you, but it's worth your time to check the resource material and see whether or not your conditions are right for them.

- The **pawpaw** (*Asimina triloba*) is a hardy native tree which grows to 20 feet on rich soils. The fruits are four to six inches long and yellowish in color; when ripe, they have a sweet, richly flavored pulp. Pawpaw trees are relatively disease free and have no major insect pests. Several cultivars are available.

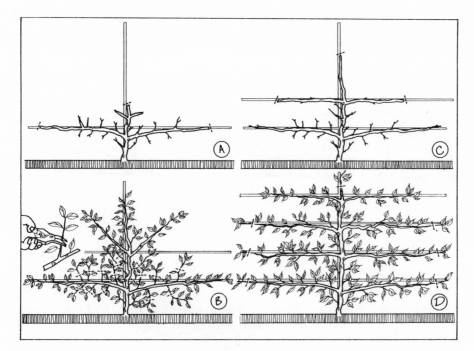

Fig. 2 Espalier fruit tree. (A) Espalier after first season's training and pruning; (B) Second season's growth and recommended pruning; (C) Espalier after second season's training and pruning; (D) Mature four-year-old espalier. Illustration by Kathy Speers.

- The **sand cherry** *(Prunus besseyi)*, a Great-Plains native, grows to about seven feet and is drought tolerant. It bears heavy crops early in the season. Named varieties are often superior to the more commonly available bush cherries.

- The **beach plum** *(P. maritima)* grows naturally along the eastern seashore from Maine to Virginia. Plants grow to 10 feet and tolerate salt and wind. The bluish-purple fruits can be eaten raw or used in jellies and preserves.

- The **Nanking cherry** *(P. tormentosa)* is a dwarf cherry from northern China. The bright red fruits can be eaten fresh and the plant is easily trained as a hedgerow.

- The **highbush cranberry** *(Viburnum trilobum)* can be found from northern New England to Pennsylvania. The fruits hang on the shrubs all winter and are an ideal jelly fruit. Selected cultivars are commercially available.

- The **saskatoon** *(Amelanchier alnifolia)* is native to the Great Plains; the berries were widely used by the Plains Indians and the early European settlers. Promising selections have been made by members of the North American Fruit Explorers. (See listing in Resources section.) A similar species, the **serviceberry** *(A. arborea)* is a small tree which produces berries that can be eaten raw, cooked, or dried.

Elderberry

- The **elderberry** *(Sambucus canadensis)* is superb for pie and jelly and can be made into excellent wine. The plants are somewhat invasive, although you can control them easily by removing suckers annually. Plant two or three cultivars for high yields. Commercial varieties are available.

- **Currants** and **gooseberries** *(Ribes sp.)* are extremely hardy shade-tolerant plants. In some areas, however, their use is restricted because they are alternate hosts for the white-pine blister rust disease. Nurseries selling these plants will also have the necessary permits.

- **Blueberries** are native shrubs and many species are found in the eastern United States and Canada. The commonly grown species is the highbush blueberry *(Vaccinium corymbosum)*. All blueberries require acid soils (pH 4-5) and high levels of organic matter. Plant two or more cultivars to ensure high yields.

- **Raspberries** and **blackberries** belong to the genus *Rubus*. Many species occur naturally throughout the eastern United States and Canada. For home gardens, the European red raspberry, the black raspberry, the wineberry, and the common blackberry provide delicious fruit. All four plants need some attention to control their spread; this is especially true for blackberries, which probably should be planted only in semi-wild areas.

- If you have plenty of yard room, then it may be worthwhile to plant some **persimmons**: either the American *(Diospyros virginiana)* or in milder climates, the Oriental *(D. kaki)*. To get good fruit crops from the females, you must also plant a male tree. The fruits are extremely astringent when unripe; delicious when fully mature.

- **Mulberries** *(Morus sp.)* are important, although often overlooked, fruit trees. The fruits are delicious either raw or preserved. The trees themselves are fairly hardy and tolerant of both shade and poor soil. Several commercial varieties are available.

Nut Trees

Nuts are often regarded as mere condiments or flavorings, when in fact many are calorie- and protein-rich foods in their own right. You'll find many nut species from which to choose. For the backyard, hazels are suitable in milder climates, whereas both walnuts and Chinese chestnuts will grow further north. The latter two make excellent shade trees. Almonds will fruit well only in mild climates. Hickories are generally large trees and slow to bear. Pecans are only marginally successful in the Northeast; many cultivars produce poorly filled nuts. In selecting nut trees, one should pay attention to the ease with which the nuts can be cracked. Some cultivars are much easier to crack than others, and all vary in the ratio of kernel to shell. The best information on nut trees has been compiled by the Northern Nut Growers Association (see listing in Resources section).

Coppices

If you have a reasonably large area available, you might like to try establishing a coppice woodlot. *Coppicing* is the process of cutting woody plants at ground level and allowing sprouts to develop from the stumps. A typical coppice woodlot is harvested on rotations of about five years—you harvest one-fifth of the area each year. Surprisingly high yields of firewood are available from small areas. Suitable species include poplar, willow, alder, hazel, and black locust.

Hedgerows

Hedges are planted for marking property lines and creating privacy. With a little planning these same functions can be provided by hedges which produce food, shelter, bee forage, and beneficial insect habitat (see Fig. 3). Suitable food-producing hedgerow plants include bush cherry, flowering quince, mulberry, jujube, hazel, beach plum, and rugosa rose. On the leeward side, you can establish herbs, wildflowers, and plants useful to honeybees.

Fig. 3 Multifunctional
suburban hedge.
Illustration by
Maia Massion.

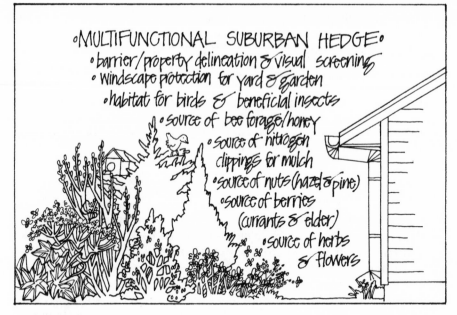

Bamboos

Though most bamboos are not native to the United States, many of the species from Japan and China will grow well here. A few are hardy in the Northeast, growing as far north as Boston. These species include *Phyllostachys aureosulcata*, *P. flexuosa*, *P. angusta*, and *P. bissetti*. Some produce edible shoots in the spring, and all will produce bamboo poles useful in gardens as fences, and for innumerable other tasks about the home. Bamboo is the plant most used by the most people on Earth.

Planting
SITE PREPARATION

Although many trees and shrubs will *grow* in less-than-ideal environments, under these conditions they tend to be less productive and possibly more susceptible to pests. Before you plant on a poor site, one or two seasons of dedicated soil improvement will be well worth your effort. The general idea is to increase the level of available and total nutrients and at the same time raise the level of organic matter in the soil. Green manuring, compost application, and the addition of rock fertilizers and limestone are all effective methods for achieving these goals.

However, if you do not have the time for this type of advance soil preparation, you can still plant trees and shrubs on all but the poorest sites. In these cases, some fertilization at the time of planting is advisable (see procedure 5 in the section that follows).

PLANTING TECHNIQUES

Usually, young trees and shrubs are purchased and then transplanted into their permanent location. They must be planted carefully if they are to survive, grow well, and give high yields. In temperate climates, the best planting time for most woody plants is the early spring, *after* the ground has thawed but *before* plant growth has begun. Alternatively, planting can be done in the late fall. Nurseries will advise you on the best planting dates. Nursery stock is often supplied bare rooted, although evergreens are always sent in containers or with their roots covered with soil and wrapped in burlap.

Bare-rooted plants should arrive with the roots still moist. They should be unpacked on arrival and placed in a bucket of water for a few hours. If they cannot be planted immediately, they must be "heeled in" on a protected site in the garden. This involves digging a trench, spreading the roots in the trench, covering the roots with soil, tamping firmly, and watering. Heeled-in plants can be kept for days or even weeks, but they will become stunted if left for a season.

Ideally, planting is done on a cloudy day after a recent rain. Once the site has been selected, proceed as follows:

1. Take the plants from their temporary site or from the water bucket and move them to the planting site. *Keep the roots covered and moist at all times.*

2. Skim off any existing vegetation and roots within a three-foot-diameter circle at the site.

3. Dig the hole with vertical sides to a diameter and depth that easily accommodates the new plant's roots. Soil at the bottom of the hole should be loosened a foot deeper than the hole itself. Roots must never be forced into a hole that is too small.

4. Trees should be planted at the same depth as they were in the nursery. If the tree has been grafted, the graft union—a swollen area typically six inches to a foot above the roots—should be kept above ground level.

5. Place the tree in the hole and add or remove soil until the tree is at the correct depth. Spread the roots carefully. (On poor sites, compost, lime, and rock powders may be added. Soluble fertilizers and manure should *never* be placed in the planting hole.) Place topsoil around the roots until the hole is about half full. Carefully firm the soil.

6. Water generously and continue filling the hole with soil. Both watering and firming are necessary to remove air pockets from the soil.

7. When the hole is filled, firm the soil so as to leave a saucer-shaped depression around the trees and water.

8. Prune the tree's branches. This compensates for roots lost when the tree was moved from its original site.

9. Stake the tree and place a protective tree guard around it.

10. Mulch around the tree with a six-inch layer of organic material.

11. Record the planting date, cultivar name, and nursery source in a notebook.

12. Label the tree. Plastic tags marked with waterproof ink can be used, but they are short-lived. Aluminum tags are preferable. Alternatively, a wood sign with enamel paint can be erected near the tree.

Newly planted trees and shrubs require regular watering for the first couple of weeks after planting, then every two weeks or so throughout the first summer.

For evergreens and trees supplied in containers, use the same planting procedure. Carefully remove the container or burlap so that the roots are not disturbed. Place soil in the hole around the root ball; firm and water as you fill the hole.

The planting of shrubs or hedgerows is not nearly as exacting as the planting of trees. The general procedure is the same, but it's not necessary to be quite so fussy with handling.

SPACING

Fruit and nut trees should be spaced sufficiently so that when they become mature, their foliage will not touch. Distance between new trees will vary according to the species you plant and the size you expect the mature trees to reach. Commonly used spacings are given in Table 2. Nurseries will also advise on spacing.

Care and Maintenance

Your trees and shrubs will require some attention if they are to produce good yields year after year.

WEEDS

Young trees and shrubs require protection from other plants, the weeds and grasses that compete for water and nutrients. Thorough mulching is an adequate solution, especially if you establish several layers of newspaper beneath your mulch material. If you run geese, these animals will effectively control grassy weeds that spring up around your trees or grow through the mulch. Mowing is another good way to control weeds and grasses.

TREE OR PLANT	SPACING	
	WITHIN ROW	BETWEEN ROWS
APPLE		
Dwarf	6 ft. (max.)	14 ft. (max.)
Semidwarf	12 ft. (max.)	20 ft. (max.)
Standard	20 ft.	28 ft.
PEACH/NECTARINE		
Dwarf	8 ft.	16 ft.
Standard	12 ft.	20 ft.
PEAR		
Dwarf	8 ft.	16 ft.
Standard	12 ft.	20 ft.
SWEET CHERRY		
Mazzard stock	20 ft.	28 ft.
Mahaleb stock	16 ft.	24 ft.
SOUR CHERRY		
Mahaleb stock	20 ft.	28 ft.
Dwarf	4 ft.	12 ft.
PLUM*	14 ft.	22 ft.
QUINCE*	10 ft.	18 ft.
APRICOT*	14 ft.	22 ft.
WALNUT	40 ft.	40 ft.
BLACKBERRIES	3 ft.	8 ft.
CURRANTS	5 ft.	5 ft.
GOOSEBERRIES	5 ft.	5 ft.
RED RASPBERRIES	2 ft.	5 ft.
BLACK RASPBERRIES	4 ft.	6 ft.
BLUEBERRIES	3 ft.	5 ft.
HEDGEROW		
Low	10–12 in.	Not applicable
Medium	12–18 in.	Not applicable
High	2–4 in.	Not applicable

Table 2 *Recommended Spacings*

*Exact spacing depends on cultivar. Consult nursery.

FERTILIZATION

Mulches of organic materials will fertilize your trees and shrubs adequately if you supplement them with rock powders and limestone where necessary. Mulching should not be done late in the season; late mulching encourages new growth, which is susceptible to winter damage. As a general guide, we suggest the *equivalent* of one-half pound of 10-10-10 fertilizer

Fig. 4 Common terms used in pruning.

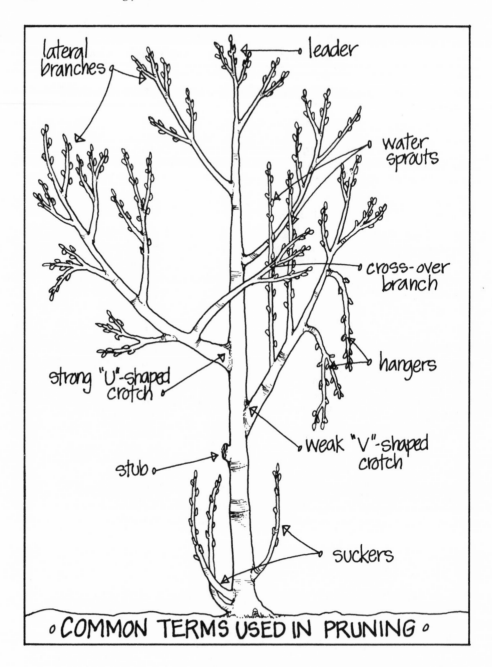

COMMON TERMS USED IN PRUNING

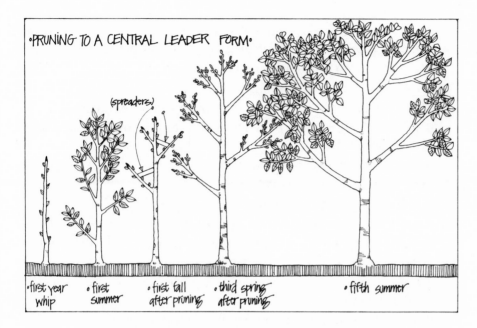

·PRUNING TO A CENTRAL LEADER FORM·

(spreaders)

·first year whip ·first summer ·first fall after pruning ·third spring after pruning ·fifth summer

Fig. 5 Pruning to a central leader form. Illustration by Maia Massion.

per inch of trunk diameter measured 12–15 inches above the ground. If you have your soil tested at a laboratory, ask them to recommend fertilizer applications that can be converted to the equivalent amounts of organic materials and compost. NPK (nitrogen, phosphorus, potassium) conversions for many organic materials are given in Appendix A in Chapter 4.

PRUNING

The pruning of fruit and nut trees is done for several reasons.

- It develops a desirable structure and shape.
- It helps maintain a desired size.
- It improves the quality and yield of fruit.
- It removes dead or diseased wood.

Pruning is easy to learn. The best possible way, of course, is to work with an experienced orchardist, but not everyone will have this opportunity. Figures 4, 5, and 6 diagram some of the basic terms and techniques of pruning. We urge you to study them closely and to familiarize yourself with the following 16 guidelines before you make that first critical cut.

1. Never make a pruning cut without some definite purpose.
2. Light pruning is preferable to severe cutting.
3. Trees well-pruned when young require less attention as they mature.

°PRUNING NEAR A BUD°

A. Correct.
B. Too steep & too close to bud.
C. Not steep enough & too far from bud.

Fig. 6 Pruning near a bud. Illustration by Maia Massion.

4. Always use sharp tools and make clean cuts. Use pruning shears on wood up to one-half-inch diameter. Use a saw on larger limbs.

5. Always prune to just above a bud (Fig. 6).

6. Always prune trees at planting time.

7. Choose main branches for even distribution and wide crotches (Fig. 5).

8. If weaker crotches must be retained, you can strengthen them with spreaders (Fig. 5).

9. Remove any crossed branches.

10. Remove any dead or diseased wood.

11. Remove water sprouts and suckers (Fig. 4).

12. Remove low branches only when there is plenty of growth elsewhere.

13. To reduce height in an older tree, you can cut back the central leader.

14. Prune older trees to allow even light penetration.

15. Treat all larger wounds with tree paint purchased from a garden supplier or nursery.

16. Prune in the early spring while the trees are still dormant.

Fruit Trees

Fruit trees, especially apple and pear, commonly are pruned to a central leader (Fig. 5). Many peach, cherry, and some plum trees are pruned to a spreading, open form (no central leader).

Nut Trees

Many nut trees are pruned to a central leader system or some modification thereof. Severe pruning should be avoided at all times. Trees that are forked can be trained correctively to a single leader. Hazels and filberts sucker profusely; for maximum nut production, remove suckers.

Berry Fruits

With the exception of everbearing raspberries, all raspberries and blackberries set fruit on wood produced in the previous season. Pruning involves removing the fruited canes in the fall and thinning and removing weak canes in the early spring. Everbearing raspberries are pruned by cutting canes to ground level after fall fruiting. Prune blueberries by thinning out some of the bearing branches each year; begin doing this in the third year after planting. Prune currants and gooseberries to remove any wood more than three years old and to retain equal amounts of one-, two-, and three-year-old wood. Prune elderberries to retain vigorous one-year-old canes together with a few that are two years old.

Hedgerows and Windbreaks

Shrubs planted as hedgerows and windbreaks must be heavily pruned at planting time in order to ensure dense bottom growth. Most shrubs are pruned to a height of about six inches. Once established, hedges may need occasional pruning to keep their desired height and form.

POLLINATION

Many fruit and nut trees will produce good crops only if more than one cultivar is planted. Your nursery will advise you of suitable combinations. Most nut trees are wind-pollinated, but fruit trees require the presence of bees for effective pollination. Usually the natural bee population will suffice. If you fear that there are not enough bees available, you can hand-pollinate a few trees. When the yellow pollen grains appear in open flowers, take a soft brush and dab it gently into as many flowers as possible.

INSECT AND DISEASE CONTROL

As Chapter 4 described, we employ several pest management strategies, ranging from prevention through organic insecticides. Whenever insects appear on your trees, identify them and try to determine whether or not they are causing damage. Once again, pest control should be based on prevention rather than on cure. Choosing varieties well-suited to your site conditions, growing resistant varieties, and fertilizing with organic materials are three excellent ways to avoid pest damage.

Sanitary measures are important, too. The eggs and larvae of many insect pests overwinter beneath loose bark, under fallen leaves, and on windfall fruits. Loose bark should be scraped off in the spring, collected on newspaper or plastic sheeting, and either composted or burned. Windfall fruits can be composted, made into ciders and juices, or fed to animals. At pruning time, all dead or diseased wood should be removed. This helps control infection and is especially important for combating fireblight, a serious disease in pears.

Physical barriers and traps coated with attractants and/or adhesive materials will help control many pests. *Tanglefoot®* is an adhesive material that can be applied to tree trunks in early spring. It will ensnare many migrating pests on their way to the foliage. Sticky traps hung in fruit trees will control other insects.

Mice that overwinter beneath mulches can severely damage young trees by nibbling their roots. In the fall, mulches should be raked back two feet from the trunks. Wire-mesh or plastic tree guards also offer some protection.

Some crops—especially cherries, mulberries, blueberries and elderberries—require protection from birds, if you expect to harvest a good crop. For the bushes, plastic netting covers are available. On fruit trees, commercial orchardists sometimes use noise-generating devices that supposedly scare birds away. However, other birds are useful in controlling insect pests. Erecting feeders and nesting boxes and planting appetizing shrubs and trees will encourage beneficial birds to settle in your backyard. (For a list of plants that attract birds to the yard and garden, see Table 4, page 151.)

When a pest becomes a problem, find out what its natural enemies are. Do any of these creatures live nearby? If not, can you encourage or introduce them?

Various biological controls can be introduced to combat pests on fruit trees. In the next section, some suppliers are listed. The bacterial diseases *Bacillus thuringiensis* and *B. popillae* are commercially available and will control some insects. Other insects are susceptible to viral diseases and if these insects are present in high numbers, you *may* be able to control them by giving them the disease. Collect a pint or two (or as many as possible) of the pests. Try to collect some that look *unhealthy*, as these are the ones that have the disease you're trying to transmit. Mash them up in a blender, add some liquid biodegradable soap, dilute the mixture with water, and spray it on the affected plants. If you've collected any pests that have the viral disease, this method will help pass that disease on to other susceptible insects.

A number of relatively safe sprays can be used against insect pests. Dormant oil sprays applied in early spring will asphyxiate many overwintering insects. Apply them to all parts of the tree and they'll be effective against many mites and the eggs of codling moths, leaf rollers, and aphids. Certain other insecticides are derived from various plants. You can use them, but be cautious; they are somewhat unselective and may kill beneficial insects as well. Rotenone, ryania, pyrethrum, quassia, and sabadilla dust are all available. Diatomaceous earth can be used against soft-bodied insects; it is unselective.

Sources of Information on Food-Producing Trees and Shrubs

In a single chapter, we can do little but brush the surface of this rewarding form of home food production. For those of you who wish to explore it further, there exists a body of information in a number of different forms. Here are some of them.

ORGANIZATIONS

THE NORTHERN NUT GROWERS ASSOCIATION
   Mr. John English, Treasurer
   Route 3
   Bloomington, IL 61701
   ($10.00/year)

This organization was founded in 1910 and has been involved ever since in the selection, propagation, and testing of nut trees. They publish the *Nutshell* (a quarterly) and annual reports.

NORTH AMERICAN FRUIT EXPLORERS
Mary Kurle, Treasurer
10 S. 055 Madison St.
Hinsdale, IL 60521
($5.00/year)

NAFEX members are involved in the selection and propagation of outstanding native fruit trees and shrubs. They have established testing groups for many fruits: hican, mulberry, paw-paw, persimmon, plum, quince, raspberry, and so on. Members are available for consultation. They publish a quarterly journal, *Pomona*.

THE PERMACULTURE ASSOCIATION
37 Goldsmith Street
Maryborough
Victoria 3465
Australia

This association was formed in response to the books *Permaculture One* and *Permaculture Two*. (Listed under General Texts in the chapter Bibliography.) They publish a quarterly journal carrying articles on permaculture, aquaculture, forestry, biofuels, etc. Subscriptions are Aus$12.00/year. U.S. currency should *not* be sent.

BOSTON URBAN GARDENERS
831 Statler Building
20 Park Plaza
Boston, MA 02116
($2.00/year)

BUG has recently formed a permaculture group, which is researching the use of perennial shrubs and trees for Boston. They are interested in fruit and nut trees as well as plants that provide shelter, block noise, require little maintenance, are long lived, and resistant to pests and disease. BUG membership is $2.00/year and includes their newsletter.

NORTH AMERICAN PERMACULTURE
P.O. Box 1100
Winters, CA 95694

NAP is the North American equivalent of the Permaculture Association in Australia. Write for current information about membership and publications. Include a stamped, self-addressed envelope.

NURSERIES AND SEED SUPPLIERS

When you order plants from any nursery, remember these things:

- Some nurseries offer guarantees and will replace any plants (mostly fruit trees) that do not survive.
- Check hardiness zones. Some nurseries may make exaggerated claims for their plants.

- With nut trees it is sometimes not apparent whether the trees are vegetatively propagated or are seedlings. If in doubt, assume the latter.
- Check pollination requirements for fruit and nut trees so that you have a compatible mix of cultivars.

The following list is not entirely comprehensive. Please bear in mind that by including a particular nursery we're *not* recommending it over others that are not listed.

Conservation Districts. Many supply seedlings for conservation plantings. Useful windbreaks, erosion controllers, and native fruits are often included. Check the Yellow Pages under Government Offices, United States, Agriculture Department. If your town or city has a conservation office, call or drop in and talk with people there.

Miles W. Fry & Son, Inc. Frysville, Ephrata R.D. 3, PA 17522. Extensive range of fast-growing hybrid poplars.

Louis Gerardi Nursery. RR 1, O'Fallon, IL 62269. Grafted nut trees. Many varieties of northern pecans, hickories, Carpathian walnuts, heartnuts, butternuts, Chinese chestnuts, filberts. Grafted pawpaws, mulberries and American persimmons. Scionwood of all the above.

Grimo Nut Nursery. RR 3, Lakeshore Road, Niagara-on-the-Lake, Ontario, Canada LOS 1JO. Seedling nut trees from superior selections. Grafted Carpathian walnut, black walnut, heartnut, butternut, sweet chestnut, ginkgo, mulberry, pecan, and hickory. Will custom graft.

Gurney's Seed and Nursery Co. Yankton, SD 57079. Large range of fruit trees and berries, house plants, flowers, herbs, hedge plants, ornamentals, shade trees, gardening aids.

Hilltop Orchards and Nurseries Inc., Route 2, Hartford, MI 49057. A major supplier to commercial growers. Common fruit trees only. Catalog contains pollination data as well as cultural recommendations.

J.L. Hudson Seedsman. Box 1058, Redwood City, CA 94064. Seeds from a truly enormous range of plants.

International Tree Crops Institute U.S.A. (ITCIUSA). Route 1, Gravel Switch, KY 40328. Persimmon and honeylocust cultivars.

Mellingers, Inc. 2310 W. South Range, North Lima, OH 44452. A huge range of plants, including unusual native fruits, hardy bamboos, shade trees, fruit trees, berries, seedling nut trees, flowers, and vegetables. They also supply tree and shrub seeds, books, gardening equipment, grafting knives, pruning shears, etc.

J.E. Miller Nurseries, Inc. Canandaigua, NY 14424. Large range of fruit trees including dwarfs and semidwarfs, antique apples. Berries and seedling nut trees. Garden aids—tree protectors, pH tester, pheromone traps, etc.

New York State Fruit Testing Cooperative Association, Inc. Geneva, NY 14456. Most fruit trees, berries, grapes. Many old varieties of apples and pears. Dwarf apples, disease-resistant varieties.

Palette Gardens. 26 West Zion Hill Road, Quakerstown, PA 18951. Bamboos.

Pataky's Nut Grove Nursery. 1116 Hickory Lane, Mansfield, OH 44905. Extensive range of grafted and seedling nut trees.

Rayner Bros., Inc. P.O. Box 1617, Salisbury, MD 21801. Strawberries, raspberries, blackberries, dwarf and standard fruit trees, blueberries.

F.W. Schumacher Co. Sandwich, MA 02563. A wide range of tree and shrub seeds.

Smith Nursery Co. P.O. Box 515, Charles City, IA 50616. A wide selection of shrubs and shade trees, including many species useful for wildlife, hedgerows, and windbreaks. Wide selection of shrub and tree seeds.

Southmeadow Fruit Gardens. 2263 Tilbury Place, Birmingham, MI 48009. Suppliers of an enormous range of unusual fruits including over 160 varieties of apples as well as many pears, plums, apricots, cherries and grapes. Also supply hardy native fruits. Price and variety list free on request. Illustrated catalog for history and description of their plants—$8.00.

Stark Bro's. Nurseries and Orchards Co. Louisiana, MO 63353. Supplies commercial growers with common fruit trees. Catalog contains useful cultural information.

St. Lawrence Nurseries. Route 2, Potsdam, NY 13676. Hardy varieties of antique apples, pears, plums, butternuts, black walnuts, Carpathian walnuts, hickories, filberts, plus native black cherry and burr oak (Ashworth).

Talbott Nursery. RR 3, Box 212M, Linton, IN 47441. Grafted Chinese chestnuts, American persimmons, Carpathian walnuts, northern pecans, pawpaws.

Weston Nurseries, Inc. East Main St., Box 135, Hopkinton, MA 01748. An extensive range of landscaping plants as well as some fruit and nut trees, herbs, and wildflowers.

Leslie H. Wilmoth Nursery. Route 2, Box 469, Elizabethtown, KY 42701. Many varieties of grafted nut trees. Will custom graft.

Dave Wilson Nursery. Hughson, CA 95326. Most fruit trees and an extensive selection of genetic dwarfs. Also jujube, quince, pecan, walnut, Oriental persimmon. Their catalog includes cultivar evaluations—each tree is described for its suitability in various climatic zones.

Worcester County Horticultural Society. 30 Elm St., Worcester, MA 01608. Scion wood from 60 varieties of antique apple.

Additional Listings

Brooklyn Botanic Gardens has published a listing of suppliers for over 1200 Trees and Shrubs. Write to *Nursery Source Guide,* Brooklyn Botanic Gardens, 1000 Washington Ave., Brooklyn, NY 11225.

The Avant Gardener 12(20), August 1980, contains a list of suppliers for vegetable seeds, herbs, fruit and nut trees, berries and specialist plant material. Write to PO Box 489, New York, NY 10028. ($15.00/yr.)

Soil Conservation Society of America's *Sources of Native Seeds and Plants* lists over 170 suppliers of native seeds and plants. The publication is available for $2.00, postpaid, from Soil Conservation Society of America, 7515 Northeast Ankeny Road, Ankeny, IA 50021.

Arboreta

Many useful plants will be available from nurseries, from your own landscape, or from exchanges with friends and colleagues. Occasionally, however, individual species may be elusive. After searching everywhere else, *and only then,* serious researchers may contact either the Bailey Hortarium at Cornell University, or the Arnold Arboretum in Jamaica Plain, Massachusetts. Both organizations have computerized access to lists of plants held by participating arboreta throughout the United States.

INSECT CONTROL MATERIALS

Here your best source will depend on the approach you're planning to take—natural enemies, biological controls, "safe" poisons, or impeding devices.

Beneficial Insects

Rincon-Vitova Insectaries, Inc.
  P.O. Box 95
  Oakview, CA 93022

Rincon-Vitova carries *Aphytis melinus,* a parasite of red scale, and *Cryptolaemus montrouzieri,* a mealybug predator. Also green lacewings, *Trichogramma* wasps, predatory mites, fly parasites, and ladybugs.

The IPM Practitioner
  Bio Integral Resource Center
  Box 28A, Route 2
  Winters, CA 95694

The October, 1982 issue of this publication (available for $2.00) contains a full listing of suppliers of beneficial organisms.

Biological Controls

B. popillae (Milky Spore Disease) is a biological method of Japanese-beetle control. It's marketed as Doom® by

Mellingers, Inc.
  2310 W. South Range Road
  North Lima, OH 44452

Bacillus thuringiensis is sold under the trade names Dipel, Thuricide, and Bactur. It's available from many garden supply centers and nurseries. If you can't find it locally, try one of the following suppliers, both of whom carry it as Thuricide.

Pratt-Gabriel Div.
  Miller Chemical & Fertilizer Corp.
  122 Sharon Rd., Box B
  Robbinsville, NJ 08691

W. Atlee Burpee Co.
  Warminster, PA 18991

Botanical Poisons

It's likely that you'll find rotenone through one of your local suppliers. If not, try Mellingers (above) or one of the following:

Organic Control, Inc.
  5132 Venice Blvd.
  Los Angeles, CA 90019
  (Combination pyrethrins,
  rotenone, and ryania)

Burgess Seed & Plant Co.
  905 Four Seasons Road
  Bloomington, IL 61701
  (Sabadilla)

Diatomaceous Earth

Perma Guard Co.
  P.O. Box 29453
  Phoenix, AZ 85034
  (Perma Guard)

Astrochemical Corp.
  Route 3, Box 345AC
  Lafayette, LA 70501
  (Earth Guard)

Traps, Barriers, and Netting

Animal Repellants, Inc.
  Lawn & Garden Div.
  P.O. Box 999
  Griffin, GA 30224
  (Durex anti-bird mesh)

The Tanglefoot® Company
  314 Straight Ave. S.W.
  Grand Rapids, MI 49504
  (Tree Tanglefoot®, Tangletrap®,
  for insects)

Zoecon Corporation
  975 California Ave.
  Palo Alto, CA 94304
  (Insect attractants and traps)

Gurney Seed & Nursery Co.
  Yankton SD 57079
  (Garden nets, traps)

Tools and Equipment

A.M. Leonard, Inc.
6665 Spiker Road
Piqua, OH 45356
(Free horticultural tool-and-
supply catalog)

Smith & Hawken Tool Company
68 Homer
Palo Alto, CA 94301
(Free catalog—superb tools)

BIBLIOGRAPHY

General Texts

CREASY, R. *The Complete Book of Edible Landscaping.* San Francisco, CA: Sierra Club Books, 1982.

Korn, Larry (ed.). *The Future Is Abundant.* Arlington, WA: Tilth, 1982.

HILL, L. *Fruits and Berries for the Home Garden.* New York: Alfred A. Knopf, 1977.

LOGSDON, G. *Organic Orcharding, A Grove of Trees to Live In.* Emmaus, PA: Rodale Press, 1982.

LOGSDON, G. *Successful Berry Growing.* Emmaus, PA: Rodale Press, 1974.

MOLLISON, B. *Permaculture Two, Practical Design for Town and Country in Permanent Agriculture.* Stanley, Tasmania: Tagari Books, 1979.

MOLLISON, B., and D. HOLMGREN. *Permaculture One, A Perennial Agriculture for Human Settlements.* Melbourne, Australia: Transworld Publishers, Ltd., 1978.

PEATTIE, D.C. *A Natural History of Trees of Eastern and Central North America.* New York: Bonanza Books, 1966.

SMITH, J. RUSSELL. *Tree Crops, A Permanent Agriculture.* New York: Harper Colophon Books, 1978.

WYMAN, D. *Wyman's Gardening Encyclopedia.* New York: Macmillan, 1978.

YEPSEN, R.B. (ED.). *Trees for the Yard, Orchard, and Woodlot.* Emmaus, PA: Rodale Press, 1976.

Nut Trees

JAYNES, R. (ED.). *Nut Tree Culture in North America,* Northern Nut Growers Association, Hamden, CT, 1979.

MACDANIELS, L.H. *Nut Growing in the Northeast,* Information Bulletin 71, U.S.D.A. Extension Service, Cornell University, Ithaca, NY, 1977.

Fruit Trees

CHILDERS, N.F. *Modern Fruit Science.* New Brunswick, NJ: Rutgers University, 1978.

McGOURTY, F. (ED.). *Handbook on Fruit Trees and Shrubs.* Brooklyn, NY: Brooklyn Botanic Gardens, 1975.

TUKEY, H.B. *Dwarfed Fruit Trees.* Ithaca, NY: Cornell University Press, 1978.

WESTWOOD, M.N. *Temperate-Zone Pomology.* San Francisco, CA: W.H. Freeman, 1978.

Species Identification

BORROR, D.J., and R.E. WHITE. *Field Guide to the Insects of America North of Mexico.* Boston: Houghton Mifflin, 1970.

BULL, J., and J. FARRAND. *The Audubon Society Field Guide to North American Birds, Eastern Region.* New York: Alfred A. Knopf, 1977.

CARR, A. *Rodale's Color Handbook of Garden Insects.* Emmaus, PA: Rodale Press, 1979.

PETERSON, R.T., and M. McKENNY. *A Field Guide to Wildflowers, Northeastern and North-Central North America.* Boston: Houghton Mifflin, 1977.

PETRIDES, G.A. *A Field Guide to Trees and Shrubs, Northeastern and Central North America.* Boston: Houghton Mifflin, 1972.

Design

BARNHART, E.A. "On the Feasibility of a Permanent Agricultural Landscape," *The Journal of the New Alchemists* 5, 1979, 73-85.

BARNHART, E.A. "Tree Crops: Creating the Foundation of a Permanent Agriculture," *The Journal of the New Alchemists* 6, 1980, 57-73.

MOLLISON, B. *Permaculture Two, Practical Design for Town and Country in Permanent Agriculture.* Stanley, Tasmania: Tagari Books, 1979.

MOLLISON, B., and D. HOLMGREN. *Permaculture One, A Perennial Agriculture for Human Settlements.* Melbourne, Australia: Transworld Publishers, Ltd., 1978.

Microclimate

ROBINETTE, G.O. *Plants/People/ and Environmental Quality.* Washington, D.C.: U.S. Department of the Interior, 1972.

SEARLE, S.A. *Environment and Plant Life.* London: Faber and Faber, 1973.

Landscape Architecture

McGOURTY, F. (ED.). *Tree and Shrub Forms—Their Landscape Use.* Brooklyn, NY: Brooklyn Botanic Gardens, 1976.

SPANGLER, R.L., and J. RIPPERDA. *Landscape Plants for Central and Northeastern United States.* Minneapolis, MN: Burgess Publishing Company, 1977.

Propagation

BROWSE, P.M. *Plant Propagation.* New York: Simon and Schuster, 1979.

LIPP, L.F. (ED.). *Handbook on Propagation.* Brooklyn, NY: Brooklyn Botanic Garden, 1976.

Pruning

BRICKELL, L. *Pruning.* New York: Simon and Schuster, 1979.

HILL, L. *Pruning Simplified.* Emmaus, PA: Rodale Press, 1978.

SUNSET EDITORS. *Pruning Handbook.* Menlo Park, CA: Lane Publishing Company, 1972.

SUNSET EDITORS, *Garden Trees.* Menlo Park, CA: Lane Publishing Company, 1975.

Pest Control

McGOURTY, F. (ED.). *Handbook on Biological Control of Plant Pests.* Brooklyn, NY: Brooklyn Botanic Gardens, 1976.

SCHWARTZ, P.H. *Control of Insects on Deciduous Fruits and Tree Nuts in the Home Orchard—Without Insecticides,* U.S.D.A. Home and Garden Bulletin No. 211, U.S. Government Printing Office, Washington, DC, 1977.

YEPSEN, R.B. (ED.). *Organic Plant Protection.* Emmaus, PA: Rodale Press, 1976.

Chapter 8

Community Gardening

Susan Ervin and Michael Greene

One answer to limited gardening space around your home is to pool resources with friends or neighbors and form a community garden. The tradition of community food plots is as old as agriculture itself, but today it's enjoying a significant rebirth across the country, particularly in urban areas.

One on-the-job benefit at New Alchemy is the chance to participate in community gardening on our twelve-acre farm. Many rewards are derived from this activity, and there's little doubt that our weekly work sessions go a long way toward maintaining our overall group spirit.

We've also worked a great deal with existing community-garden projects in Boston, Hartford, and New York, and on county prison farms throughout the Northeast. Not long ago we built an irrigating windmill for a community garden in Boston.

Susan Ervin and Michael Greene are by far our most knowledgeable and experienced community garden people. Susan coordinates our own community gardening project, and Michael earned his green thumb in community projects in Santa Barbara, California, and the South Bronx. In this chapter, they team up to provide some personal guidelines for starting a community project in your area. To avoid reinventing the wheel, do consult your local garden groups first; however, this chapter will be helpful whether you're kicking off a new project or looking to join an existing cooperative.

THE EDITORS

Community Cooperation

A COMMUNITY GARDEN is a garden area shared by a group of people who don't have a place to garden at home. Usually such a garden is divided up so that each person or household has an individual plot. Gardening consortiums form in different ways and for different reasons. A group of neighbors cooperating with one another is probably most common, but many community gardens are organized by food or energy coops, gardening classes, fellow employees, senior citizens, and parent groups.

Community gardens are very common in other countries. At the entry point into mainland China near Macao, for example, customs officials have a big garden where they work when they're not tending to official duties. Hotels, schools, and factories in China all have community gardens.

Community gardens are also becoming quite popular here in the United States—especially in cities, where people are converting vacant lots and public or institutional land into thriving plots.

Locating a Site

Finding and arranging for a site will be your primary concern. Look around for viable public or private land and see if the owner will donate or rent it to the project. Local civic groups sometimes sponsor community gardens and even provide some services, such as plowing, fencing or the water supply. Or, a group of coworkers can get together and ask their employer for the use of company land for gardening.

Local departments of conservation, parks and recreation, and also redevelopment and housing authorities can assist in your search for land, so don't hesitate to call them.

Community Organization

Division of Responsibilities

Once a gardening group is formed, members must decide which activities and equipment will be individual responsibilities and which will be shared. Often a coordinator is chosen or appointed. Coordinators usually help things go more smoothly, but fellow gardeners should be prepared to share some responsibilities and pay the coordinator for her or his time (unless you have a real saint in your group). The coordinator might assume any or all of the following tasks.

1. Find a site and arrange for water, plowing, and security (a fence).

2. Handle fees, funding, and budget.

3. Call and organize meetings.

4. Organize division and assignment of plots and pathways.

5. Act as liason between the group and cooperating agencies, such as town officials, community action programs, etc.

Expenses

Your project may save you quite a bit of money over time, but there will be some start-up investments and a few routine expenses along the way. Ongoing costs to be shared by the participants might include these:

- Rototiller rental in the spring.
- Bulk purchase of rock minerals as soil supplements.
- Bulk seed purchases.
- Mulch and compost collection work.

Estimate your expenses and divide by the number of participants. The result will be your annual membership fee. Money left at the end of the season can be returned, carried over to the next year, or used for special improvements. It can also contribute to a fine harvest party.

Choosing Plots

A method for plot assignment should be decided in advance. You don't want to start out with conflicts, and certain plots are bound to be more convenient. Some may get better sunshine, easier water access, or even healthier soil. It's also preferable to let people keep the same plots year after year so that they can overwinter some vegetables and benefit from their work of soil improvement. Some form of name drawing may be the most equitable solution, unless the garden is small and the participants are easy to please. Perhaps the coordinator should be given a priority in return for his or her work.

New Members

If there is space for new gardeners, the group should think about how to choose them. A first-come first-served waiting list seems reasonable enough. Neighborhood garden groups may choose to accept only neighborhood residents.

Rules and Regulations

In the long run, we've found that a community garden code of rules can help to keep all participants happy. Be sure that specific responsibilities and rules are well defined from the beginning. Prepare *written* rules for participation, and ask each new gardener to sign the agreement. You'll want to specify whether or not the use of chemical fertilizers, pesticides, or herbicides, is acceptable and you may want to limit the time of day and length of time for watering.

Clearly describe the kind of appearance that's expected of the plots, and reserve the right to condemn and reassign neglected gardens.

End-of-season cleanup standards should be established, too. Clearing dead plants, green manuring, cover cropping, or mulching can be specified ahead of time.

A sample set of rules and regulations is included as Appendix A at the end of this chapter.

Tips for Success

Group Meetings

Occasional group meetings will help keep things moving. You can schedule pot-luck dinners, group food preservation, and even guest speakers. Be sure to meet in midwinter to gear up for the coming growing season. This is the ideal time to study the seed catalogs together and plan bulk purchases.

Continuity

It's most desirable to obtain access to your site for more than one year, since the benefits of soil improvement will increase over time. Be sure to secure a formal, legal agreement with the owner or donor. Include duration of use, agreed-on activities, and any special provisions, such as returning the site to its former condition or the right of access to water. The owner of the land, whether public authority or private individual, will be liable for damages if anyone is injured, so you'll need to obtain a waiver of responsibility to protect them. Appendix B at the end of this chaper is a sample liability release and agreement with landowners.

Water

Your water supply is important. You may be able to get permission to use fire hydrants for water. If there is water on the site, you'll probably share the water bill, setting rules to limit water use. If there is no water source, you'll have to raise the money for a water system and share the cost. If you have a sponsoring organization—civic, employee group, or community-action agency—they may pay for the water.

Technical Advice

Try to find some source of technical advice for beginners, especially if you don't have experienced gardeners in your group. Look around for a good local gardener who'll agree to provide workshops at different seasons. Contact other community gardening groups, and learn from their

experiences. Share your books and source materials. Don't overlook your public library, either.

Security

The security of your garden from theft and damage is another consideration, often more serious in urban areas. As a general rule, the more active the garden site, the less of a problem vandalism will be. The frequent presence of gardeners is a definite asset. Likewise, it's good to locate the garden within view of neighboring houses whose occupants are familiar with your normal activities. A sign explaining the project should increase human appreciation of what you're doing and thus minimize vandalism. You may have to fence the whole garden site, however, if dogs, serious vandalism, or thievery threaten to be a problem.

Pollution Control

If your garden is near a busy street or road, particles of exhaust pollution will bring lead into your garden and onto your vegetables. By all means retain any existing barrier of shrubs, vines, or high weeds along the highway. Even if they're ugly, they'll absorb some of this pollution. You can plant a barrier of tall annual flowers the first year and add perennial flowering shrubs for a permanent barrier, if you plan to continue the project indefinitely.

Parting Advice

Plant lots of flowers around the garden!

Resources

Many of the suggestions in this chapter comes from two excellent pamphlets produced by the Massachusetts Department of Food and Agriculture: *The Downtown Farmer—A Guide for City Farmers* (also available in Spanish) and *How to Organize a Community Garden in Massachusetts.*

Both publications may be useful to a new community garden. You can get them free, by writing to Division of Agricultural Land Use, Mass. Dept. of Food and Agriculture, 100 Cambridge Street, Boston, MA 02202.

Other useful sources of information are:

Boston Urban Gardeners, *Handbook of Community* Gardening, edited by Susan Naimark and published by Scribner and Sons.

The American Community Gardening Association, PO Box 8645, Ann Arbor, MI 48107

Project Resource Library, Gardens for All/The National Association for Gardening, 180 Flynn Ave., Burlington, VT 05401.

APPENDIX A
Sample Rules and Regulations

RULES FOR COMMUNITY GARDENERS ON STATE LAND*

Garden plots and adjoining aisles must be kept neat and free from mature weeds and overgrowth.

Priority in the allotment of state land garden plots is given to low-income elderly, low-income families and youth ages seven to sixteen (with adult supervision).

Horticultural uses only are permitted, and food production is encouraged over other forms of gardening.

No permanent fixtures can be installed on any plot.

If gardening activity has not started in your assigned garden plot by June 1, it will be given to someone else.

Liability: The owner of the land including the state institution where the gardens are located, and all its employees and agents cannot be held liable for accidents or damages to person, property, or plants that might occur relative to gardening activities on state land.

Use of herbicides (weed-killers) in any form is not permitted on state land. Use only those pesticides that are registered for home vegetable garden use (insecticides, fungicides, bug-sprays and powders). Use them sparingly and on wind-free days when they will not blow into the neighboring garden plots.

No drug producing or illegal plants can be grown.

Produce grown on state land cannot be sold.

Fall clean-up is the responsibility of each gardener. The land must be left in at least as good a condition as it was at the beginning of the season.

No fee shall be charged for use of a garden plot; however, gardeners may want to assess themselves for materials or services (water, plowing).

For answers to specific questions about plants, gardening advice, and gardening information, use the local resources. Ask your garden coordinator, the other community gardeners (some are quite experienced) or the County Extension Service (home garden publications).

Check with your volunteer community garden coordinator for any other rules about hours, parking, water, costs, etc.

*From a summary of typical state regulations for community gardens.

APPENDIX B
Sample Liability Release

TOWN/CITY OF _____

I, _____ of _____
for good and valuable consideration given to me by the Town/City of
_____, specifically the use of city-owned land for a garden
plot during the summer of 19_____ located at _____
the receipt of which is hereby acknowledged, do hereby release and discharge the
Town/City of _____ from any and all claims, demands,
actions and causes of action of every name and nature which I now have or might
have upon or against said Town/City of _____
its agents, servants or employees, and especially from all claims arising out of any
and all personal injuries, damages, expenses, and any loss or damage whatsoever
resulting or to result from the Town/City's allowing me the use of said property for
gardening purposes. It is also understood and agreed that I will hold harmless the
Town/City of _____ from all claims, demands and suits for
damages, costs, loss of services, expenses, or compensation which I, my heirs, next
of kin, executors, administrators, successors, assigns have or may have on account
of or in any way growing out of said use of Town/City property for gardening purposes or its results by the Town/City of _____ or its agents,
servants, or employees.

I further understand that this release is to compromise and terminate all claims
for injuries or damages of whatever nature, known or unknown, including any
damages known or unknown to the fruits, vegetables, or flowers which I have
planted.

Signed _____

Date _____

Chapter 9

Food Preservation

Susan Ervin

If you want to eat home-grown food all year long, greenhouses and season extenders will help, but still you'll need to preserve and store food for times of low production. You can plant a larger summer garden for the specific purpose of preserving food, or you can simply preserve excess amounts of the inevitable few crops that overproduce. You can also buy large quantities of produce during harvest season (when it's fresh and inexpensive) and preserve it for future use.

In any case, no book about gardening and food would be complete without a discussion of preservation techniques. Plenty of useful guides are available, but somehow Susan has a special knack for taking you right into the kitchen and sharing in this busy fall activity. Wintertime readers will find themselves licking their lips as they envision juicy strawberries in January, crisp beans in February, or zesty hot peppers in March. Susan Ervin is one of our premier food preservers. In April, after everyone else's supply of summer produce has dwindled away, you can always count on a visit to Susan's kitchen for an endless treasury of canned or frozen summer treats. Her savory preserves and her canned peppers in their tart brine are nothing short of inspiring!

THE EDITORS

T O PUT BY is an early nineteenth-century term meaning to "save something you don't have to use now, against the time when you'll need it."[1] We still hear this expression today from old-time country people, who apply it to prudence and planning. "Putting food by" is the antidote for uncertainty about your future food supply and personal welfare. But even if you have a steady income and a handy supermarket, it's very satisfying as winter settles in to look over your jars of bright red peppers and deep purple jams, bins of potatoes and squash, containers of dried beans, and freezer full of assorted vegetables.

There are several methods of food preservation, but one rule applies to all of them: The food to be preserved should be of as high a quality as you would want to eat fresh.

Whatever method of food preservation you're using, fresh high-quality produce is essential. Beginners often make the mistake of being overly ambitious and then not carrying through, or they think they can get by preserving produce of lower quality than they would eat fresh. If you pick two quarts of beans when they're young and tender and get them into the freezer an hour after they're picked, you'll have some really nice beans to eat in the winter. If you pick a bushel of beans that have grown big, tough, and stringy, then let them sit on the back porch for two days, and finally do a slipshod job of freezing them at midnight, you'll have a plentiful supply of low-quality beans frowning at you all winter. Young, crisp cucumbers make crisp pickles; old, hollow, soggy cucumbers make hollow, soggy pickles. And, as all of us know, one rotten apple will spoil the whole barrel.

Blanching and Freezing

Freezing is probably the most popular way to preserve food today. Frozen foods have a taste, texture, and color that most closely resembles fresh ones, and the freezing process is quick and simple. However, a freezer is quite expensive, and its annual electricity consumption usually is very high. Modern freezers are designed to be compact, but as a result they're often underinsulated. This means that the motor puts out hot air underneath the space you're trying to keep cold. We sincerely hope someone starts designing energy-efficient freezers soon. A chest freezer is a bit more efficient than an upright, which allows the cold air to fall out when you open the door. However, uprights offer convenient access to food and they're easier to arrange.

Most vegetables are blanched before they are frozen. *Blanching* means dipping them into boiling water briefly to slow down enzyme activity. That means they don't ripen any further.

To prepare foods for blanching, cut them into small pieces so they'll heat through quickly. As a general rule, things should be cut to the size at which you intend to use them—green beans broken or frenched, squash cut in thin slices, and broccoli heads divided up into smaller pieces.

Bring a pot of water to boil. It should be deep enough so that you can immerse a colander or strainer of the vegetables in it. Blanch only a small amount at a time so the produce will heat evenly and quickly. Most preserving instructions give a precise time for blanching each vegetable. We don't time ours—we go by appearance. Green vegetables are ready when they turn a clear, bright green. Non-green things, like carrots, squash, or cauliflower, take on a slight transparency when they're sufficiently blanched. Blanching time ranges from about one to four minutes.

Standard procedure is to dip the blanched vegetables into ice water to cool them quickly. Making a lot of ice takes forethought and fuel energy, so we usually just run very cold water over the vegetables. If you aren't cooling with ice, be especially sure not to over-blanch the vegetables. Shake the colander or sieve to remove excess water and spread the vegetables on a clean towel to dry. We like to have two colanders or sieves in service at once. One can be in the pot blanching while we are working with the newly blanched vegetables in the other.

An alternative to immersing the vegetables in boiling water is steam-blanching. The vegetables are elevated above an inch or so of boiling water, covered with a lid, and steamed until the desired color change takes place. Steam-blanching takes longer, but you don't have to bring so much water to a boil and no nutrients are left behind in the water. We always steam-blanch greens, edible pod peas, and summer squash, because it keeps them drier. Metal vegetable-steaming baskets are quite common now, and there are beautiful Chinese bamboo steamers that stack up to allow a lot of steaming at one time. Check often throughout the process to make sure you don't run out of water.

Pack blanched, cooled, dried vegetables into sealable plastic cartons or new freezer bags. Don't try to use recycled plastic bags. They often have little holes in them and aren't airtight. Freezer bags are stronger and come in various sizes. Beginners tend to package things in excessively large quantities. Pints are often more convenient than quarts, unless you plan to feed a large household.

Certain vegetables and most fruits are better if they're *not* blanched. We prefer to freeze tomatoes, pepper, corn, celery, okra, and all fruits raw. Tomatoes are just washed, chopped, and bagged. Pepper and celery do best if they're diced. Corn should be cut off the cob to save space. Lots of people blanch the corn on the cob before cutting it off, but we think it's better uncooked; certainly it's easier. Cut okra into quarter-inch slices. We like to fry eggplant lightly in hot oil instead of steaming or blanching it. Beets should be cooked whole and packed.

As for fruits, we pack dry berries (e.g., cranberries, blueberries, elderberries) without sugar. Juicy fruits, like peaches and strawberries and raspberries, retain their texture better if they're sweetened. Apples, pears, and rhubarb are fine raw or blanched. Frozen fruit juices are a special treat.

Don't think you have to assemble bushels of produce and spend all night putting things up. We like to pick double the amount of whatever we are picking for dinner and freeze the extra. Sometimes we don't even bother with separate blanching. We'll just put all the beans or broccoli or whatever in the pot with a little bit of water. Then, when the color clarifies, we take half out, cool it, dry it, and freeze it. Be fairly careful about procedures until you get a feel for preserving; then you can be more easygoing.

Keep track of what you've put in the freezer and be sure to include the date on the label. Try to arrange things so they're accessible. If you bury all of your early-season crops *under* the late ones, you'll just be getting down to the peas when it's almost pea season again. Don't keep frozen foods longer than a year. Long-term storage is energy *in*efficient, and the nutrient content and quality does decline over time.

You can freeze special baby foods, too. Prepare the foods as if they were to be eaten right away—that is, cook, blend, strain, or whatever. Then spoon them into ice-cube trays. When the cubes are frozen, crack them out and pack in freezer bags. You can take out single cubes as you need them. Of course, you can freeze fully prepared dishes for adults, too. But just getting the food into the freezer in the busy growing season is usually enough work. You'll have more time for cooking in the winter.

If the sad day comes when your freezer gets unplugged or the power goes off for a long time, check to see whether or not any ice crystals remain in the food. (Remember—things at the front or on top will warm up first.) If there *are* ice crystals, you can refreeze the food, although the texture may suffer somewhat. If some things are still quite cold, but not icy, we suggest making a big soup or a fruit sauce and then freezing *it*. Don't take chances, especially with meat or fish.

Canning

Canning is the other form of food preservation that's familiar to most people. Once canned, foods can be set on the shelf, ready to use. Canning equipment is less costly than a freezer, and, needless to say, it uses less fuel energy. But canning is a lot more work than freezing. Some canned foods are tasty, but many lose a lot in texture and flavor. Foods we like to can are tomatoes; fruit sauces; apple, pear, and peach slices; green beans; sauerkraut; and, of course, pickles, jams, and jellies. Any vegetable can be

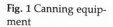
Fig. 1 Canning equipment

canned. The books recommended at the end of this chapter will give you instructions for anything you want to try.

In canning, the food is sterilized and stored in a vacuum. Jars of food are either submerged in boiling water or processed under steam in a pressurized canner. The heat sterilizes the food and forces air out of the jars.

BOILING-WATER CANNING

The simple boiling-water method is suitable for high-acid foods—tomatoes, acid fruits, pickles, sauerkraut—and for jams, jellies, and fruits in sugar syrup. The higher temperatures of a pressure canner are necessary for all other foods if you are to prevent spoilage from bacterial growth.

Equipment and Preparation

Standard canning jars are essential. They are heat resistant and have special lids designed to form a vacuum seal. The inner portion of the lid is a flat metal disk with an attached rubber ring that will be in contact with the glass-jar rim. The inner rubber rings can't be reused; the outer rings can. The jars come in various sizes and with regular or wide mouths. Wide mouths are easier to fill with bulky things. Jars cost over $3 per dozen now; but if you take care of them, they'll last a long time.

If you plan to can with the boiling-water method, you'll need a big, deep canning pot. You can buy canners that hold either seven or nine quarts at a time. Be sure your canner allows for a couple of inches of headroom above the jar tops. Some newer canners are really too shallow and boil over all over the place. In addition to this annoying fact, the jars won't seal if they're not fully submerged. Your canner will contain a metal basket to hold the jars and enable you to lift them in and out of the water bath. (See Fig. 1.)

Jars and lids must be sterilized just before they're filled. For jars, put several inches of water in the canner, place washed jars *upside down* in the metal basket, and steam them vigorously for ten minutes. Or you can fill the canner about one-third of the way up, fill the jars with water, and boil them. The first method is quicker. Save the hot water for later processing. Remove the jars from the pot and place them upside down on a clean cloth until you are ready to use them. Strong tongs are almost essential for handling hot canning jars. Check all jar rims for nicks or cracks. Imperfect rims will prevent sealing. Rings and lids can be put into hot—but not boiling— water.

Extra hints: (1) While the jars are sterilizing, you can prepare the food to go in them. (2) When you fill the jars, always leave one-half inch of headroom; make this a full inch for fruit sauces.

Here are specific preparation steps for some of the things you may plan to can.

Tomatoes   Raw packing is the easiest method. Wash, core, and chop into a bowl. Pack into jars—you may not want to use all the juice. Sometimes we puree the tomatoes in a blender. Of course, you can cook them down or strain them and make sauces if you prefer. Tomatoes are so good and useful canned that there's no need to waste freezer space on them.

Fruit sauces   We don't peel apples, pears, or peaches. Cook them until tender with a little water and sugar or honey to taste. Puree in the blender and pour into sterilized jars.

Fruit slices   Make a syrup of 2½ cups sugar (or slightly less honey) to 5 cups of water and hold at a hard boil for several minutes. This amount of syrup will probably be sufficient for seven quarts of fruit—but we won't guarantee it! Put sliced-up fruit into the syrup and cook until tender. Cherries and rhubarb are good this way, too. Fill sterilized jars. These slices are good plain or for making pies, shortcakes, and cobblers.

Green beans   Since green beans aren't very acidic, it is strongly recommended that you use a pressure canner. The risk of botulism runs higher with low-acid foods. However, some folks have canned beans via the boiling-water-bath method for years and are still alive and well to talk about it. If you're willing to take the chance, process beans for an extra-long time (45 minutes). Wash and break beans, bring them to a boil in a pot of water, pack them into sterilized jars, and cover them with the boiling liquid.

Pickled peppers   Pack whole, raw cherry peppers—or slices of banana peppers, or Cubanelles, or any other interesting pepper—into sterilized jars. You can mix sweet and hot peppers. Put one or one and one-half teaspoons pickling salt in each jar. Bring two parts vinegar and one part water to a boil—probably you'll want 2½ cups total for each quart of peppers. Fill the jars with boiling vinegar-water mixture.

Pickled beets   Cook whole beets until they're tender; small ones are best. Leave an inch of stem, and don't cut off the root end or the color will bleed as they cook. Cool and peel. Small beets can be packed whole; larger ones must be sliced or hunked. Put one and one-half teaspoons of pickling salt in each quart jar. Fill the jars with three parts boiling vinegar to one part boiling water. You can sweeten the vinegar if you want, and you can add spices, too.

Processing

After the jars are packed, run a knife around inside each one to release air bubbles. Wipe the rims carefully with a clean, wet cloth, making sure there is at least one-half inch of headroom. Place a clean, hot lid on each jar. Screw on the rings (but not too tightly) as you go along.

At this point, you should check once again to make sure your canner is two-thirds full of water. If not, add more water to the canner and heat until it's very close to the boiling point. Try to warm your jars just a bit before submerging them, as cold jars will break in boiling water. There should be an inch or more of water *above the tops of the jars.* If not, add hot water. Place the lid on the canner, and bring the whole works to a boil.

The exact length of processing time depends on the food. As a general rule, the more acidic the food, the less processing time it takes. Measure the time from when the water begins to boil again, not from when you put the jars in. We process raw, packed tomatoes and sauerkraut for 15 minutes, all pickles for 10 minutes, fruit and fruit sauces for 15 minutes, jams and jellies for only 5 minutes, and green beans for 45 minutes.

When the appropriate time is up, lift the basket and remove the jars. Set them out to cool, leaving some space between the individual jars. Don't mess with the lids. Some rings may be quite loose, but you may lose your seal if you tighten them now.

After they've cooled, check all jars for proper sealing. The lids will be depressed in the center and give off a solid sound when you tap them. Unsealed lids will have some give in the center and sound hollow when you tap them. Often the jars aren't sealed when they come out of the canner, but a vacuum forms as they cool. You'll come to appreciate the little "ping" a lid makes as it seals.

If a jar doesn't seal, it can't be stored, and it's contents must be used or refrigerated. Anything that is supposed to have a firm texture—pickles, beans, fruit slices, sauerkraut—will suffer from a second processing. Soft things can be reprocessed if you want. If few of your jars seal properly, it may be that you're not cleaning the rims thoroughly, or perhaps you're filling the jars too full. On the other hand, you may have purchased some poorly made jar lids, like the ones we bought this summer. For a while we thought we had lost our touch; but when we bought a new batch of lids, every jar sealed nicely.

It's best to store your jars in a cool, dark place . . . but don't let them freeze. We like to keep some of ours visible—they're so pretty!

Inspect your canned goods occasionally to see if anything is noticeably spoiling. Before you open a jar, always check to see if it's still sealed. If not, dispose of the contents. Always smell the food. If it smells bad, if you see any mold or bubbles, or if it seems slimy or overly soft, throw the food away.

PRESSURE CANNING

We can give you some general instructions for pressure canning here, but the most important one is that you follow the directions that come with your own pressure canner. These devices provide much higher temperatures and allow you to can many more foods safely, including meat and fish. Pressure canners are rather expensive. Very often we find that our jars don't seal properly or that a lot of the liquid is lost. If you learn how to use a pressure canner correctly, that shouldn't happen.

The basic procedure goes something like this: Put about an inch and a half of water in the canner, put the jars on the rack provided, cover, and place on high heat. Let steam come out of the vent for seven minutes. Then put the pressure cap on and let the pressure rise to the proper level. Ten (10) pounds of pressure is standard. Reduce the heat slightly to maintain the pressure. *Never leave a pressure canner unattended.* Try to keep the pressure constant and don't bump the kettle around. Uneven pressure or disturbance of the jars can cause the liquid to come out. Remove the canner from the heat when the time is up. Let it cool. Don't remove the pressure cap, and don't try to open the canner until the pressure has dropped to zero. If you do, you'll encounter scalding steam. When the pressure has dropped, out come your goodies, ready for your cupboard shelves.

Pickles

There are two basic approaches to making pickles: brined, which takes a long time, and short-brined, which doesn't.

Brined pickles are fermented for several weeks in crocks. Traditional kosher dills are an example. Often no vinegar is used. At their best, these pickles truly are delicious, but success is not so guaranteed as it is with short-brined or quick-processed pickles.

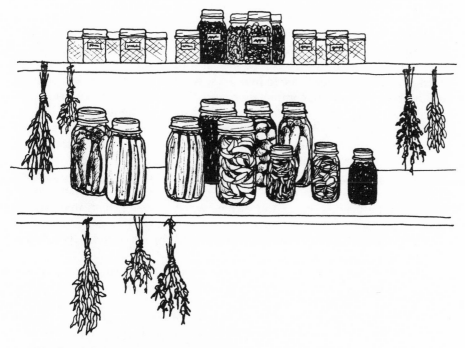

Traditional Brined Pickles: a Recipe

The following recipe was developed from one that appeared in a USDA bulletin, *Making Pickles and Relishes at Home.*

BRINED DILL PICKLES

(Yield: 9 to 10 quarts)

Ingredients

Cucumbers, 3 to 6 inches long, 20 lbs. (about ½ bushel)
Whole mixed pickling spice, ⅔ cup
Dill plant, fresh or dried, 2 to 3 bunches
Vinegar, 2⅓ cups
Kosher or pickling salt, 1¾ cups
Water, 2½ gallons

Cover cucumbers with cold water. Wash thoroughly, using a vegetable brush; handle gently to avoid bruising. Take care to remove any blossoms. Drain on rack or wipe dry.

Place half the pickle spices and a layer of dill in a five-gallon crock or jar. Fill the crock with cucumbers. (Garlic may be added, if it's desired.) Thoroughly mix the vinegar, salt, and water, and pour this mixture over the cucumbers.

Cover with a lid or a plate of heavy china or glass that fits *inside* the crock.

Use a weight to hold the plate down and keep the cucumbers under the brine. (A glass jar filled with water makes a good weight.) Cover loosely with a clean cloth. Keep pickles at room temperature. When scum starts forming in about three to five days, remove it daily. Do not stir pickles, but be sure they are completely covered with brine. If necessary, make additional brine, using original proportions specified above.

In about three weeks, the cucumbers will have assumed an olive-green color and should have developed good flavor. Any white spots inside the fermented cucumbers will disappear in processing.

The original brine is usually cloudy as a result of yeast development during the fermentation period. If this cloudiness is objectionable, fresh brine may be used to cover the pickles when packing them into jars; to make fresh brine, use ½ cup salt and 4 cups vinegar to a gallon of water. The fermentation brine generally is preferred for its added flavor, but it should be strained.

Pack the pickles, along with more of the dill, into clean, hot quart jars. Avoid too tight a pack. Cover with boiling brine to one-half inch from the top of the jar. Adjust jar lids.

Process in boiling water for 15 minutes (start to count the processing time as soon as hot jars are placed into the actively boiling water).

Remove jars and complete seals, if necessary. Set jars upright, several inches apart, on a wire rack to cool.

Processing time will be shorter if you use a pressurized canner. Again, please check your instruction booklet and follow its guidelines carefully.

The Short-Brined Method

Our favorite approach to pickling is the short-brined method, in which the vegetables are brined for only a few hours.

Always use pickling salt or kosher salt. Regular table salt has additives to make it ''free-running''; that's fine for popcorn, but it will cloud or darken your pickles. We prefer cider vinegar for pickling, but some like white vinegar better. Wine vinegar *isn't* suitable. You'll find that vinegar is cheaper by the gallon.

Always use small, firm cucumbers for pickling. Pickling cucumbers are better than slicing cucumbers, because they tend to have denser, less watery flesh. Pickle the cucumbers within hours of harvesting. Wash them carefully, removing the spines and blossom remnants by gentle scrubbing.

If you don't have enough cucumbers at one time to make a full canner of pickles, you can save several days' harvest in a brine. Put the washed cucumbers in a crock (don't use metal) and cover with a salt solution, about ⅔ cup of pickling salt to a gallon of water. Hold the cukes under with a weight, such as a plastic bag filled with water. Add each day's harvest, skimming off any scum that has formed on the brine surface before you put in fresh cukes. If you go on adding cucumbers for more than four or five days, you'll need to add more salt. If things begin to look questionable, pour out the old brine, rinse the cucumbers, add fresh brine. When you have enough cucumbers saved up, rinse and proceed as with fresh ones, eliminating any obvious repetitions.

Here are a few of our favorite recipes. (*Hint:* Allow more than a quart of cucumbers to make a quart of pickles, because they pack together more compactly after they're heated.)

Dill pickles If you have enough small cucumbers (4½ inches maximum), you can make whole dill pickles. Put the scrubbed cucumbers in a brine of ¼ cup pickling salt to a gallon of water and leave them overnight. If the cucumbers are larger, quarter them lengthwise and layer with salt (about ½ cup per 7 quarts of cucumbers) in a large bowl. Cover with ice cubes and let stand for three hours or refrigerate overnight. Drain and rinse.

For 7 quarts of pickles you'll need about 5½ cups of vinegar. Sugar or honey should be to taste—we use only a cup for sour dills. Bring vinegar and sugar or honey to a boil. Put in the brined cukes and heat for five minutes. Pack the cucumbers and brine into sterilized jars, layering with a few fresh dill heads, or add a teaspoon of dill seed per jar. Cap according to our general canning instructions and process for 10 minutes.

Bread-and-butter pickles Slice cucumbers and onions about one-eighth inch thick. For seven quarts of pickles, six quarts of cucumbers and two of onions is about right. You can include bits of cauliflower, broccoli, sweet peppers, or carrots, if you like. Put the vegetables in a large bowl, sprinkling each layer with salt, using about one-half cup in all. Cover with ice cubes and let stand for three hours. It's okay just to refrigerate them without ice, but the finished pickle may not be quite so crisp. Drain. Bring almost to a boil a mixture of vinegar (5 or 5½ cups), brown sugar or honey to taste (we use ½ to 2 cups), turmeric (2 teaspoons), and pickling spices (2 tablespoons). Heat the vegetables in the hot vinegar for 5 minutes, pack in jars, cover with hot vinegar mixture and process for 10 minutes. We sometimes add a few fresh grape leaves, which supposedly make the pickles crisper.

Pickled peaches To make 7 quarts, you'll need about 10 quarts of whole peaches. Peel the peaches raw. For easier peeling, you can dip them into scalding water for a minute. Boil 2 quarts of vinegar, a quart of water, and 4 to 6 cups of sugar for about 15 minutes. Spice with 2 tablespoons whole cloves, if desired. Add the whole peeled peaches a couple of quarts at a time to the boiling syrup, heat for five minutes, and pack into sterilized jars. Cover the fruit with boiling syrup, cap, and process for 15 minutes.

Sauerkraut   Traditionally, sauerkraut is made by the long-brined method in a large crock. We've had more success using quart jars and a *modified* brining method. Discard outer leaves and slice cabbage into very fine slivers. Pack into sterilized jars, adding a tablespoon of pickling salt per jar. Cover with boiling water. Cap with rings and lids, but put the lids on *upside down*, so the rubber seal isn't touching the jar rim. Store for about two weeks in a place where the temperature remains around 70°F. Then open a jar and see if the kraut is tart and tangy. If not, let it ferment for another week. But don't let it rot. When the fermentation is complete, remove any soft or dark cabbage at the surface, wash the lids and rims, and cap the jars properly. Put into hot (not boiling) water, bring to a boil, and process for 15 minutes.

Fruit Preserves

From most fruits, we prefer to make jams rather than jellies because jams give you more volume for the amount of fruit you preserve. The exceptions are those small, seedy fruits that require lots of preparation—grapes, beach plums, rose hips, currants, cherries.

Usually we cook the fruits down until they gel instead of using additional pectin, which causes quicker gelling. But there's an exception here, too: you will get brighter, fresher-tasting preserves from delicate berries (like strawberries and raspberries) if you do use pectin, thus reducing cooking time. We think apple, grape, quince, blackberry, and pear all are better when cooked down, but that's personal preference. If you don't use pectin, always include some underripe fruits; normally they're higher in natural pectin. In this section you'll find three of our favorite recipes. You can find good recipes for jams and jellies in nearly every cookbook, although most of these turn out to be too sweet for our tastes.

If you use commercial pectins (Sure-Jell® and Certo® are two), follow their instructions. Ones intended for dietetic jellies let you get by with a lot less sugar, and they taste better.

To make homemade pectin, cover unpeeled, uncored apple slices or hunks with water and cook until they're soft. Line a colander with a double layer of cheesecloth or a thick kitchen towel. Strain the juice out of the apples; you can stir and mash a little, but not too much. Boil the juice down to make a strong syrup; three quarts of juice should be reduced to about two *cups* of syrup. This boiled-down syrup is your pectin. Freeze for future use, or process for five minutes in ½-pint jars. Use ½ to ¼ cup of the prepared pectin to help low-acid fruits to gel. Add the pectin to the fruit or juice before you add the sugar.

You can use honey instead of sugar for preserves, but try to find a light one that doesn't completely overpower the taste of the fruit.

For proper gelling, always cook fruit in small batches—no more than four or five cups per pot. And use a pot with a capacity at least double that of the amount you're cooking, because you must have enough room for a rolling boil. The possible exception is when you preserve things like pears, apples, or quinces; you actually just simmer these fruits down until they're thick.

We favor the use of pint jars for preserves. Quarts are okay for big households; half-pints are good for special treats, like wild strawberries.

Some preserves produce a lot of foam while they're cooking. As children, some of us loved to eat the foam as it was skimmed from the jam.

Here are the recipes we promised.

Grape jelly We're fortunate enough to have lots of wild grapes on Cape Cod. They make very good jelly. Pick the grapes off the bunches, including a few underripe ones. Put about a cup of water into a big pot full of grapes. Mash and squeeze the grapes with your hands to release the juices. Bring the grapes to a pretty high heat, but don't boil them. (The seeds seem to give off a bitter taste when they're boiled.) Simmer for about 10 minutes. Strain through a colander. For a clearer jelly, line the collander with a cloth. Put four cups of juice in a large pot with two cups of sugar. Bring to a rolling boil and keep it there until the mixture gels when you drop a bit on a cold plate. A jelly thermometer will show a temperature of about 220°F at this point. It usually takes 15 minutes for our grape jelly to gel, but it really depends on the quality of the fruit and the amounts of water and sugar. Pour the hot jelly into sterilized jars. Because it's clear, grape jelly doesn't require processing. You can cap the jars and then turn them upside down for a few minutes. Right the jars and the lids should click down as they cool.

An excellent apple jelly can be made by this same method, using just the peels to make the apple juice. The flesh can be used for sauce, pies, or whatever.

Quince jam We use the fruits of the flowering quince or japonica to make our favorite jam. A nearby arboretum has a large collection of flowering quinces and some varieties produce fruits as large as small lemons. We're fortunate to have access to them. This jam is time-consuming, but worthwhile.

Pare off all unblemished portions of the hard fruits. We don't peel them. Put about five cups of good fruit into a pot with just enough water to see it through the surface of the cut-up fruit. This fruit is extremely sour and will devour frightening quantities of sugar before it's sweet enough; probably you'll want to start with equal parts sugar and fruit, and you may add more. Cook until the fruit is a clear orangish color and there is very little liquid. It will burn quite easily as it gets thick and sticky, so stir frequently and turn the heat down.

Pack into sterilized jars; process for five minutes. If you have a good bit of jelly around the fruit pieces, you can just turn the jars upside down, as we described in the grape jelly recipe. For blackberries, pears, and peaches, use the same method of cooking down the fruit with sugar until it's thick, but the jars should be processed.

Beach-plum jelly   Beach plums are native to Cape Cod and are found along our roadsides and places with poor soil, as well as near the beaches. There are good cultivated varieties, too; beach plums are not reserved for seacoast dwellers only.

Wash the beach plums and place them in a large pot with just enough water to show through. Mash them up, bring to a boil, and cook about 10 minutes. Strain through a colander lined with a cloth, squeezing to get the last of the juice out. Put four cups of juice in a large pot and add one-half cup of homemade apple pectin. Bring to a boil; after a couple of minutes, add two cups of sugar. Boil until gelling state is reached—that is, 220°F or when the juice "sets-up" when a bit is dropped on a cold plate. Fill sterilized jars, process for five minutes, or use the upside-down-jar method.

Drying

Sun drying is no doubt the oldest and most obvious way to preserve food. Many familiar foods dry naturally—grains, beans, and seeds, for example.

Drying removes water from the food, which means that decomposition can't proceed. Dry foods are greatly reduced in bulk, are light in weight, and are easy to store. Logically, foods that are low in natural moisture are easier to dry than high-moisture foods are.

Commercially manufactured electric dryers are available. It's possible to build one yourself or simply use your oven. The form of drying that interests us most is sun drying. The sun is a free energy source—it's up to you to take advantage of it. Of course, sun drying means you are dependent on good weather for successful preservation. A series of cloudy days will foil your efforts and you may have to resort to the oven or wood stove or hot attic to finish your current batch of food.

Even though drying is one of the simpler methods of food preservation, you may find it more limited in appeal than canning or freezing your

crops. The success in drying lies in knowing which foods respond well. Certain foods are a sure success; apples, pears, apricots, onion rings, hot peppers, mature beans and peas, corn, seedless grapes, and herbs for spices and teas. Stick to these at the beginning. They don't demand any additional steps, such as blanching. Chips of many other vegetables are nice for camping, for soups, and for use with dips: zucchini, carrots, beets, sweet potatoes, pumpkins, and even tomatoes. These vegetables (except tomatoes) should be blanched before drying, however, to prevent further ripening. So should juicier fruits, like peaches and plums. Generally, steam blanching is better than submerging in boiling water because the steam doesn't get the food as wet. Blanch until the color clarifies; ten minutes is standard blanching time.

All foods should be sliced as thinly as possible, so they'll dry quickly and evenly. It's not necessary to peel most fruits. Removing herb leaves from the stems before drying makes for easier flaking or powdering later. Sometimes stems can become so brittle after drying it is hard to keep from breaking them up with the leaves.

The simplest form of sun drying is just laying things out in the sun. They can be spread on clean sheets of fabric or put between two screens. To keep flies and animals away, cover things that are drying outdoors. (A well-known herbal tea company once held a heated staff meeting to determine whether or not they were ''mistreating'' their customers by having such a high content of chicken manure in their teas. The teas were being dried on the ground in African villages. We're not sure what they finally decided. . . .)

Hot peppers can be strung and dried whole.

As night falls, be sure to bring your semidried produce inside or it will reabsorb a lot of moisture.

For many foods, screened or slatted shelves in a dry outbuilding will provide adequate drying conditions. We've hung old window screens in our sheds and always complete the drying of beans there. Probably you won't get total drying for the really hard-to-dry foods this way. After three days of inside drying, food should be put in the oven for a short time, just to make sure it's completely dry. When you turn the oven off after baking, there's enough heat left for this kind of final drying.

Herbs should not be dried in direct sunlight. A cheesecloth covering is adequate; herbs also dry well stuck into a paper bag with the mouth of the bag tied around the stems. Hang up the bag in a dry, well-ventilated place. Greens can be dried like herbs. One New Alchemist makes large quantities of vegetable seasoning for salads and soups by drying all types of greens (kale, chard, beet greens, and parsley), powdering them, and storing them in jars. It's rather salty, even though no salt is added.

The surest method of sun drying is using a solar dryer. You can build your own; the Rodale Press has published plans that include actual blueprints along with step-by-step instructions (see Resources at the end of this chapter).

One visitor to our farm told us that in summer she uses her cold frame for drying. If you do this, be sure to vent the frame during the day to let the moisture escape; then close it up at night. The vents on solar dryers should be closed at night, too.

Most foods take two to four days to dry, depending on the weather. Fruits and vegetables will tend to be pliable but tough when they're dry. They shouldn't stick together when you squeeze a small handful. Onion bits will be crispy. Herb leaves should powder readily. If they don't seem ready after three days, finish them in a warm oven or they may lose their strength. Cool before packing. Foods should be stored airtight. Plastic bags really aren't adequate; jars or tins are best.

Root Cellaring and Storage

Root cellaring, sometimes known as "common storage," is the simplest of all food-preservation methods. A root cellar is any cool, moist place where vegetables can be stored unprocessed. It doesn't have to be a "cellar" in the basement sense. The broad spectrum of common storage includes outdoor pits and mounds; barrels buried in straw; vegetables left in the ground, well-mulched with hay, straw, or leaves; barrels or boxes in the garage, with vegetables buried in sand or sawdust; cellar storage rooms; and even a sauna.[2] See Fig. 2 for an example of a typical root cellar.

Crops suitable for common storage include potatoes and sweet potatoes, turnips, carrots, beets, parsnips, winter squash and pumpkins, cabbages, apples, pears, green tomatoes, and onions. Only undamaged, unblemished specimens are candidates for this type of storage.

Store only late crops. Storage life is limited, and food stored early will not last throughout the winter. Plus, common storage relies on the natural occurrence of cold weather for cooling the storage area. It's best to do some late plantings, targeted especially for storage. Plant these crops in confined areas where they won't interfere with your fall field preparation. Certain varieties are especially adaptable to storage; catalog descriptions will help you choose the right ones.

The simplest method is to leave root crops in the ground and mulch them heavily to prevent freezing. Carrots and parsnips and leeks store well this way. Beets don't do as well, because their tops protrude from the ground and freeze. Use 9–12 inches of mulch and make sure it will stay in place. Fresh leaves must be covered with some other material or they will blow away. Eventually the ground will freeze too hard for you to dig the vegetables out; but after it thaws, you'll still have some usable food. Jerusalem artichokes are sweet and crisp in the early spring, even without mulching.

A garbage can or wooden barrel or box can be buried in the ground below the frost line. It's easiest to do this by digging back into a hill. Make sure there is good drainage away from the container. Tip barrels forward. Put in a layer of clean straw or leaves or shredded paper first, then a single layer of vegetables, then another layer of packing material, and repeat the process until the storage container is full. Close the lid and cover with an easily removable mulch bag of leaves or bales or straw. All root crops that need cool, moist conditions do well this way, as do apples.

Cabbages and celery can be stored in insulated trenches in the garden, though we've never done it ourselves. This will preserve them only until deep-freezing weather. Dig a trench about two feet deep. Replant celery or cabbages close together in the trench. Make a slightly pitched roof by leaning a wide board over on the side of the trench and mulch heavily with an easily removable mulch.

An ideal root cellar has a fairly constant cool temperature (just above freezing) and a moist, dirt floor. A house cellar that has a furnace in it may be too warm. You could solve that problem by partitioning off one section and insulating to keep it cooler. On the other hand, your cellar can also get too cold. In some cases, a cool upstairs storage room is perfect. The entry stairway from the outside to an otherwise too-warm basement may be just right; so may an unheated room or a closed-in porch.

Here are some of the guidelines we follow at New Alchemy for root cellaring:

Apples and pears Wrap individually in paper and store in boxes or baskets. Choose late storage varieties.

Beets Store in boxes with clean, damp sand or sawdust. We use an old refrigerator liner. Alternate single layers of beets with enough sand (or sawdust) to cover completely.

Cabbage To store in a root cellar, pull late cabbages up by the roots, "paper" the outer leaves by sunning them directly for a couple of days and covering them over at night. Hang them by their roots in the cellar. Or, cut and remove damaged outer leaves and wrap individual heads in paper; or layer with clean, dry straw in airy bins or baskets. Cabbages often have a strong smell (which becomes especially unpleasant if they rot) so you probably won't want to store them in a spare room.

Cauliflower Store like cabbages, individually wrapped, in bins and baskets.

Fig. 2 Root cellar

Carrots If not mulched in the ground, store in clean, damp sand or sawdust.

Onions Dry for several days to a week in direct sun, a warm outbuilding, or an attic. Remove to a cooler place and store in net bags or airy baskets. You can braid the tops together to form a beautiful bunch to hang. Yellow-skinned varieties tend to store better.

Parsnips Best after a frost. Mulch in the ground or store in sand or sawdust.

Potatoes Dry in an attic or other warm place for several days before removing to cooler storage. Keep away from light or they'll turn green and be mildly poisonous. Store in airy baskets or bins. Some people bury them in the cellar with straw or sawdust between layers.

Table 9.1 *Freezing Points, Recommended Storage Conditions, and Length of Storage Period of Vegetables and Fruits*

COMMODITY	FREEZING POINT °F	PLACE TO STORE
VEGETABLES:		
Dry beans and peas		Any cool, dry place
Late cabbage	30.4	Pit, trench, or outdoor cellar
Cauliflower	30.3	Storage cellar
Late celery	31.6	Pit or trench, roots in soil in storage cellar
Endive	31.9	Roots in soil in storage cellar
Onions	30.6	Any cool, dry place
Parsnips	30.4	Where they grew, or in storage cellar
Peppers	30.7	Unheated basement or room
Potatoes	30.9	Pit or in storage cellar
Pumpkins and squashes	30.5	Home cellar or basement
Root crops (miscellaneous)		Pit or in storage cellar
Sweet potatoes	29.7	Home cellar or basement
Tomatoes (mature)	31.0	Same as above
(green)		Same as above
FRUITS:		
Apples	29.0	Fruit storage cellar
Grapefruit	29.8	Same as above
Grapes	28.1	Same as above
Oranges	30.5	Same as above
Pears	29.2	Same as above

Reprinted from: *Home Storage of Vegetables and Fruits* by Evelyn V. Loveday, Garden Way Publishing, Inc., Charlotte, VT, 1972. With permission.

Squash and pumpkins   Harvest after a light frost. Cure for several days in a warm dry place before removing to cooler storage. Storage life is shortened by temperatures below 50°F. Check carefully for borers before storing.

Sweet potatoes   Frost will cause sweet potatoes to rot. Should be cured at 85°F for a week for best storage. A solar dryer may do it; so may a spot near the wood stove or above the furnace. Store in baskets or bins.

Green tomatoes   Pick before frost; frost-damaged ones will rot, not ripen.

STORAGE CONDITIONS		LENGTH OF
TEMPERATURE °F	HUMIDITY	STORAGE PERIOD
32° to 40°	Dry	As long as desired
Near 32° as possible	Moderately moist	Through late fall and winter
Same as above	Same as above	6 to 8 weeks
Same as above	Same as above	Through late fall and winter
Same as above	Same as above	2 to 3 months
Same as above	Dry	Through fall and winter
Same as above	Moist	Same as above
45° to 50°	Moderately moist	2 to 3 weeks
35° to 40°	Same as above	Through fall and winter
55°	Moderately dry	Same as above
Near 32° as possilbe	Moist	Same as above
55° to 60°	Moderately dry	Same as above
55° to 70°	Same as above	4 to 6 weeks
Near 32°as possible	Moderately moist	Through fall and winter
Same as above	Same as above	4 to 6 weeks
Same as above	Same as above	1 to 2 months
Same as above	Same as above	4 to 6 weeks
Same as above	Same as above	4 to 6 weeks

Store in single layers where you can check them easily for ripening. Bring in a few at a time to ripen in sunny windows. (Fried green tomatoes are delicious. Slice your completely green fruits about one-quarter inch thick, dredge in flour, and fry until nicely brown.)

No matter how careful you've been, there's always the possibility that some rotting may occur. Check often for this. Be prepared also to deal with any rodents that take a liking to your storage area.

Table 1 shows at a glance the recommended storage conditions for common fruits and vegetables.

REFERENCES

---

1. HERTZBERG, RUTH, *et al. Putting Food By*. New York: Bantam Books, 1975, p. 303.

2. LOVEDAY, EVELYN V. *Home Storage of Vegetables and Fruits*. Charlotte Vermont: Garden Way Publishing Co., 1972.

RESOURCES

For additional details on preserving fruits and vegetables, and for information for preserving meats, fish and dairy products, we recommend the following books:

HERTZBERG, RUTH,*et al. Putting Food By*. New York: Bantam Books, 1975.

Loveday, Evelyn. *The Home Storage of Vegetables and Fruits*. Charlotte, VT: Garden Way Publishing Co., 1972

Rombauer, Irma, and Marion Becker. *The Joy of Cooking*. New York: New American Library, 1974.

Stoner, Carol (ed.). *Stocking Up*. Emmaus, PA: Rodale Press, 1974.

Wolf, Ray (ed.). *Solar Food Dryer*. Emmaus, PA: Rodale Plans, Rodale Press, 1981.

The U.S. Department of Agriculture Extension Service offers a number of useful food-preservation bulletins.

Hang braided garlic and onions in a cool place.

Chapter 10

Recycling Nutrients in Your Home Food System

Earle Barnhart

Throughout the previous nine chapters, we have presented a number of techniques designed to help you produce more of your own food. We don't expect that you'll plunge immediately into the process of implementing all of them. We do hope that you'll select and try out the systems and approaches that are appropriate to your home site and your family's preferences. We believe that if everyone produces even a small fraction of their own food, the net national and global result will be dramatic—and that ultimately our nation's dependence on an ecologically unsound and shortsighted agricultural industry will be reduced.

As a home food producer you'll do more than just provide a few calories or grams of your family's food. You'll be responsible for effecting a subtle change in the disaster-bound course that is our current national food system. You'll be taking steps to ensure that something will be left on this planet for your children and grandchildren.

Using the basic techniques we've described in this book may be only the beginning of a greater adventure. When you begin to combine and integrate individual food-growing methods, your apartment or home can be even more productive. As you produce increasing amounts of your own food, you'll become more aware of the nutrient and energy flows that are vital to a home food system. And as your proficiency develops, you'll find that you can recycle these basic materials to reduce your net costs and increase your production. A classic example of this is our current work with hydroponics. Our original solar-algae pond aquaculture system produced about one pound of fish for every pound of fish feed. Now, as we are learning to reuse the fish wastes as fertilizer for hydroponic vegetable growing, we find we can produce one pound of fish *plus* two pounds of vegetables for every pound of fish feed we use.

In this chapter, Earle Barnhart describes how the notion of recycling nutrients and energy can enhance your food-production system. Earle is eminently qualified to write about this subject. A New Alchemy staff member since 1971, he has worked in almost every area of research here. He is a true believer in and practitioner of the fine art of integrated food systems. Earle's and Hilde's backyard is a veritable edible landscape: solar greenhouse, chicken yard, tree crops, bamboo patch, perennial plot, vegetable garden, and beehives. Earle has designed integrated food systems in urban and rural locations around the world, from Boston to Barbados and the Philippines. And perhaps most important, he possesses an intuitive ability to see the "wastes" of one system as the "fuels" for another—a sense that we all must work hard to develop.

THE EDITORS

Guidelines

ANY FOOD-PRODUCTION SYSTEM requires a constant supply of nutrients to help sustain food plants and animals. In addition, every system creates wastes. The key to self sufficiency lies in knowing how to recycle those wastes to provide your nutrients. In a well-designed system, nutrients move from plants, to animals (including human consumers), to organisms that break down organic materials, and then *back* to plants to complete the cycle. It is crucial to remember that the wastes from one process are often the raw materials for another. Once you're aware of this, you can establish your own nutrient cycles.

The key to efficient nutrient recycling is a careful examination of the various pathways by which food and wastes move through your home.

Think about your many daily activities involving food and wastes:

- You spend time working to get money to buy food.
- You spend time and money to travel to stores and transport food home.
- You collect kitchen scraps in a garbage can, which you carry out to the street periodically.
- Your own wastes are piped away through the sewer or a septic system.

The challenge is to use the same (or less) effort and energy to keep nutrients in home food cycles where they contribute to food production.

One way to start is by considering the costs of *transportation* in the conventional home food system. We often import nutrients and export wastes. For example, here on Cape Cod many people expend time and money to have garden and lawn fertilizers brought from half-way around the world to provide their gardens, shrubs, and trees with nutrients. Simultaneously, they expend additional time and money to have their daily food wastes, summer grass clippings, and annual autumn leaves hauled to the dump and buried. This is ecological madness! The same or less effort could be used to compost or otherwise recycle local garbage, leaves, and grass clippings.

Converting wastes to resources in your home food system depends on relatively *short-term nutrient processing*. Consider some of the options from which you can choose:

- Clean food scraps can be used in soups for an immediate recovery of nutrients.
- Food scraps can be fed to chickens to produce eggs within a day or two.
- Vegetable scraps and some lawn clippings and leaves can be added to worm beds. Worms can be fed to chickens, which in turn produce eggs. This process takes one or two months.
- Worm castings can be added to greenhouse or garden soils and the nutrients recovered as vegetables within a few months.
- Vegetable wastes, lawn clippings, leaves, and animal manures can be composted. Fresh vegetables can be harvested a few months to a year later.
- Compost and worm castings can be used to fertilize food-producing trees that provide fruit a few years after planting.
- Nutrient-rich water from fish ponds can be used to irrigate vegetable and tree crops.

Sometimes the recycling of useful nutrients is not easily separated from the recycling of unwanted materials. Not all organic materials are interchangeable. In fact, some materials within your home ecosystem may be toxic to one component of your system but not to others. *Toxic* may mean deadly, but it may also imply merely a negative effect, such as poor seed germination, slowed plant growth, or poor appetite in an animal. Toxins may be produced industrially—heavy metals, pesticides, pollution in rain—or they may occur naturally in the form of highly acid or alkaline products, disease pathogens, and natural poisons.

As we stressed in earlier chapters, it's essential to use nontoxic materials and paints for worm boxes, planting containers, and fish-tank equipment. Some preservatives will not only kill the plants, worms, or fish in the container, but also gradually release toxins that eventually end up in *your* food and *your* body.

As for natural toxins, you can avoid most problems by learning from the experiences of others. Examples of natural products that must be carefully recycled include the following:

- Tree leaves, such as those of the black walnut, which will stunt or damage many other plants.
- Wood ashes, which in high concentrations will damage plants and salt the soil.
- Fresh, nitrogen-rich manure, which causes some vegetables to be soft and more prone to aphid damage.

Since human wastes contain a special group of toxins—human disease organisms—they are more difficult to use in the home food system. Urine may be diluted and applied safely as a supplemental nitrogen-rich fertilizer. Research on composting toilets continues, and some people successfully use the end-product of the composting process as fertilizer for fruit trees. Still, one can't be certain that disease organisms have been destroyed. Human-waste composting remains an important problem of ecological agriculture, and until an effective small-scale waste-treatment method is proven, nutrients in human feces are generally unavailable for home recycling.

Much useful information is available in *The Integral Urban House* written by staff members of the Farallones Institute in Berkeley, California. They detail various techniques for recycling plant materials, human wastes, lawn clippings, water, and so on. (This and other useful books are listed in the Resource section at the end of the chapter.)

Examples of Integrated Home Food Systems

The extent to which you close up nutrient cycles depends on a few variables. The most important of these is your own creativity in learning to turn your wastes into resources and in designing systems that truly integrate your home food production.

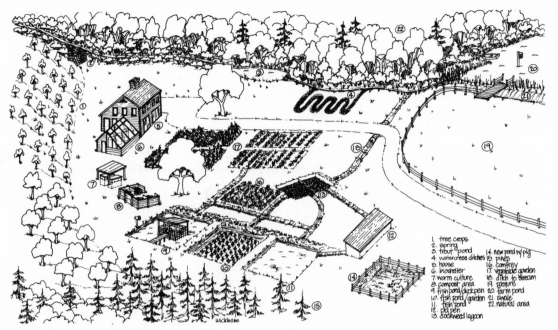

1. tree crops
2. spring
3. trout pond
4. watercress ditches
5. house
6. bioshelter
7. worm culture
8. compost area
9. fish pond/duck pen
10. fish pond/garden
11. fish pond
12. pig pen
13. duckweed lagoon
14. new pond w/pig
15. pines
16. comfrey
17. vegetable garden
18. ditch to stream
19. pasture
20. farm pond
21. swale
22. natural area

Fig. 1 Rural integrated aquaculture/agriculture farm

Another important variable is where you live. If you live in an urban setting, your options will be very different from those of a farm dweller. In this section, we'll describe ways in which diverse food production can be designed to take advantage of careful nutrient cycling and special *polycultures* (more than one species). It's likely that one of them will make sense in your area. To gain a full understanding of the many ways in which integrated agricultural ecosystems can be fabricated for various climates and soils, study the conceptual models presented here and seek out some real-life examples, as well.

RURAL HOMES

Figure 1 shows a farm-sized landscape that integrates aquaculture, agriculture, and livestock production. This farm, conceptualized by William McLarney, is designed to take particular advantage of the nearby stream of water (keyed as area 2 in the figure). The purest water from the stream is used to grow trout (area 3) and watercress (area 4). Fertilizers are added at other locations to grow fish and animal foods in special nutrient-rich ponds (areas 9, 10, and 11). The pigs, chickens, and gardens are shifted from one pond site to another to do automatically the work of distributing manures and collecting feeds. Other animal feeds are grown—note the comfrey (area 16) and duckweed (area 13). Finally, aquatic plants are used to extract excess nutrients from the intensively used water before it is returned to its natural course.

Fig. 2 Suburban agri-
cultural landscaping.
Earle Barnhart, illus-
trator.

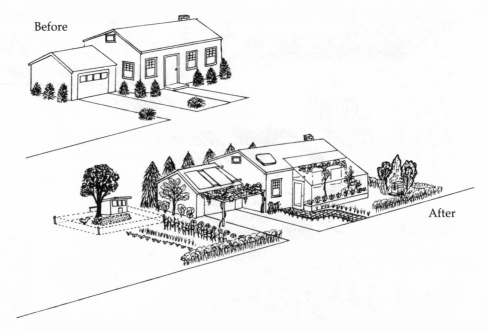

Fig. 2 Suburban agricultural landscaping. Earle Barnhart, illustrator.

For a more complete description of this farmscape, see the *New Alchemy Quarterly No. 11,* ''The Integration of Aquaculture and Agriculture in the Northern United States.''

SUBURBAN HOMES

Nearly *all* of a suburban landscape can be devoted to home food production. Don't base the extent of your efforts on how much open yard space exists. Suburban food production can be increased dramatically by using available space above driveways and against buildings. Figure 2 shows how these areas can be planted with climbing vines and tree crops. (Note also that this model provides some year-round solar and wind-insulation features.)

Chickens are the primary recyclers of food and plant wastes in this landscape. These wastes are placed in the chicken yard to be eaten immediately or composted gradually into the soil. Periodically, the enriched topsoil in the chicken yard is moved to the garden vegetables or landscape plants as fertilizer. Alternatively, every two years the chickens could be moved to the garden plot and the old chicken yard could be used for gardening. Managed this way, a standard-sized suburban landscape can provide a significant percentage of a family's basic food needs.

The Village Concept

Not every suburbanite lives in a single-family house set on a substantial lot, nor does every city dweller inhabit a high-rise apartment building.

Fig. 3 Village food production: ecological integration. Paul Sun, illustrator.

Somewhere between these extremes are vast numbers of neighborhoods, developments, and condominium settings that lend themselves perfectly to the concept of community gardens and greenhouses. Here, of course, you need more than just food-production expertise: You must be willing to work cooperatively with others and, if necessary, to organize a project.

A village model such as the one shown in Fig. 3 can take control of a commonly overlooked resource—the street. Here, alternate street or neighborhood cores have been redesigned to house small fish farms, raised-bed vegetable and berry production plots, plus fruit and nut trees. Some of the space may be used for community food gardening, while trees, aquatic facilities, and growing beds can be leased to urban farmers who tend and locally market the crops. Obviously, this type of system takes time, dedication, and cooperation. But it can be done, and its rewards are well worth the effort.

URBAN HOMES

In an urban situation you may feel that your food-production options are limited. The fact is, they're simply less obvious. Community gardens thrive on vacant lots and rooftops in many cities, and there are plenty of ways in which wastes can be turned into resources. For example, there is no shortage of materials to be composted or fed into worm beds. You can accumulate restaurant scraps, street leaves, horse manure (try police stables), and grass clippings, in addition to your own kitchen garbage.

Urban areas do tend to have higher concentrations of air pollution and industrial debris than found elsewhere. This includes toxic lead from paint chips and automobile exhaust. Special precautions can be taken in your choice of food plants, preparation of crops, and long-term soil management to minimize the amount of lead and other pollutants that are ultimately eaten. Contact your local urban gardening association for advice.

IN CONCLUSION

Anyone (rural, suburban, or urban dweller) can preserve food and practice indoor gardening and worm culture. As you become conscious of both your resources and your wastes, you'll begin to see them as interchangeable. That's when the nutrient flows become nutrient cycles—and the challenge of self-reliance, for everyone, for all seasons, becomes a possibility.

RESOURCES

FARALLONES INSTITUTE. *The Integral Urban House: Self-Reliant Living in the City.* San Francisco: Sierra Club Books, 1979.

McCLARNEY, WILLIAM., and PETER BURGOON. ''The Integration of Aquaculture and Agriculture in the Northern United States,'' *New Alchemy Quarterly No. 11,* Spring, 1983. New Alchemy Institute, 237 Hatchville Rd., East Falmouth, MA 02536.

MOLLISON, BILL, and DAVID HOLMGREN. *Permaculture One, A Perennial Agriculture for Human Settlements.* Melbourne, Australia: Transworld Publishers Ltd., 1978.

TILTH INFORMATION SERVICE, 13217 Mattson Rd., Arlington, WA 98223.

TODD, JOHN, and NANCY JACK TODD (EDS.). *The Village as Solar Ecology.* New Alchemy Institute, 237 Hatchville Rd., East Falmouth, MA 02536, 1980.

Afterword

Well, you're on your own now.

In this book, we have tried to give you enough information to get started on the road to food self-reliance. If our Resource suggestions and Bibliography listings don't provide answers for the inevitable questions that will arise, please don't hesitate to write us—or better, to *visit*—at our Cape Cod center. Our full-time research and educational staff host internships, offer tours, and teach courses on these and many other topics year round. If it's not convenient to drop in, our membership program provides a handy and accessible way to keep in constant touch.

This book summarizes many years of research and practical experience at New Alchemy Institute. We hope you have found it useful and that, in time, you will pass along your ideas and knowledge about home food production to your neighbors and friends. The power to sustain ourselves and to meet our basic needs is within us all. If we work together, we can regain control of our food systems before it is too late. And let us all be mindful of that simple Chinese saying: *You can give someone a fish, and feed them for a day—or teach someone to fish, and feed them for life.*

Good luck!

THE EDITORS

About the New Alchemy Institute

The New Alchemy Institute is a small, nonprofit organization with twelve years of experience in the research and education of renewable resource technologies. Our goal has been to design and test human support systems—food, energy, shelter—that are environmentally sound and economically efficient. We favor strategies that minimize reliance on fossil fuels and that operate on an economic scale accessible to families and small enterprises.

Our Cape Cod Center is comprised of 22 (more or less) full-time researchers, educators, designers, and craftspeople. Many of us devote part of each year to working in other parts of the world, including our Costa Rica Center (NAISA). Our international work is carried out in the hope that our research and our experience can be used by large numbers of people in diverse regions of the world.

Our first decade of work has focused largely on the research and development of technologies that support low-cost, year-round food production and energy-efficient shelter design. Our work in biological agriculture, wind technology, and solar design is well known and has been supported by the U.S. Departments of Energy and Agriculture, the Environmental Protection Agency, the Solar Energy Research Institute, the National Science Foundation, and a broad range of private foundations. Our solar aquaculture research is widely reported in U.S. and international scientific literature and has been the focus of visits by senior scientists and dignitaries from all parts of the globe.

Perhaps the most dramatic aspect of our work has been the integration of these sciences, as in our bioshelters. Bioshelters are solar-heated buildings that link a variety of biological elements in new, productive ecosystems. We were among the first to develop solar greenhouses that incorporated both aquaculture and agriculture.

Our small, twelve-acre Cape Cod Center has been visited by over 100,000 people. Recently, the Institute has been pressed to provide comprehensive technical information to large numbers of energy-conscious regional, national, and international constituents. We have responded by broadening our research focus to include an extensive agenda of outreach and educational activities. In addition to our summer Saturday workshop program (over 7000 visitors in 1980), we now run a year-round group tour program that serves students, senior citizens, and others. Our recently introduced summer series of full-day specialty courses is a booming success, providing information on all of our work for people of all ages. Our apprenticeship program serves approximately 40 people each year.

The decade ahead will be a difficult one. Fuel costs continue to rise as fossil fuel reserves dwindle. Each day we are reminded of serious new toxic threats to the environment and to human health. The New Alchemy Institute is convinced of an urgent need to create new support systems that are inexpensive, productive, and environmentally sustainable.

The Institute is nonprofit and tax-exempt and derives its support from private contributions and research grants. Grants for our scientific research are often available, but adequate funding for general support remains uncertain. The success of the Institute will depend on our ability to address ourselves to the genuine needs of people working on behalf of themselves and the earth, and on the realization by our friends that financial support of our research is essential if the task ahead is to be accomplished.

The New Alchemy Institute has an Associate Membership available to those interested in helping support our work. Upon joining, Associates receive the *Journal of the New Alchemists* No. 7. The Institute Quarterly and other special interest mailings sent throughout the year keep Associates further informed of the work in progress. Over the years, the support of our Associates has been critical to the continuance of the Institute and its work.

Associate Membership for individuals and families is $35 per annum (tax deductible). Contributions of larger amounts are very much needed and appreciated. Contributing Membership is $50 per annum; Sustaining Membership is $100 per annum; Sponsor is $250 per annum; Patron is $500 per annum; and Life Membership is $1000.

Friends wishing to have their membership payments qualify as a deductible contribution under the tax regulations of Canada should make Canadian dollar payments payable to The New Alchemy Institute (P.E.I.) Inc. All other membership contributions should be made payable to The New Alchemy Institute. Because of the costs involved with collection charges and currency exchange, we ask that all payments to The New Alchemy Institute, except for Canadian membership, be in the form of United States dollar instruments, preferably International Money Orders.

We invite you to join us as members of The New Alchemy Institute. A company of individuals addressing themselves to the future can, perhaps, make a difference during these years when there is waning reason to have hope in the continuance of human history.

Gary Hirshberg, Executive Director
The New Alchemy Institute
237 Hatchville Road
East Falmouth, MA 02536

Contributing Staff

Merryl Alber, contributing editor and co-author of Chapters 1 & 5 grew up in New York State and received her B.S. in Zoology/Botany from Duke University in 1981. She came to New Alchemy that year as part of our Education program. Merryl has worked in all Institute program areas, but her primary responsibilities as Education Coordinator involve directing our tour, course, and intern programs, and assisting the publications program. Her interests include outdoor gardening, biological pest control, and telling horrible jokes.

Colleen Armstrong is New Alchemy's premier Bioshelter Horticulturist and a renowned expert on biological pest control in solar greenhouses. She grew up in suburban Detroit and studied at the University of Michigan. In 1975 she traveled to Massachusetts for a two-year Jekyll-and-Hyde existence at a large greenhouse-nursery complex: by day she sprayed insecticides and fungicides on ornamental plants, and by night she gardened organically in her own backyard. She joined the Institute in 1977. When not managing the New Alchemy bioshelters, she teaches courses, gives lectures, and writes articles and books. Colleen lives with her beautiful son, Linden, and loves to dance.

Denise Backus grew up in rural Maine, attended a one-room country schoolhouse for seven years, graduated in 1955 from Northfield School, and received her B.A. in English from The Women's College of the University of North Carolina in 1959. After 10 years in various cities, she and her two children moved to Woods Hole, where she worked at the Woods Hole Oceanographic Institute, first as a laboratory assistant in the Biology department and later in the Education office. In 1979 she came to New Alchemy Institute to manage the office, and since 1982 has been serving as Administrative Director. She lives in Woods Hole with her husband, some of their five children, and a colorful assortment of chickens.

Earle Barnhart, contributing editor and author of Chapter 10, has worked at New Alchemy since our first Cape Cod summer in 1971. He grew up on his family's Ohio farm and graduated from New College in Florida. Earle is accomplished in all of our research areas: agriculture, aquaculture, tree crops, bioshelter design and management, windmills, and renewable energy technologies for developing countries. In recent years he has focused on permaculture and bioshelter design, and is currently designing a bioshelter exhibit for Boston's Museum of Science. Earle lives in Woods Hole with his wife, Hilde Maingay, in their own diverse and magical food landscape. Earle's hobbies are writing, woodcarving, toymaking, and plant propagation.

Tracy Calvan was born and raised in Manhattan, where she thought that grass was the stuff that grew up only between cracks in pavement. She studied writing at Hampshire College in Amherst, Massachusetts, and became a full-time New Alchemy staff member in 1980. Tracy has worked as the Institute's Publications Coordinator and as Editor of the *New Alchemy Quarterly*. In addition to this text, she edited the *New Alchemy Water-Pumping Windmill Book* and the *Backyard Fish Farming Book*. Along the way, she has become a talented organic gardener. Her other interests include filmmaking and dance.

Susan Ervin was born and raised in western North Carolina. She was educated at the University of North Carolina at Chapel Hill. After university she worked at a folkschool in rural North Carolina, where she began to garden, worked in a greenhouse, and learned to weave and dye. She lived on small farms in Virginia and New York and in Boston before joining the Institute in 1974. At New Alchemy, Susan worked in experimental intensive agriculture, greenhouse agriculture, and demonstration gardening. She also taught and wrote about her work and managed our community gardens. Her winters were spent at the New Alchemy farm in Costa Rica, working with agriculture and community development. Susan left the Institute in 1982 to set up a market garden in North Carolina with husband (and New Alchemy co-founder), Bill McLarney, and daughter, Rosie.

Michael Greene worked at New Alchemy from 1979 to 1981 before joining the Cape and Islands Self-Reliance Corporation as a community development specialist. He grew up in Queens, New York, and graduated Empire State College with a major in Environmental Sciences. Before coming to New Alchemy, he worked with community gardening and waste recycling projects at the People's Development Corporation of the South Bronx, and in Santa Barbara, California. In the South Bronx, he helped develop methods of using worms to recycle residential solid wastes, and worked on efforts to reclaim urban land for agricultural use. At the Institute he worked in all aspects of aquaculture research plus our gardening and education programs. He is now pursuing graduate study and lives in Manhattan.

Gary Hirshberg, co-editor and New Alchemy Institute's Executive Director, grew up in New Hampshire before traveling "south" to Massachusetts in 1972. He majored in Environmental Studies at Hampshire College and directed environmental education programs in Maine before joining the Institute in 1977. At New Alchemy, Gary worked in the wind and education programs, and was a co-founder of the Cape and Islands Self-Reliance Corporation. In addition to his fundraising and overall administrative responsibilities, Gary has a strong professional interest in rural economic development and economic development in the People's Republic of China, where he occasionally travels and lectures. When he is home, Gary loves to write, garden, and raise chickens.

John Quinney was born in New Zealand and spent his first 20 years there, frequently working on the family sheep and cattle farm. He was educated at Canterbury University and Imperial College in London, where he earned a PhD in Organic Chemistry. For the next five years he held various jobs in New Zealand and England: farm worker, rigger on a pipe-laying barge, roustabout on oil rigs, and a construction worker in the North Sea. He came to the United States in 1979 and graduated the Masters program in Social Ecology at Goddard College in Vermont with a thesis entitled "Agriculture, Shelter and Village: The Nature of a Sustainable Landscape." After volunteering at the New Alchemy Institute for a year, he joined the Tree Crops program staff in September 1980. His work at the Institute centers around tree crops: planting, propagating, and maintaining a collection of food-producing trees and shrubs. As a permaculture consultant, John teaches workshops and lectures throughout the country and abroad.

Greg Watson grew up in Cleveland, Ohio, and attended Tufts University and Campus-Free College. He has taught and developed curricula in alternative schools in Boston and Cambridge, Massachusetts. As a marketing consultant to the Massachusetts Department of Food and Agriculture, Greg worked with inner-city community groups and farmers throughout the state to organize the Boston Farmers' Markets. He is a board member of the Boston Urban Gardeners and the Cape and Island Self-Reliance Corporation. As Director of New Alchemy's Community Outreach Program, Greg is currently facilitating the development of a bioregional economic development plan that has as one of its major objectives the preservation of prime agricultural land on Cape Cod and the islands of Martha's Vineyard and Nantucket. He lives with his wife, Debbie, and their daughter, Brooke, and is a serious student of Bucky Fuller.

Ann Wickham is the illustrator for this text. She was born in southern New Jersey and graduated from Rhode Island School of Design with a degree in architecture. Before working for a year as a New Alchemy illustrator in 1981, Ann was employed in Vermont and California on a number of solar and other technical projects. At present, she is working toward her architectural license in New Jersey and is designing and building a house for her parents.

Index

Intensive beds, 98–101
Interplanting
    for pest control, 150
    purpose of, 117, 118
Iron, 5
Irrigation, 146–147
    and backyard ponds, 192
    with water from solar-
        algae ponds, 198
*It's All on the Label: Under-
    standing Food, Additives
    and Nutrition* (Block), 7

J

Japanese beetles, 150, 155
Jars, growing sprouts in,
    15–19
Jerusalem artichoke, plant-
    ing suggestions for, 132
Jordan, William, 72

K

Kale
    double transplanting for,
        30–31
    insect–resistant varieties
        of, 172
    planting suggestions for,
        132
    planting table for, 164
    in solar greenhouses, 69,
        82
Kohlrabi, planting sugges-
    tions for, 132

L

Ladybugs, 71, 72, 73, 151
Lamb's quarters
    control of, 145
    companion planting
        guidelines for, 166
Lappé, Frances Moore, 5
Leaf miner, plant varieties
    resistant to, 174
Leaf mold, as mulch, 112
Leaf rot, 63
Leeks
    planting suggestions for,
        132
    in solar greenhouses, 82
Lentils, sprouting, 16
Lespedeza, as green
    manure, 111
Lettuce

disease-resistant varieties
    of, 178
double transplanting for,
    30–31
grown indoors, 35–36
planting schedules for, 84
planting suggestions for,
    132
planting table for, 164
price revenue for, 84
in solar greenhouses,
    68–69, 82, 83
Lice, and chickens, 219
Light
    for growing vegetables
        indoors, 31–34
    for home greenhouse,
        76–77
    in large solar green-
        houses, 59
    for outdoor gardening,
        89–92
Lima beans
    disease-resistant varieties
        of, 177
    planting suggestions for,
        128
    planting table for, 165
Lobelia, 71
Logsdon, Gene, 95
Lumbricus rubellus, 40

M

McCullagh, James C., 54
McLarney, William, 190
Macronutrients, 93
Malabar spinach, 138
Manure
    for composting, 106, 109
    hotbed, 58
    NPK percentages in, 162
Marek's disease, 219
Marigolds
    companion planting
        guidelines for, 166, 167
    in insect control, 71
Mealy bugs, 71
Melons
    double transplanting for,
        30–31
    harvesting of, 157
    mulching for, 114
    planting suggestions for,
        133
Mexican-bean beetles, 150
    characteristics of, 155

plant varieties resistant
    to, 169, 170, 171, 172,
    173, 174, 175
Micronutrients, 93
Milky spore, 152
Mimosa, disease-resistant
    varieties of, 178
Minerals
    function of, 3
    sources of, 5
    storage of, 4
Mint
    companion planting
        guidelines for, 166
    in insect control, 71
Mites
    in chickens, 219
    spider, 71
    two-spotted, 175
Mollison, Bill, 101
Mollison-mulch method, of
    soil preparation, 101,
    102–103
Mulberries, 235
Mulch
    defined, 112
    for late planting, 279
    living, 114–115
    materials for, 113–114,
        144
    permanent, 114
Mulching, 112–113, 143–145
Mung beans, sprouting, 16
Muskmelon
    disease-resistant varieties
        of, 178
    insect-resistant varieties
        of, 172
Mustard
    disease-resistant varieties
        of, 178
    grown indoors, 36
    insect-resistant varieties
        of, 172
    planting suggestions for,
        133
    in solar greenhouses, 83
Myzus persicae (Sulzer), 73

N

Nanking cherry, 233
Nasturtiums
    companion planting
        guidelines for, 166
    in insect control, 71, 74
Natural Organic Farmers
    Association (NOFA), 95

*Nature and Properties of Soil,
    The* (Brady), 95
*New Alchemy Back Yard Fish
    Farm Book, The* (McLar-
    ney and Parkin), 190
New Alchemy Institute,
    295–300
Newcastle disease, 219
Newcomb, Duane, 119
Newspaper, as mulch, 144
Nitrogen
    in common organic mate-
        rials, 162–163
    for composting, 106
    sources of, 93
Noise control, tree crops
    for, 226
NPK percentages, in com-
    mon organic materials,
    162–163
Nutrients
    essential, 3, 95
    recycling of, 288
*Nutritive Value of American
    Foods*, 6
Nut trees
    examples of, 235
    pruning of, 242

O

Okra
    harvesting of, 157
    planting suggestions for,
        134
One-Straw Revolution, The
    (Fukuoka), 115
Onions
    disease-resistant varieties
        of, 178
    planting suggestions for,
        134
    planting table for, 164
    storing, 281, 282–283
Organic gardening, 87
Organic Plant Protection
    (Yepsen), 64, 156
Outdoor gardening, 87
    choosing site for, 89–92
    different crops, 122–138
    direct seeding, 140–141
    harvesting, 156–158
    planning for, 115–122
    soil for, 92–95
    soil-building techniques,
        105–115
    soil preparation for,
        96–105

Other books of interest from the New Alchemy Institute:

The New Alchemy Back Yard Fish Farm Book
Growing Fish in Floating Cages

William McLarney and Jeffrey Parkin

$8.95 paper
ISBN 0-931790-21-2

96 pp   8 × 8

From the very beginning the New Alchemists have felt that the cultivation of fish as a low-cost, high-quality protein food is a tool that should be made available to everyone. This book on the method of raising fish in wire cages placed in natural bodies of water provides a fish culture system analogous to vegetable garden systems which produce abundant healthful food for home consumption with low economic cost and space requirements. topics covered include: building your own cage (a complete how-to manual), how to stock, feed, care for, maintain, and harvest your cage.

William McLarney is a cofounder of the New Alchemy Institute. Coauthor of a text on aquaculture, McLarney holds a PhD from the University of Michigan.

Jeffrey Parkin participated in the cage culture, fish feeds, and earthworm experiments at NAI.

The New Alchemy Water Pumping Windmill Book

Gary Hirshberg

$8.95 paper
ISBN 0-931790-23-9

128 pp   8 × 8

This do-it-yourself construction guide to inexpensive water-pumping windmills, offers comprehensive information on selecting, building and operating practical and attractive windmills. It is written for homeowners or landowners who want to increase their independence of commercial power sources. Hirshberg gives complete plans and directions for building and installing the New Alchemy Sailwing windmill, the product of over seven years research and field analysis. This is the definitive book on modern water-pumping windmill technology.

Gary Hirshberg is the director of the New Alchemy Institute and is also a consultant for both the U.S. Fish and Wildlife Service, and the National Audubon Environmental Institute.

"This manual reads like it should have a greasy thumbprint on every page! . . ."
J. Baldwin, Co-Evolution Quarterly